THE THIRD WORLD

Premises of U.S. Policy

(Revised Edition)

Edited by

W. SCOTT THOMPSON

ICS PRESS

Institute for Contemporary Studies
San Francisco, California

Inquiries, book orders, and catalog requests should be addressed to ICS Press, Suite 811, 260 California Street, San Francisco, California 94111—415—398—3010.

Library of Congress Cataloging in Publication Data
Main entry under title:

The Third World, premises of U.S. policy.

    Includes index.
    1. Underdeveloped areas—Addresses, essays, lectures.
2. International economic relations—Addresses, essays,
lectures. 3. United States—Foreign economic relations
—Underdeveloped areas—Addresses, essays, lectures.
4. Underdeveloped areas—Foreign economic relations—
United States—Addresses, essays, lectures. I. Thompson,
W. Scott (Willard Scott), 1942–
HC59.7.T456 1983   337.730172'4   83–8426
ISBN 0–917616–58–8
ISBN 0–917616–57–X (pbk.)

THE THIRD WORLD

CONTENTS

PREFACE   xi

I

Introduction

1   THE THIRD WORLD REVISITED   3
    W. Scott Thompson

    Dynamics in the International Order:
    1978–1983 4   Revising Reality 8   Coda 17

2   THE THIRD WORLD AND THE CONFLICT
    OF IDEOLOGIES   19
    Max Beloff

    Defining the Third World 20   Ideology as
    Instrument 23   American Naiveté 25
    Excuses for Development Failures 28   Guilt and
    Fear 29   No Role in Nation-Building 31

3   MYTH VERSUS REALITY IN
    "NORTH-SOUTH" NEGOTIATIONS   35
    Allan E. Goodman

    Origins and Significance of the Myths 36
    Myth v. Reality 38   Implications 47

II

Social and Economic Realities

4   PROSPERO'S ISLAND   55

Dennis Austin

Colonial Rule 60   Artificiality 62
Resources 63   Political Order 66   The View
from Amnesty 68

5   THE MILITARY AND POLITICS IN THE
     THIRD WORLD   75

S. E. Finer

Military Intervention in the Third World 76
The Military Regimes 94   The Future of
Military Intervention 111

6   FOREIGN AID: WHAT IS AT STAKE?   115

Peter T. Bauer
Basil S. Yamey

The Creation of "North" and "South" 116
Anomalies of Aid 119   Aid and Economic
Growth 120   How Aid Can Inhibit
Development 123   Between Aid and the Poor:
Third World Rulers 125   Failed Analogies and
Justifications 128   Aid and Restitution 131
Reshaping Aid Policy 133   The Central
Question 135

III

International Affairs

7   THIRD WORLD VOTING PATTERNS AT THE
     UNITED NATIONS   139

Kenneth L. Adelman
Marc F. Plattner

The World of the United Nations 141   Theory
and Practice in the United Nations 142   The
Top Ten 146   The Need for Awareness 149

8   THE THIRD WORLD PEOPLES OF SOVIET
     CENTRAL ASIA   155

Daniel Pipes

Historical Background 156   Colonies or
National Republics? 160   Prospects and United
States Policy 170

9   MILITARY BASES IN THE THIRD WORLD   175

Robert E. Harkavy

Changes in Geopolitical Value of Forward
Bases 176   Changing Technological
Requirements for Basing Access 181   Changing
Costs of Facilities Acquisitions 185   New Terms
for Old Relationships 190   Sovereignty versus
Security: Base Denial Diplomacy 193   The
Future of Basing Diplomacy in the Third
World 198

IV

The Economic Problem

10   THE CASE OF DEPENDENCY THEORY   203

Tony Smith

Dependency Theory 204   Theoretical
Assumptions 206   Moral Fractures 208
Accounting for Economic Fluidity 212   Rising
Strength of the South 217   Reconciling
Differences 219   Conclusion 222

11   POLITICAL ORIGINS OF THE NEW
      INTERNATIONAL ECONOMIC ORDER   223

Richard E. Bissell

Historical Background 224   The New Third
World Leadership 226   The Search for
Stability 233

12   BEYOND THE NEW INTERNATIONAL
      ECONOMIC ORDER   239

Nathaniel H. Leff

Commodity Agreements 240   Increased
Resource Transfers 242   Improved Access to
Technology and Markets 243   Multinational
Corporations 247   The Overall Economic
Impact 249   Political Relations 250   Learning
from Experience 252   U.S. Policy and the Third
World 254   Economic Shifts Since
Promulgation of the NIEO 255   Possibilities for
an Exit 258   The Changing International
Context 260   The Need for
Nonintervention 263

13   THE ROLE OF PRIVATE CAPITAL IN
      DEVELOPING THE THIRD WORLD   267

      Wilson E. Schmidt

      The Possibility of Mutual Gain 268   The
      Burgeoning International Capital Market 269
      Multinational Corporations 273   The Problem
      of Subsidies and Mutual Gain 279
      Development Strategies and Obstacles 282

V

Conclusion

14   A WORLD OF PARTS   287

      W. Scott Thompson

      Political Order 288   Economic
      Management 291   Military Factors 295
      Geopolitical Ramifications 296

NOTES   303

CONTRIBUTORS   311

INDEX   315

PREFACE

In the five years since the first edition of THE THIRD WORLD appeared in 1978, many important changes have been reflected in the Third World itself and also in Third World relations with the developed countries. This period has witnessed, in addition to a number of regional conflicts, the Soviet invasion of Afghanistan, the fall of the Shah in Iran and the subsequent rise of Islamic fundamentalism in the Persian Gulf states, the rise of conflict in Central America, two major changes in world oil prices, and the change of presidential administrations in the United States.

In light of these and other changes, the Institute decided to bring out a new edition of the book, revising some chapters and adding several to reflect recent events. This edition maintains the broad perspective of the first, exploring economic, social, and political issues in both the Third World itself and in North-South relations. We are pleased again to have W. Scott Thompson as editor.

Among the new papers, Bauer and Yamey have drawn on the experience of the last five years to present here more of a critique of foreign aid than they could in the earlier book. And we have also added two papers dealing with the broad arena of international affairs—one by Kenneth L. Adelman and Marc F. Plattner on international organizations as the principal instruments establishing and developing what the authors herein conclude is the myth of the Third World; and the other, by Robert E. Harkavy, on military bases as the fulcrum of power for the superpowers.

This new edition of THE THIRD WORLD fits into a publication program that includes several recent and planned Institute studies on international economic and political issues. Among these are our broad assessment of U.S. foreign and defense policy in NATIONAL SECURITY IN THE 1980s (edited by W. Scott Thompson) and our forthcoming study of development in both First and Third World countries in WORLD ECONOMIC GROWTH (edited by Arnold C. Harberger).

We hope this book in its new form will continue to make an important contribution to the contemporary debate on these important issues.

Glenn Dumke
President
Institute for Contemporary Studies

I

Introduction

1

W. SCOTT THOMPSON

The Third World Revisited

During the United Nations Second Special Session on Disarmament, the right of the peoples of the world to demonstrate publicly in favor of disarmament —regardless of the position of their respective governments —was a difficult and contentious issue. Communist countries, predictably, fought hard to have the particular clause referring to this right removed from the text of the resolution at hand.

At a critical moment in that debate, in the final hours of the conference, a Pakistani delegate, not generally known for his support of Western positions in UN forums, rose to a stilled audience and reminded his colleagues that the resolution could not be adopted without a consensus. He assured the gathering that, without the clause pertaining to public demonstration, there would be no consensus, and thus no communiqué. There was little doubt in the minds of the other delegations that his statement represented the predominant "Third World" position. Even more acutely, there was no doubt in the minds of the Communist delegations that their bluff had been called.

Over a month earlier, when the special session had begun, close to one million Americans gathered in Central Park for what was later billed by the prestige press as the largest demonstration "for the cause of humanity" in the history of the modern world. Clearly, the clause in the resolution was not directed at the United States. Finding themselves in the position traditionally occupied by the U.S. in such United Nations debates, the Soviets and their allied delegations were faced with a Hobson's choice: they could demand removal of the clause, risking the sort of defeat to which they were wholly unaccustomed in Third World circles; or, they could concede to the "Third World" bloc and save a resolution essential to sustaining their program of encouraging an anti-American schism in the Atlantic alliance. Once again proving the sophistication of their geopolitical designs, they opted for the latter course.

This example of procedural politics is not, by itself, evidence of a major shift in the disposition of the Third World toward the West. To be sure, there remains much painful rhetoric in Third World oratory. But far more impressive is other evidence coming from the developing world that indicates a new sense of clarity in their collective perception of reality—economic, political, and ideological. It is in marked contrast to the perceived reality of 1978, when the first edition of this book appeared.

Dynamics in the International Order: 1978–1983

The central tenet of the first edition held that our subject was a differentiated, multifarious, and heterogeneous political entity. It was difficult at that time to discern a single voice among the cacophonous statements, proclamations, and manifestos that, with some pretention, constituted a collective position. Indeed, the introduction to that volume stated:

Although, in its official rhetoric, the Third World speaks of itself as an undifferentiated mass, these leaderships realize that their interests differ from region to region, indeed, from state to state. . . . We would probably all prefer not to use the term "Third World" at all, had it not come to be so convenient. . . . For its use, to an extent, has the effect of a self-fulfilling prophesy, endowing those most radical leaders with a sense of mission.[1]

The contributors to that first volume detected great diversity and, with some prescience, growing sophistication in the foreign policy of the individual states in the "marriage of political convenience" referred to as the "Third World." In spite of the rhetorical semblance of unity, it made no sense, they agreed, to consider the Third World an *analytically* coherent entity. Today, a mere five years later, they have found it is not even possible to consider the Third World a *politically* coherent entity.

Much has transpired since the publication of that first edition. First of all, the American political context in which the book was originally written is now very different. To some extent, the first edition was a critique of the Carter administration's idealistic designs for the Third World in "a new age" in which both Americans and citizens of the less-developed countries (LDCs), having overcome their "inordinate fear of communism," would work together to advance the cause of universal and inalienable human rights. As the contributors to that first edition then realized, such a policy, noble and enlightened as it appeared, could not be imposed upon a complex international system in which leaders of lesser principle freely exercised absolute power over their own large constituencies and threatened the existence of other sovereign LDCs less willing to resort to the use of force to advance the cause of "national liberation." The American public, sympathetic to Jimmy Carter's experiment but tempered by the experiences of a second oil shock, genocide in Southeast Asia, occupation in Afghanistan, bloody proxy wars in Africa, aggressive combat brigades ninety miles from Miami, and national humiliation in Teheran, rejected this idealistic approach in the 1980 election with a decisive confirmation of a new realism. The American public implicitly recognized the criterion that, according to Lord Beloff, has long animated Soviet policies toward the Third World; namely, that "Third World regimes want to know, not who is going to be nicer to them, but who is going to come out on top."

Moreover, this new American realism is also found elsewhere; the political context of the developing world also changed dramatically since 1978. Two kinds of events contributed to a new sense of "realism" among the LDCs.

First were the events that revealed the true origins of Soviet international conduct, both at home and abroad: *inter alia,* the Soviet-supported war in Southeast Asia (with its concomitant extermination of a substantial portion of an entire people); the various examples of Soviet-executed coups (directly and indirectly) in Afghanistan, Cambodia, and Nicaragua; the Soviet-Ethiopian alliance to snuff out the highly principled and popularly supported Eritrean revolution standing between Ethiopia and its designs on Somalia; the massive Soviet arms transfers to terrorist and revolutionary movements such as al-Fatah, the Sandinistas, SWAPO, and Colonel Qaddafi's private armies; the use of Soviet-supplied Cuban troops to advance the cause of "liberty" and stifle prospects for a political settlement in Southwest Africa; and most recently, the highly significant revelations in Southwest and Southeast Asia of Soviet violations of the conventions proscribing the use of chemical and biological weapons. While significant in themselves, all these events augured a more precise understanding among the

LDCs of the motivations behind the conduct of Soviet foreign policy and the unstated, but now better understood, ramifications of Soviet aid.

Second were the events that indicated that the American alternative to Soviet aid and support was decidedly uncompetitive in the nasty, brutish, solitary, and short-lived international arena in which the LDCs found themselves. The United States was completing its recognition of the People's Republic of China which, however much a response to geopolitical reality, was done in a way to dismay the leaders of many small states already worried by the long string of American abandonments of politically unfashionable regimes; President Carter was signing the Panama Canal Treaty, exposing that formerly protected international thoroughfare to the vicissitudes of a politically turbulent region, where it also chose to abandon the corrupt Somoza regime to the Soviet/Cuban inspired and funded Sandinistas; and Americans were passively observing the sacking of an American embassy in Iran and failing to execute the sort of simple rescue operation that Israel performs with efficient and, one might add, distressing regularity. Finally, the uneasiness with which the LDCs witnessed the Western alliance, in the absence of a leader, fall into disarray led to the conclusion in some Third World capitals that there was no concrete alternative to the Soviet camp: they would be forced to fend for themselves in an increasingly volatile world or come to terms with Soviet power.

World events demanded that the LDCs rethink their foreign policies as well as reconstitute their domestic ideologies, and their intelligentsia searched for innovative models accordingly. The decomposition of the bipolar world order, which had previously offered LDCs clear-cut binary alternatives for aid, leadership, and models for their own development, forced upon Third World leaders the responsibility for their own future and the requirement of creative and imaginative policymaking to realize it. At the same time, it forced those same policymakers to take stock, many for the first time, of the international order in which they operated and of the political, economic, and military realities that confronted them. Needless to say, the picture that emerged was far different from the misty, impressionistic, and romantic canvas that many had previously thought represented the international system.

Revising Reality

Political realities. Politically, the Third World saw that it could afford neither to be overwhelmed by the draconian conditions of Soviet alliances, nor to be underwhelmed by the episodic commitments from the United States. Yet the traditional middle ground between the two superpowers—the international organizations—steadily eroded as well. Even the Non-Aligned Movement (NAM) was in turmoil at the hands of would-be leaders such as Fidel Castro, forcing it for the first time toward a more realistic posture, and thereby was becoming inert. Without such institutional collectives to act as conduits for material and ideological aid, even the relatively developed LDCs found it increasingly difficult to maintain their long-term programs and cultivate a reasonable and orderly system of governance against the tide of anarchy and threats to their legitimacy endemic to the Third World.

Moreover, the conceptual foundations of political development, often referred to as "ideologies" in the common currency, have never been effectively developed in the Third World countries. This has presented a perpetual problem for those builders of nation-states in the developing world. As Lord Beloff points out,

the major ideologies are themselves products of the conditions and mental attitudes of the advanced world. They have been imported into the Third World, which has not so far developed bodies of ideas complex and all-embracing enough to be dignified by the title of "ideology."

Conditions and events have amplified the problem of ideological development even further. The recent emergence of new "hybrid" ideologies—liberation theologies of Eastern and Western origin, anti-historical versions of Marxism, regional political doctrines, and various strains of nationalistic socialism, for example—has further fractured the Third World as a political entity.

The mythological aspects of the major terms of reference in the developed/developing world conflicts are illustrated in Allan Goodman's chapter on the North-South negotiations. There, he now points out, the recent failure of the agendas these myths generated—for example, the New International Information Order, the New International Economic Order, or the Law of the Sea Treaty—has left these programs operationally empty for both the developed and less-developed countries.

Yet the future of the equally mythological "North-South dialogue," which previously atrophied as a result of unrealistic LDC demands and Western intransigence, could become fruitful if, argues Goodman, the LDCs develop more realistic postures relative to their requests; and if the U.S. economy expands to provide the international liquidity for developing countries to absorb more U.S. exports.

There was no need to revise the literary allusion so eloquently put forth in Dennis Austin's thoughtful chapter on Shakespeare's *The Tempest:* the metaphor still applies to the variety of LDC ideologies described by Beloff, and to the inability of such doctrines to supply operational paradigms for policymaking. The LDCs find themselves playing, often alternately, the parts of Caliban and Ariel. The interchangeability of the roles is caused, in large part, by the fact that Prospero (also played alternately by the U.S. and the USSR) moves in and out of the drama without regard to stage direction. Austin's conclusion in 1978 is even more apparent today: "Prospero's island is now too crowded and too complicated to bring all its difficulties under a pseudodoctrine of a belief that, since it no longer carries conviction, dangerously darkens counsel."

Economic realities. The economic developments in the last five years have been so often rehearsed in the general press that it hardly seems necessary to recite the details anew. Nonetheless, the contributors who studied economic issues found many reasons to revise their conclusions by further asserting the verity of the free market above and against the inefficiencies of planned centralized economies, and private commercial development above and against government-sponsored aid programs. These points are best illustrated by the economies in countries such as Taiwan and South Korea, which experienced little if any growth during the periods in which they received large aid packages (the 1950s and 1960s), yet prospered and grew at phenomenal rates when aid was cut off in the 1970s. They were forced to reorder once stagnant, protectionist economies. These and other countries liberalized their economies, allowing market forces to reallocate their productive capacities for export to the world economy and instituting tax policies that attracted foreign investment. Because of these reforms, LDCs that pursued sensible policies found themselves better equipped than their industrialized counterparts to manage themselves through the throes of recession while avoiding the instability that continues to plague such other developing countries as Tanzania, Ghana, and India, which are still receiving large infusions of aid.

As this volume goes to press, the oil glut that has developed over the past two years heralds the imminent demise of OPEC. In its wake, states such as Mexico and Nigeria—to mention just those with the most ambitious development programs—have been forced to postpone or cancel the massive welfare and infrastructure projects that had been initiated when oil receipts made extravagant spending possible.

Moving from the practical to the theoretical, no paradigm of Third World dilemmas has proved more enticing than "dependency theory," which analyzes purported Third World subservience to First World economic necessities as a structural phenomenon. Tony Smith's reassessment of dependency theory provides good cause not only for retiring it once and for all, but also, by inference, for developing a new model of economic development. Dependency theory has "obscured" the details of the North-South relationship. By now it is clearly impossible to construct a credible economic model, predicated by dependency theory, that accounts for the natural, historical dynamism in the world economy without

making imperialism more all-pervasive and self-perpetuating than is the case. [Dependency theory] may serve the political needs of certain groups to see the power of the North in this light, but there is no reason those of us without such needs should subscribe to a world view so distant from reality.

Without supplying a new economic model (see the Institute's forthcoming *World Economic Growth,* by Arnold C. Harberger), Professors Bauer and Yamey assert in their new chapter that "foreign aid is the source of the North-South conflict, not the solution." Indeed, we have repeatedly reviewed the case for making the "Third World" little more than a semantic fiction; yet Bauer and Yamey strike a counterintuitive note in locating a common denominator:

The diverse components of the Third World do indeed share one characteristic. This is not poverty, stagnation, exploitation, brotherhood, or skin color; it is the receipt of foreign aid. *The concept of the Third World and the policy of official aid are inseparable. Without foreign aid there is no Third World.* Official aid provides the only bond joining together its diverse and often antagonistic constituents.

The irony that foreign aid, traditionally viewed as a catalyst to development, now presents itself as an obstacle to modernization is redoubled when one considers the fact that, notwithstanding Tony Smith's argument herein, the majority of the LDCs still use some form of dependency theory in their political rhetoric if not in their economic planning. It is difficult to understand the persistence of arguments about Western "imperialism and exploitation" when, during the period 1977—79, many oil-rich nations as well as those nations with political systems and ideologies antithetical to the United States—Cuba, South Yemen, and Viet Nam—all received foreign aid. At such a time of accusation about imperialism and exploitation, OPEC dominated the Western economy, Vietnam practiced systematic genocide, Cuba dispatched troops to Africa, and political refugees (many of whom were fleeing the aforementioned countries) required the United Nations to appropriate a special assistance fund of some $560 million.

In addition to evidence of the negative effects of aid programs in themselves, over the past five years the Western economies have become even less able to sustain their own domestic social programs, let alone large foreign aid projects. This points to a structural change—perhaps not yet quantitatively detectable—for both donors and recipients of aid. Increasingly, the trend will move toward development of private sector solutions to development problems in the fashion so well described by the late Wilson Schmidt. His principle of maximizing "mutual gains" is merely a reiteration of the market practices followed in private sector financing with much success. Mutual gain between the rich and poor countries is possible when LDCs borrow in the world capital markets. "As long as the rate of return on capital in the poor countries is higher than in the rich countries," he writes,

there is a possibility for mutual gain by the transfer of capital from the rich to the poor countries. By offering a tangible return to the rich, the poor can co-opt the private sectors of the rich countries into their progress, gaining the benefits of their capital and know-how.

The possibility of real economic development among the LDCs presumes the expanded use of these private sector mechanisms. As new practices in the international capital markets provide borrowers increasingly flexible, yet unartificial, financing mechanisms, the LDCs will discover arrangements through which development projects may be financed in a mutually beneficial way for both the creditor and debtor parties. This increasing move to private markets will involve a concomitant shift in political rhetoric; but this shift will come more slowly. The political origins of the New International Economic Order remain the same, although as Richard Bissell has pointed out, the techniques of the LDCs often betray their stated political principles. He lists a number of "sleights of hand" devised by the Third World, such as the Enterprise body of the Law of the Sea Treaty and new Special Drawing Rights (SDRs) for one-time LDC contributors to the IMF, both used to finance otherwise uneconomic projects.

The ultimate reconciliation of political and economic realities will be a long and difficult transition. It is here that the truly ideological development and ultimate maturation of the Third World will take place. Because that path will undoubtedly be an uneasy one, it will require a strong and continuing role for the military; thus, examining that role in greater detail becomes essential for understanding the broad nature of problems in the Third World.

Military realities. In general, political scientists consider military problems to be a constituent part of the political analysis of individual countries. In the case of the Third World, however, there is a special reason to consider them as discrete and to consider them last.

Military power and other fundamental aspects of political power are more important in the Third World than in the developed countries for two reasons. First, the greater frequency of political transition in the LDCs and the consequential instability explain why political legitimacy in those countries tends to derive much more directly from the fundamen-

tal aspects of political power—including military power—
than in the West. Second, the tendency to rely on military
power to provide order and legitimacy is augmented by the
fact that many LDCs do not share the tradition of reason
that has long marked political development in the West. Partially because of the idealistic strand in U.S. foreign policy
thinking, American elites tend to deny the significance of
the political power matrix in dealings not only with the Third
World but also with Western allies and even with America's
principal political adversary. The majority of Third World
leaders, on the other hand, possess a more highly refined
understanding of the often rarefied elements of Machtpolitik
than their Western counterparts. Thus they better understand the most basic manifestation of Machtpolitik—
military force. The lack of such understanding on the part
of the American intelligentsia and much of its leadership
played a very large role in the U.S. tactical victory/
strategic defeat in Southeast Asia.[2]

There have been many examples of the exercise of military
power in the Third World since the initial publication of this
book. Such engagements have been of three kinds. First are
those that manifest assertions by ideological and quasi-
religious movements—often fueled by external supplies of
arms and politics—to destabilize or restabilize a regime's
legitimacy. This variety of military force has been evident recently in Angola, Chad, Ethiopia, Nicaragua, Salvador, and
Vietnam.

The second type represents a correlative defeat, victory, or
stalemate for the sponsors of the respective LDCs (American
or Soviet in most cases, but including French, British,
Chinese, and even other LDC sponsor/allies as well). Examples include many of those listed above because of the
multidimensional character of those engagements: without
both an indigenous as well as East-West component, they frequently would not have occurred. Israel's war in Lebanon,
because it represented a major shift in the balance of power

in the Middle East, and Iran's revolution, for the same reason, would fall into this category.

The third type represents wars fought in the Third World by developed countries. The two best examples are the Falklands campaign (a necessary but costly engagement for the British) and, so it increasingly appears, the Soviet engagement in Afghanistan, with its growing costs. Although it is actually an indirect conflict, bearing some of the characteristics of our second category, the circumstances of Soviet involvement in Poland allow us to categorize the imposition of martial law there as an instance of direct aggression through power projection. Although the results are not fully in for any of the examples cited, it is safe to say that most victories in these types of wars tend to be pyrrhic.

The chapter that deals specifically with singular examples is Daniel Pipes' revised study of the Third World peoples of Soviet Central Asia. He concludes that the problems of Afghanistan are representative of the far larger problem of maintaining control of the Soviet empire, which, according to his demographics, will deteriorate as the ethnic Russians decline relative to other groups in the population. The war in Afghanistan, then, became necessary to preserve the myth that "joining the Soviet Union [is] an enlightened act of benefit to the society as a whole . . . breaking away [is] counterrevolutionary, merely the selfish response of the bourgeoisie." This Soviet perspective of war in the Third World is a classical Clausewitzian extension of policy by other means. Understanding it is essential in constructing adequate Western strategy to "contain" (to use an antiquated word) Soviet aggression in the LDCs.

More generally, but equally essential as a prerequisite to the constitution of a Western military strategy, is the largely revised chapter by S. E. Finer on the military and politics in the Third World. Noting that "armed forces are the single most important political actor in the Third World," Finer considers the implications of the ongoing involvement of the

military in Third World political transitions. He concludes
that "the principal way in which liberal democracy has been
subverted in the Third World . . . is by military intervention."
He continues:

> For the military to become neutral requires two conditions: in the
> first place, that they do not fear their civilian successors; and in the
> second, that these civilian successors do not need the military to
> keep themselves in power.

This seemingly simple conclusion is, unfortunately, more
easily stated than realized, as the long historical development required of all civilized political societies attests. Given
these historical conditions,

> the outlook for a majority of states is the gloomy one of the first
> military regime to be succeeded by a second, with the interval filled
> by alternative bouts of indirect rule, monopartism, or feebly func-
> tioning party-competitive systems backed up by martial law or
> states of siege.

In light of this prognosis, we have added a chapter in this
edition on power projection in the Third World by the major
powers. In its latest incarnation, this means forward basing.
Robert Harkavy's careful study of forward basing in the
LDCs reveals that this tactic, while essential to the operational side of current Western strategies, remains a difficult
and unsure quantity. In reexamining the geopolitical foundations of our forward basing, although he remains convinced
the subject will remain "a crucial feature of global diplomacy," Harkavy highlights a number of questions that must
be answered before any kind of rapid deployment strategy
can be considered reliable. These questions include con-
sideration of the traditional nature of such bases, the *quid
pro quo* for access, the influence of multipolarity, the struggle
over raw materials, and even the most fundamental assumptions of geopolitical principles.

Coda

Although the events that have predicated the analysis in this book have changed, the principal purpose of the book has not. This new edition is not so much a prescription for policy as an attempt to understand the underlying premises. Its purpose is to ask questions about the assumptions on which our Third World policies have been founded. Our contributors represent, now as then, no more one school of thought, as such, than a political persuasion. Intellectual curiosity, our contributors have found, has the advantage of being honest, while also serving the interests of both the West and those diverse countries of Africa, Asia, Latin America, and the Middle East that we have so long—and so incorrectly— referred to as the Third World.

2

MAX BELOFF

The Third World and the Conflict of Ideologies

The "conflict of ideologies" is, of course, only a metaphor. Men or groups of men engage in conflict, and ideologies are systems of ideas that have no existence outside the minds of individuals. The role of ideologies may be to justify men engaging in conflicts over issues that they might otherwise seek to resolve by peaceful means, or to furnish them with a picture of the world within which their own struggles become more meaningful and hence more satisfying. The element of ideology in past conflicts has tended to loom larger in the minds of those actively engaged than in the reflections of later historians. Crusaders may have believed that they were going off to rescue the Holy Places of their faith from the grasp of the infidel; later historians talk about land-hunger and Mediterranean trade. Philip II may have launched the Armada hoping to restore England to the Catholic Church; we look at the logistical problems of the Spanish empire.

From the outbreak of the French Revolution, the principal conflicts in the world have always had an ideological flavor, however important the material elements may have appeared. Radical republicanism, socialism in its Marxist and other guises, and fascism in a variety of forms, have inspired peoples, parties, and states to remold society in the light of their value systems. In turn, conservatives and liberals have tried to halt or reverse such changes.* Most important of all, nationalism has proved the most potent of ideologies, and the one most likely to prevail in an ideological conflict—if we may return to the metaphor.

Defining the Third World

When we apply these general lessons from the past to the Third World at the present time, we have to add some further considerations. In the first place, there is a problem of definition. The Third World can be regarded as simply a residue: what is left when one has subtracted from the world as a whole the industrialized West—mostly living under a system of capitalist or mixed economies—and the Communist empires of Russia, China, and their satellites. But that residue contains countries of very different degrees of economic advancement and with a vast number of different types of social and government organization. One could, therefore, argue that the phrase "the Third World" itself is a kind of abbreviated ideology. Those who use it in the Third World do so to justify claims for assistance in moving towards a higher degree of economic organization and greater material

---

*I use "liberal" in the European sense as equally antithetical to the absolutism of the *ancien regime* and to socialism. As commonly used by Americans, it becomes hard to distinguish from (non-Marxist) socialism.

wealth; those who use it in the West implicitly concede these claims.

It is also, of course, a fact of great importance that most Third World countries have populations that are wholly or mainly nonwhite. The notion of the Third World thus contains some distinctly racial overtones. One could almost say that there has grown up—as a kind of counterideology to the nineteenth-century ideas of the superiority of the white "race," which reached their culmination in the Nazi "Aryan myth"—a black racism that sees the "emancipation" of colored peoples as the overriding issue of our times and that recognizes no limits of prudence or humanity in pursuit of this end.

How deeply rooted such an ideology can become is expressed in another ideological key word: "nonaligned." Originally a nonaligned country was one whose government regarded the conflict between the Soviet Union and the West as none of its business and refused to take sides with either. In that sense, it was merely a slightly different version of classical "neutrality," as exemplified by Switzerland. But in actual practice, the nonaligned have become a group of countries that, while forming part of neither the Western Alliance nor the Soviet bloc, are nevertheless very close to the Soviet position in most of the issues that arise—particularly issues in or relating to the Third World; the "nonaligned" in relation to the Israeli-Arab conflict, for instance, are clearly nonaligned against Israel. Indeed, a Soviet bloc country like Rumania takes (no doubt, for good reasons of its own) a much more neutral stand than such "nonaligned" countries as Yugoslavia or India. Again, there is the curious fact that Cuba, which is even more dependent on and more subservient to the Soviet Union than some of the East European satellites, is admitted to the ranks of the "nonaligned."

All this would point to some confusion, a confusion shared by some Western statesmen and diplomats, particularly in the United States. The reasons for this confusion demand further probing. It is clear, to begin with, that the major ideologies are themselves products of the conditions and mental attitudes of the advanced world. They have been imported into the Third World, which has not so far developed bodies of ideas complex and all-embracing enough to be dignified by the title of "ideology," although Gandhi's peculiar blend of nationalism and "nonviolence" and rejection of the machine age came close. Nor, on the whole, have any but the most sophisticated Third World countries—which means mainly those with a long history of European contacts— been able fully to absorb the complex doctrines of the major Western ideologies.

What one gets in the Third World in place of ideology are a number of words and phrases believed to be progressive in character—such as "socialism," "democracy," "equality," "nondiscrimination," "peace-loving"—which are then combined in various ways to give an impression that the ruling party or government has its heart in the right place. The result is the creation of a confused syncretism that can be no guide to practice, since it is not based upon analysis of either the material conditions or the mental attitudes of the peoples concerned. Words like "socialism" that have, whether one likes what they stand for or not, perfectly concrete and definable meanings, become transmogrified when one finds talk of "African socialism," which is no more meaningful than, say, "African mathematics."

In seeking appropriate words in which to clothe their political aspirations, many Third World leaders have understandably found the concepts of Soviet communism easier to manipulate than the more subtle demands of Western political traditions such as liberalism. What Soviet communism appears to offer is a ready-made excuse for failing to produce the economic goods that independence has been supposed to guarantee—the failure can be put down to the survival of capitalism or to "neocolonial" exploitation. The idea of the "class struggle" is helpful when it comes to finding a good reason for the "liquidation" of traditional authorities, of the educated classes, or of any other obstacle to those who wield power in the name of "the people." The horrors of Cambodia since liberation, and the only slightly less horrific aspects of what has gone on in Uganda and Ethiopia, are testimony to the ample power of verbiage to cover up massacre.

Ideology as Instrument

It is not only against their own peoples that the present-day tyrants wield their ideological as well as their more lethal weapons; they also use ideology as a method of disarming the international community and preventing any reaction on its part, for the governments that do react are assailed as reactionary and racist—not merely by the other Communist or nonaligned governments, but even by elements among their own peoples whose minds are equally unready to unravel the deceptions and conclusions of the Third World ideologies.

Indeed, one could almost go so far as to say that the ideological aspects of the conflicts in the Third World are relevant not to the Third World countries themselves, but to the governments and peoples of the superpowers and their allies and satellites.

The Soviet Union can justify its military assistance and its armed intervention by proxy in the name of "anticolonialism" and respect for the rights of nationalities (not respected at home). Because the nation-state and its boundaries are, in much of the Third World, relatively recent and artificial, the Soviet Union can select the doctrines it applies according to the particular situation with which it is dealing. It can support the Somalis, whose national identity is not coterminous with the frontiers created by Ethiopian or European conquests. (From 1935 until after the fall of Mussolini's empire, the Ogaden was administered with Somaliland.) It can then change sides, and deny the Somalis as well as the Eritreans self-determination in order to tighten its grip upon

the Communist inheritors of the Ethiopian empire. Western
and Central Africa—notably Zaire—present similar possibilities in areas where there are important material resources that could be denied to the West, with serious consequences for the world balance of industrial and military
power. Even in Southeast Asia, where the indigenous na-
tionalisms are more deeply rooted and based upon more advanced and complex civilizations, both the Soviet Union and
the People's Republic of China have been able to manipulate
ideological appeals in competition with each other and to the
general detriment of the West.

The rulers of the Soviet Union—speculation about China
in this respect may be unwise—are, of course, ultimately inspired by an ideological commitment, but they have avoided
allowing their activities in the Third World to be robbed
of flexibility by considerations of ideological purity. Khrush-
chev may have gone further in the direction of accepting
ideological idiosyncracies than his successors, but the point
remains valid. Since the Soviet rulers preserve at home a
highly structured bureaucratic regime, frozen almost into
immobility, and since they can prevent their foreign instruments from being exposed to Soviet realities or the Soviet
people from being enlightened as to the cost of overseas expansion, they are in a strong position to cultivate the advantages that the conflict of ideologies confers upon them. These
advantages lie not in the Third World itself, but in the confused consciences of the West.

In Western Europe, inhibitions on acting to protect the
West's own interests in the Third World, and to protect its
peoples from both Soviet exploitation and the frightfulness
that accompanies the imposition of totalitarian rule, are encouraged by political parties actively sympathetic to the
Soviet cause and by other circles that respond readily and
uncritically to fashionable talk of "neocolonialism." On the
other hand, West Europeans are still too close to the past,
and have too many real contacts with their former imperial

possessions, to accept totally without question some of the claims put forward for the Third World, its regimes, and its political movements.

The real victim has been the United States where, until quite recently, much of the Third World—particularly Africa—has been watched without the benefit of first-hand experience or understanding, and interpreted in the light of slogans that derive from external ideologies. It is not simply a question, as in Europe, of the follies of the Left. In America both Left and Right, in their different ways, have subscribed to the same cardinal illusion—that the imperial or colonial period was a negative factor in the development of Third World countries, and that, freed from their imperial masters, Third World peoples would do as well as did George Washington and his contemporaries when they attained political independence.

American Naiveté

This ideological curtain prevented Americans from seeing how ill-equipped most of the newly independent nations were to prove themselves able managers of their own economic inheritance, and to protect themselves against externally aided Communist subversion. Least of all could they perform these functions through American-style democratic institutions, or the fashionable "mixed" economies of the post-Keynesian world. Their need was not for American democracy, which their social arrangements and traditions made impossible—the earlier experience of Latin America is very cogent in this respect—but for American-style capitalism. In countries facing a population explosion, increased production and increased trade were what mattered most. The successes in the Third World—Singapore, South Korea, Taiwan—did not conduct their affairs with Jeffersonian rectitude, nor would they have been as successful if they had.

It might have been hoped that the Vietnam misadventure

would have produced a greater sense of realism—that Americans would have come to realize that the objective of stemming the Communist advance was not an ignoble one, and that even the much-derided "domino" theory was not in itself absurd. They might even have taken comfort from the fact that, after some false starts, they did learn to cope with the internal war of subversion, guerrilla activity, and terrorism. What vitiated their intervention in the end was that the Communists had no intention of treating the frontier between the two Vietnams seriously, and were prepared to invade South Vietnam with the full panoply of conventional forces at a time when the domestic circumstances in the United States made any military response impossible. The fact that the United States had entered the war in a fog of intellectual confusion proved irremediable. Having lost their nerve and their national unity, they accepted withdrawal as a prelude to the defeat of their ally, with catastrophic consequences for the people of all Indochina and perhaps all Southeast Asia.

History suggests that nations often learn from their defeats. What is important is that the lessons be the correct ones. It is not clear that the United States has fully assessed the political, as distinct from the military, lessons of Vietnam. It seems too readily taken for granted that because "intervention" failed, "nonintervention" will succeed; that "progressive" forces (as defined in Soviet-inspired ideologies) will always come out on top and must, therefore, be accepted or even supported unless very cogent material reasons suggest the contrary (as in the Middle East). It has also been assumed that the Soviet Union, which, after all, won the war in Vietnam through its own style of intervention, would accept a self-denying ordinance. Again, it was assumed that "race" would invariably be a more decisive factor in the choice of sides in a postcolonial situation than any other, and that the Russians would therefore be subject to the same suspicions as the West if their intervention was too visible.

There is of course something in this argument, but it can be pressed too far. The Russians have been able to mitigate the consequences of racial feeling against them by using surrogates such as the Cubans. The belief that the United States could make positive political gains in Africa by identifying itself with "decolonization" reached its apogee under President Carter. It has not produced significant results, because the transformation of Rhodesia into Zimbabwe has shifted the focus of "nonaligned" attention to Namibia and only strengthened the determination to destabilize South Africa, which has important strategic implications for the United States.

The Carter administration attempted another use of the ideological divide by stressing "human rights" as the principal issue to be taken into account in the United States' external relations. In respect to Poland, where the Helsinki agreements have most clearly been violated, and in respect to Afghanistan, the implications are obvious even if the correct course of action is not. But in the rest of the Third World this is by no means the case, as regimes that themselves show no respect for "human rights" may at the same time demand support as bulwarks against the further advance of communism—which would itself not enhance the "human rights" position. The result has been particularly confusing in Central America, where under the present administration there have been differences of opinion between the president and Congress as well as between the United States and some of its European allies as to what should be done.

In all Third World countries—as indeed in the rest of the world—it is the economic achievements of governments that most affect the lives of their peoples. But Third World economies have been deleteriously affected by the political instability that has so often been the result of the granting of independence to former colonial territories.

While some Third World countries have done well, others through the effects of misconceived socialist planning, inefficiency, or corruption have done very poorly. The result has been that former exporters of foodstuffs have found themselves obliged to buy food abroad, with adverse consequences for their balance of payments and the incurring of further burdens of debt. In such circumstances the original indigenous leadership is especially vulnerable to groups trained in Soviet methods of government and repression.

Excuses for Development Failures

It is natural that the ideologies with most appeal are those that allow failures to be blamed on external factors, while suggesting that it is possible (provided the right formula is adopted) to reach the levels of consumption of the advanced countries without undergoing the long and painful travail— not merely of the industrial revolution, but of the long centuries of state- and nation-building—that preceded such success in Europe. It may be said that much Western investment before and since independence was based upon the needs of the capital-supplying country rather than those of the country in which the investment was made, and that its contribution to general growth was, therefore, limited. But the same is even more true of government-to-government "aid." If a country has not developed its nationhood to the extent that it can rely on its rulers—whether civil or military—to place their country's betterment above their own, their family's, or their tribe's, neither trade nor aid will benefit the majority. Moreover, the degree of political instability caused by the frustration of the revolution of rising expectations will imperil even the bare hope of national survival.

It is neither a question of the degree of civilization attained by a people, nor the length of its recorded history—the record in South and Southeast Asia is sufficient testimony to that. Nor is it a matter of "race." On the contrary, the poor performance of even the most promising African countries, such as Ghana or Nigeria, and their inability to produce elites able to cope with the demands of a modern economy, are highlighted by the individual successes in the New World of men of African descent. What African countries need is an infusion of Western and Asian skills; they should be, in their own interest, hospitable to the skilled immigrant, as were European cities in the Middle Ages and later.

Instead, under the impulse of nationalist and racist ideologies and sentiments, many Asians have been expelled or otherwise forced out of East African countries and Zambia; political uncertainty makes the future of white expertise dubious in Zaire; and in Zimbabwe, the originally proclaimed intention of the postindependence regime to maintain a multiracial society has been undermined both by some of the actual policies pursued and by the endemic violence that accelerates the process of white emigration.

Guilt and Fear

These are harsh words, words rarely spoken in academe or in the political arena. And there are obvious reasons. In the first place, the guilt complex that Europeans—and Americans since Vietnam—evince over "colonialism" makes it conventional not to criticize the rulers of Third World countries, and to refrain, above all, from disputing matters with them that could be classed as "ideological." Indeed, in a rather patronizing way, it is thought proper to flatter them and to extol their enlightenment unless, like Idi Amin, they pass the bounds of minimal decency—and even in Amin's case, it was left to the Israelis to show him up for the bully and braggart that he was. In the second place, there is the fear that any criticism will tend to shift such rulers and their countries into the Soviet camp. And this fear that the Russians will profit by any strains between Western countries and Third World governments is used by the latter for material as well as emotional blackmail.

Fears of this kind have little foundation in reality, since

they rest upon a misconception of the nature of the Soviet appeal and of the sources of Soviet strength. The Russians are quite capable of making the necessary distinction between their long-run aim of extending the area of Soviet control—which is the way they interpret world revolution—and the more immediate objective of strengthening their own state and their own economy. Because of the nature of their economy and the resources available to them in the Soviet Union itself or in Eastern Europe, they do not need many commodities from Third World countries. In that sense, when they say they are disinterested in Africa, for instance, they are speaking the truth. However, they can reap benefits from a denial of such resources to the West. They have little, if anything, to lose from upheavals and anarchy, provided they can secure for themselves or deny to others important staging points in the world's sea and air routes. Their thinking is strategic, not economic. This fact explains the relatively small part that "aid," in the Western sense, plays in the Soviet handling of Third World issues. It is reckoned that the Soviet and East European contribution (if the military aspect is excluded) comes to about 4 percent of that of the Organization for Economic Cooperation and Development (OECD) countries. The Russians have realized that Third World regimes want to know not who is going to be nicer to them, but who is going to come out on top. The clumsiness of Soviet diplomacy at a personal level is counterbalanced by the growing conviction that the West can be trusted not to resist Soviet advances, and that the path to safety lies in maintaining or extending links with Moscow.

The question of racial feelings hardly comes into it. By definition, Marxism is an international doctrine that should apply equally to all men. But, like its founders, its modern adherents remain wedded to their prejudices. Accusations of "racism" are something with which to tax the West; they have no bearing on the Russians' own conduct. As a people, they seem to be less affected by accusations of prejudice than are other peoples; moreover, their own commitment to the values of a materialist culture makes them less, rather than more, ready to make allowances for other cultures. They maintain presence in Third World countries through groups deliberately and effectively insulated from the local population, just as those who are brought to Russia for education or training are kept separate from the indigenous student body. To get the point, one has only to try to imagine a Russian "Peace Corps." But although this form of *apartheid* may be an irritant, it will not affect interstate relations so long as the Third World countries concerned are getting what they want—which may simply be arms, and the arms may be for their local battles rather than for the pursuit of ideological aims.

No Role in Nation-Building

When ideology is involved in overthrowing existing foreign or traditional rulers, and where "liberation" or revolutionary movements have been powerfully assisted by Leninist ideas of party structure and Maoist ideas of guerrilla warfare, the role of ideology should be distinguished from that involved in the actual construction of new states. For these latter purposes, Communist ideology is as irrelevant as Western democracy. Both presuppose a high degree of authority on the part of the state, and a governmental machine that has a conception of common goals and is not simply a means for personal enrichment or social promotion; they also presuppose already existing cadres of skilled workers and professional people. Over a large part of the Third World these preconditions are not met. Where they exist at all, they result from the legacy of the imperial or colonial period in both the civil and the military fields. Unless the imperial power failed to train the local population in technical and administrative skills and relied too exclusively upon expatriates, it would seem to follow that the longer a country was under European rule or influence, the better its chances of making a success of independence.

For these reasons, neither liberal-democratic nor Communist outlooks fit easily into most Third World countries, which are more likely to regard them as the way in which the superpowers dress up their own rivalries. Their choice between them will depend, as has been said, upon which side offers the most in their own terms, and, above all, on which side they think is going to win. One must not, however, omit the fact that the choice itself may be denied by military strength. In the case of Afghanistan, the pro-Soviet alignment of the country, with all its strategic implications, has been brought about by a government imposed on the country by a Soviet-inspired conspiracy and maintained in power only by Soviet military might. That the Indian government can still maintain that Soviet troops are there "by invitation" is a telling example of the effects of ideological prejudice.

It took a thousand years for an embryonic European civilization to emerge out of the ruins of the Roman Empire in the West. A thousand years is not very long in a historian's perspective, but for those living through Dark Ages and Times of Trouble, that is no consolation. We can certainly see the possibility of a long period of violent anarchy descending on parts of the Third World. How long will it take for Uganda to recover from Amin? Who will be left to administer the recovery? In Ethiopia and Cambodia we have seen the same use of massacre as an instrument of policy, in the former case putting an end to hopes once entertained that it might peacefully transcend some of the handicaps of its inheritance.

It would not be surprising if peoples so afflicted were to accept indirect rule by instruments of Soviet power as preferable to total uncertainty. Each successive step towards establishing Soviet power will make the subsequent ones easier. From Afghanistan to Angola, the omens are, therefore, bleak. Unless the Western world can recover confidence in its own ideas, and cease to rely on some imaginary innate resistance to Soviet power in the Third World, the so-called conflict of ideologies may yet contribute to the West's isolation and eventual ruin.

3

ALLAN E. GOODMAN

Myth versus Reality in "North-South" Negotiations

Ever since the 1973 Arab oil embargo, three myths have dominated multilateral negotiations between the industrialized nations and the developing countries of the so-called "Third World":

1. LDCs' (less-developed countries') development prospects have been seriously hurt by the global economic disorders since 1973.

2. The LDCs have a clear view of the relief they want: a "New International Economic Order" (NIEO).

3. The LDCs, acting through their negotiating bloc—the
   Group of 77 (G—77)—constitute a cohesive force that
   makes them influential in international affairs.

These myths have had enormous significance for multilateral diplomacy. In brief, they have encouraged LDCs to demand radical and often poorly thought-out changes in the international economic system, and they have encouraged
responses from industrialized countries in which concern for
political appearances has outweighed concern for bringing
the LDCs down to earth. The result has been nearly a decade
of desultory "North-South dialogue," which has brought the
LDCs little in the way of concrete results and has complicated relations between industrial and developing countries
on important international and bilateral issues.

How did these myths arise? What accounts for their currency today? What is the reality? These are the central
questions to be explored in this chapter. They are designed to
set in context some of the key issues—and their implications—with which this book is concerned.

Origins and Significance of the Myths

Before these myths can be exposed, it is essential to understand the political events that gave rise to them and that led
policymakers in industrialized countries to take them
seriously.

In October 1973, a few developing countries did with one
bold stroke what many had sought to do for years. The Arab
oil embargo "proved" to LDCs that their joint actions could
influence, if not determine, the course of international
events. It was a powerful tonic, and it led to a sharp rise in
LDC militancy and assertiveness, especially in UN politics.

The chief result of these tendencies was the injection into
the UN's work on economic development of a political attitude that stressed, not the positive contribution that the international economic system had made and could make to

the developing countries, but its inequities. The demand for an NIEO amounted, in effect, to a call for "reparations" for the alleged exploitation (primarily in the area of raw materials) of LDCs by industrial countries and multinational corporations.

What some LDC leaders had in mind was the specter "one, two, . . . many OPECs"—a slogan frequently heard in UN corridors at the time—and the effect it could have on the attention paid to LDC demands for changes in the international economic order. With the example of OPEC still fresh in mind, the LDCs called *en bloc* for a special session of the UN devoted to the problems of development. When the session was held in April 1974, LDC militancy had been transformed into an unprecedented degree of bloc cohesion. This, in turn, facilitated the adoption by the UN General Assembly of a statement of the LDCs' most radical demands, those embodied in the NIEO "Action Program."

Little was substantively new about these demands; in fact, many dated from the founding of the United Nations Conference on Trade and Development (UNCTAD) in 1964, and had been pushed—with modest success in such areas as trade preferences, compensatory financing, and new SDR (special drawing rights) allocations—throughout the 1960s in UN circles. What gave the NIEO such prominence was its political impact on multilateral diplomacy. Of greatest significance has been the tendency of some key leaders of the G—77 (especially Venezuela, Nigeria, Algeria, Mexico, Indonesia, and India) to link their cooperation in global negotiations—over the law of the sea, energy prices and supply, the quality of the environment, the regulation of the export of nuclear technology, and international measures to combat terrorism—to progress toward an NIEO.[1] Consequently, it was widely believed in Western government circles that progress on the key global issues mentioned above would not be possible without the support and active cooperation of the G—77.

In addition, it was also widely believed that engaging the LDCs in a North-South dialogue could serve as a means of "bringing the LDCs into our system." The hope was (and still is) that involving LDCs in discussions of complex trade and development problems would dissuade many from insistence on the NIEO.

This dialogue has taken place in two main arenas. Of primary importance in 1975—76 was the twenty-seven-nation Conference on International Economic Cooperation (CIEC), which dealt with energy, development, trade (especially LDC commodity exports), and finance. The CIEC was plagued from the outset by the inability of the nineteen participating LDCs to act as representatives of—or actually bargain over—the G—77's bloc demands. When the CIEC formally ended in June 1977, the communiqué listed some twenty areas where agreement had been reached, and twenty-one on which it had proved impossible. Most LDCs have branded the CIEC a failure, on balance, and there is little prospect that it will be revived.

Currently, the bulk of the North-South dialogue is conducted in the Geneva-based United Nations Conference on Trade and Development. While in UNCTAD all LDCs are represented, they have proved no more able to reach an accommodation with the industrial countries over the NIEO than they did in the CIEC. Nevertheless, at least two things have been achieved: a "common fund" to help stabilize some commodity prices, and a soft-loan window at the World Bank and the International Monetary Fund (IMF).

These developments have not translated into momentum toward reaching "global bargains," however. This is true in large part because the premises on which the rhetoric of the North-South dialogue is based are more myth than reality.

Myth v. Reality

Myth No. 1: LDC development prospects have been seriously hurt by the global economic disorders since 1973. The quadrupling of oil prices and the recession of 1974–1975 have been singled out by the LDCs as having dealt a major blow to development prospects. Particularly hard hit, it is claimed, were the poorest LDCs and those that depended on earnings from exports of raw materials, the prices of which plummeted because of the global recession. The longer-term consequence of these events, UN–sponsored studies now suggest, is that without major resource transfers and fundamental changes in the international economic system most LDCs will not achieve even the relatively low target of $500 gross national product (GNP) per capita (set by the UN General Assembly in its International Development Strategy) by the end of the century.

In contrast to this myth, one must ask: what is the reality? The answer to this question depends on what one holds responsible for LDC development problems today. The global economic disorders of the 1970s have unquestionably had a profound effect on LDCs, adding billions to the costs of their imports of oil and manufactured goods. But as successive editions of the World Bank's *World Development Report* have pointed out: "During the 1970s the developing countries adjusted reasonably well to the more turbulent conditions in the world economy. Since 1973, they have grown roughly twice as fast as the industrial countries."[2] Even in the face of the deepening recession in the industrialized countries in the late 1970s, the "slowdown in [LDC] growth rates in 1980–81 was less marked than in 1974–75, suggesting that previous adjustment actions had created more resilient economic structures."[3]

In the rhetoric of the North-South dialogue, moreover, one theme frequently neglected is that LDC development problems today result more from government policies and performance than from the operation of the international economic system per se. Since the 1950s, LDCs have been important beneficiaries of freer international trade and capital movements. The steady, vigorous expansion of the economies of the industrialized countries has permitted LDCs to make impressive economic progress. For example, their real GNP growth —5.5 percent per year between 1960 and 1973—represents a sustained expansion that surpassed that of any other region or country during any previous period.

There have, of course, been considerable differences in performance among the LDCs. Countries like Korea, Taiwan, Brazil, and the Ivory Coast have sustained a growth of between 7 and 10 percent annually, while for many African and Southern Asian countries economic growth rates have scarcely stayed ahead of population growth. Despite differences in size and natural resource endowments, those countries doing well clearly have several important common characteristics: a skilled and literate populace, political stability, and export-oriented development strategies. The important point to note here is that these characteristics depend on what a government does for its people, not on the magnitude of resource transfers from rich countries. For, as World Bank President Robert McNamara observed in his 1977 address to the Board of Governors, "what is required [for development] . . . is that developing country governments adopt policies that will assist the poor to enhance their own productivity, and that will assure them more equitable access to essential public services."

There is, of course, a substantial body of world opinion maintaining that the rich countries (whether of the North or OPEC) have moral as well as security reasons for ameliorating even self-inflicted development problems. These reasons are extensively discussed in the Brandt Commission report, and the literature is so immense and complex that it is beyond the scope of this chapter to evaluate it. At the risk of being accused of dismissing the findings of the Brandt Commission in a footnote, I refer readers both to its partisans and to its critics, whose views are contained in a compendium resulting from a recent project of the Friedrich Ebert Foundation for a full and frank exposition of the main lines of current debate over whether and how the commission's findings should be implemented.[4]

It is also important to note that the international economy has generally helped—particularly in times of crisis—those LDCs whose governments have set policies to take advantage of it. Without serious tampering, for example, the present system brought many LDCs through the oil crisis and the recession. Of greatest significance has been the development of new oil resources and the expansion of LDC access to capital markets, including enlarged facilities at the IMF for compensating exporters of primary products in bad years, and greater access to private lenders. Today, in fact, foreign private sources meet over half of the Third World's financial needs. This development has meant a greater role for foreign bankers in establishing standards of economic performance and shaping stabilization policies in the LDCs. The resulting interaction has promoted greater understanding on both sides of LDC development problems.

These important facts are all but forgotten in the rhetoric of the Group of 77's various declarations and statements of demands at international negotiating sessions. There are two reasons for this. The first is the quiescence at such negotiations of the LDCs who have benefited most from the present international economic system. While these LDCs are ambivalent about many of the G−77 demands, they are also unwilling to be perceived as a source of division within the LDC bloc. The explanation for this behavior will be discussed below. The second reason for the tendency to downplay the positive contribution that the present economic system has made to development is the attractiveness of the NIEO itself. As a political manifesto, it appeals to deeply held, anti-colonial, anti-imperial emotions of LDC leaders. If enacted, the NIEO proposals would eliminate any tinge of dependency or inferiority in LDC dealings in the international economic system (e.g., aid would no longer be dependent on political or economic performance), and LDCs' status in—

and power over—international institutions (especially financial ones) would be substantially enhanced. The case of
dependency theory and its appeal among LDC leaders is well
covered by Tony Smith in chapter 11. The important point to
keep in mind here is that the NIEO is as much about politics
and political power and status in international affairs as it is
about economics.

This brings us to the issue of the ever-widening (or never-
narrowing) income gap between developing and developed
countries. Despite the pace of LDC economic growth over the
past two decades, it seems to all LDC leaders that the rich are
simply getting richer. And, if the calculations of David
Morawetz of the World Bank are correct, even if they were to
grow at twice their present rates, it would take most LDCs
more than a century to close the income gap. By the end of
this century, many LDCs may not even achieve a level of
growth that would permit them to match the minimum per
capita income target set by the UN General Assembly.

There is still considerable debate—even among LDC economists—about the appropriateness of such targets and the
use of the gap as a rationale for LDC demands on the international economy. As one LDC spokesman has argued, "The
concept of catching up must be rejected. Catching up with
what? Surely the Third World does not wish to imitate the
life-styles of the rich nations? It must meet its own basic
human needs within the framework of its own cultural
values."[5]

As I have attempted to indicate, moreover, the present international economic system appears on balance to have contributed more to development than is commonly assumed. It
will continue to do so. What has made the most critical
difference between governments that have succeeded in
meeting their development objectives and coping with reces-
sionary times, and those that have not, has been government
policy. Governments that put development first, and that
take advantage of the international economic system, will

continue to have the best prospects of achieving the growth they desire and raising their standards of living. Governments that are unable to do this will not be able to deliver on their development promises, just as they have not been able to do so in the past, despite the help of massive resource transfers. Even if the NIEO became a reality tomorrow, the development of those countries that have been most vociferous in the North-South dialogue would still depend primarily on the effectiveness of their governments and not on the transfer of resources from North to South.

Myth No. 2: The LDCs have a clear view of the relief they want: a "New International Economic Order." LDC spokesmen have supported the NIEO Action Program with unexpected tenacity through more than a decade of international conferences and negotiations. Despite diversity in outlook, economic philosophy, and political objectives among the LDCs, numerous studies, working groups, and intrabloc ministerial conferences have consistently supported the basic resource transfer schemes and proposals contained in the NIEO Action Program. This process has transformed many elements of the program into powerful political symbols. But such symbolism has had relatively little effect on the economic policy of most LDCs, or on their trade and aid relations with individual industrialized countries.

Over one and three-quarter billion people live in the LDCs. Of this number, roughly a third live in some twenty-four countries that either are resource-rich (e.g., the OPEC states, Zaire, Zambia, Jamaica, Morocco, Malaysia), or have reached a level of development and possess the human resources essential to attracting foreign investment (e.g., Taiwan, Singapore, South Korea, Mexico, Brazil). The basic objectives of these states are to maximize revenue from the sale of their resources and manufactures and to secure access to stable sources of commercial capital and technology in the industrial world.

Roughly one-half of the inhabitants of the developing world live in some seventy-two countries that have only some of the ingredients necessary for economic growth and development. These countries (e.g., India, Peru, Jordan, Liberia, Thailand) seek trading preferences, technical assistance, and government-sponsored "soft" development loans from the industrial world. Finally, those in the third segment of the LDC population live in extremely poor countries that basically lack the resources (ranging from human to economic to agricultural to energy resources) to sustain economic growth. These countries (e.g., Bangladesh, Ethiopia, Laos), as constituted at present, are wholly dependent on external assistance to survive.

Given such profound differences in objectives and capabilities, most LDC support for the NIEO Action Program has been superficial, and probably reached its high point in 1976 when the G−77 agreed on the Manila Declaration in preparation for the fourth ministerial meeting of UNCTAD. This manifesto contains the most extreme formulation of the LDCs' demands, and was adopted to paper over substantial differences between the Asian, Latin, and African regional groups that plagued G−77 strategy and tactics throughout 1975. Since its adoption, the bloc leadership has not deviated from it for fear of fracturing unity, despite substantial differences among the LDCs over the desirability of many key elements of the NIEO program, especially in the areas of commodity trade and debt relief.[6]

Myth No. 3: The LDCs, acting through their negotiating bloc (the G−77), constitute a cohesive force that makes them influential in international affairs. Thus far, the leadership of the G−77 has been remarkably successful in subordinating the differences among the LDCs—over both the appropriate tactics to use in the North-South dialogue and the desirability of particular demands—for the sake of confronting the industrialized countries with a unified bloc. Created at the first ministerial meeting of UNCTAD (Geneva 1964), the G−77 has served as the LDCs' United Nations caucusing group in New York, Geneva, Rome, and Paris, and has surpassed in influence any other LDC bloc.

But it is essential to view the relative influence of the G−77 from the perspective of its components. Of central importance is the fact that only a handful of LDCs can actually influence international affairs. The major actors are those LDCs whose actions directly affect world trade and financial flows. Aside from the oil-rich members of OPEC who possess substantial financial reserves (Saudi Arabia, Kuwait, the United Arab Emirates), the ranks of the group of export-oriented countries, sometimes referred to as "upper-tier" LDCs, are small (Mexico, Brazil, South Korea, Singapore, and Taiwan), likely to remain so, and far from monolithic or unified in outlook on international affairs.

The fact that such countries are not viewed as "LDCs" by many members of the G−77 complicates their relations with the Third World. Especially in the context of international economic negotiations and UN multilateral diplomacy, upper-tier countries are clearly ambivalent about identifying with the New International Economic Order, particularly when it would adversely affect investor confidence or threaten to disturb already satisfactory trading relationships. Nevertheless, each has been able to move with ease in multilateral diplomacy by rhetorically siding with the G−77, and by privately assuring industrial countries and multinational corporations that their respective interests are hardly threatened by the inchoate resolutions and actions likely to result from such bloc politicking.

The momentum behind the North-South dialogue, moreover, is largely due to the efforts of a small, fluid group of activist countries. They derive their influence primarily from their ability to control institutions of multilateral diplomacy (e.g., the UN General Assembly, UNCTAD, the G−77), rather than from their economic importance.

The activists (e.g., the Philippines, Indonesia, India, Algeria, Venezuela, Nigeria) argue that there should be a redistribution of both wealth and political power in international affairs. To that end, they contribute resources that are in perpetually short supply in international organizations — i.e., capable diplomats and technicians who can devote their full time and energies to running caucus meetings, staffing ad hoc drafting groups, and lobbying. Their influence is enhanced, consequently, not only because they provide what many Geneva- and New York-based Third World diplomats lack (expertise, staffing assistance, social occasions, and the prestige of occasional chief-of-state endorsements), but also because the latter often operate in the absence of any firm instructions—other than to avoid jeopardizing LDC bloc unity—from their national capitals.

Because they are explicitly concerned about power relations, and especially about increasing their authority in regional and international affairs, the activists tend to evaluate the policies and preferences of industrialized countries in terms of their impact on national prestige. What matters to the activists seems to be the degree to which the initiatives and preferences of the United States and other industrial countries reinforce or detract from such immediate objectives as the consolidation of regional status and influence and the expansion of authority over international institutions and affairs.

Most activists are more realistic in private about prospects for changes in international affairs than they are in G−77 and UN arenas, and they are increasingly pragmatic about the progress that can be made. Some have even privately agreed with World Bank President A. W. Clausen's contention that the North-South dichotomy "has reached a point of diminishing returns."[7] However, events to date—especially the unity of the G−77 and the continued (albeit grudging) attention the industrialized countries have paid to bloc demands—have only caused the activists to scale down their short-term expectations, rather than to revise fundamentally their basic demands for systemic change.

The continued North-South polarization of international economic and political issues will thus complicate the conduct of multilateral diplomacy, and could generate strains in U.S. relations with some of the LDCs who are among the most influential in UN politics. Aside from the Arab oil-producing states, however, the nonindustrial states do not have the leverage to extract any of their basic demands against the will of the major industrialized countries. And they clearly wish to avoid any net loss of support for their modernization efforts.

Nevertheless, the need to manage the problems of scarce resources will require the active cooperation and support of key LDCs. Some will continue to see the arenas in which solutions to their problems are discussed only in North-South terms, evaluating U.S. diplomatic initiatives in terms of political power balances in international organizations. Others, while they may be realistic about the utility of dealing with such problems on a global basis, will continue to find rhetorical support of LDC bloc approaches useful for enhancing their status within the context of regional rivalries and ambitions. And still other LDCs will continue to insist that the problems mentioned above can be handled only on a case-by-case basis, and in the context of specific bilateral relationships. Sensitivity to these differences in outlook among the LDCs, and to their preferences for dealing with what are nominally called "North-South" issues, will thus remain a challenge to U.S. diplomacy for the foreseeable future.

Implications

It would be erroneous to conclude from the foregoing discussion that to do nothing about the demands of the developing countries for an NIEO is the wisest course. The issues of aid and trade policies toward the LDCs, as well as their role and authority in international institutions, show no signs of disappearing from the international scene. The LDCs, singly and as a bloc, are likely to continue to be assertive—and to speak with increasing confidence—when their interests are at stake.

In addition, the North-South dialogue has uncovered differences in approach and outlook among the industrialized countries that have complicated and burdened the agenda of OECD (Organization for Economic Cooperation and Development) relations. France, Italy, and the Scandinavian countries, for example, support the LDCs' overall program to protect purchasing power in the international commodity trade; the U.S., Germany, and Japan do not. Differences also exist over the appropriateness of specific negotiating arenas, the institutions and mechanisms through which resources should be transferred from North to South, and responsiveness to LDC pressures for increased power and authority in international organizations generally. The coordination of OECD policies on North-South issues will, therefore, be a continuing problem.

Should the U.S. anticipate such a resurgence of confrontation with key LDCs over North-South issues in the next three to five years? And, if so, should it be feared?

The answer to the first question is almost certainly "yes," especially from a policy planning perspective. The Reagan administration is presently viewed, as an LDC foreign minister recently told me, "as downright insensitive to the problems of the developing countries." After factoring out "aid" for "developing" countries that really don't need it (e.g., Israel), the U.S. foreign assistance budget is lower today— and buys less for LDCs—than ever before. In addition, the Reagan administration has opposed creation of a World Bank energy affiliate to fund LDC energy development programs, cut its support to all multilateral development banks, refused to sign the Law of the Sea Treaty, and repeatedly signaled its disdain for starting global negotiations with the LDCs that the latter pressed for at the Cancun summit.

But present aid budgets and policy priorities reflect a deeper mood in American politics that is likely to outlast Ronald Reagan. LDC aid, or even the case for a basic human needs approach, is not going to receive high priority in Washington, probably, for the the remainder of this decade. So the developing countries will continue to have a *causus belli* against America that will lead them to oppose the U.S. when and where they can (e.g., in the UN) and to renew their pressure for the NIEO in appropriate multilateral forums (e.g., the General Assembly, UNCTAD). This state of affairs would exist even if LDC development prospects were bright because—and here is the important point for policy purposes—such confrontation is a *political reaction* to American decisions and priorities rather than to the so-called "objective conditions" that NIEO true believers and activists hold responsible for world poverty. As such, the problem for the foreseeable future is as much American policy (and the domestic political constraints shaping it) as it is the gap between the rich and the poor countries per se.

Confrontation with the U.S. is also likely to be encouraged by the attitudes, overtures, and actions of our OECD partners. For as U.S. policy toward LDC demands has hardened, our European and Japanese allies have sought to strike an even more responsive posture. It makes good political sense (at home and abroad) to be seen lecturing American presidents on the importance of taking the NIEO seriously, and European leaders especially have sought to use such rhetoric to win commercial advantages over U.S. firms for their citizens' business enterprises in the Third World.

So, in short, the seeds of confrontation have a fertile soil in which to germinate for the rest of this decade.

The specific causes of conflict are difficult to anticipate and the consequences for U.S. interests are, therefore, harder to forecast. Hence it is less easy to answer the second question posed above.

There *are* good and sufficient reasons to fear—and to try

to avoid—a resurgence of confrontation in North-South relations. U.S. power projection capabilities now depend, for example, on the good will of LDCs (who host training exercises and provide military facilities essential to U.S. security in response to crises) who have played activist (and anti–U.S.) roles in the North-South dialogue before (e.g., Egypt and the Philippines). There is always the specter of another oil embargo, and there is a growing potential for (significant, albeit temporary) squeezes in other critical imported minerals to be denied the U.S. in time of extraordinary need. Finally, LDCs could soften their policies on terrorism and, coupled to the PLO diaspora, this could pose very direct and bloody threats to the personal security of Americans worldwide.

At a minimum, therefore, the present administration should rethink its policies toward the Third World for the simple reason that it would be in our own self-interest—in economic, moral, and security terms—to do so.

The hallmark of such a policy should be a strategy aimed not at the redistribution of wealth (à la NIEO) but at its generation, as called for recently by David Rockefeller in a key speech before the Council on Foreign Relations.[8] Making this the object of policy, moreover, invests arguments over such matters as the appropriateness of bilateral versus multilateral aid agencies, or the setting of targets for official development assistance, or the reduction of nontarrif barriers to trade, with considerably less importance and would reduce substantially the significance, if not the potential, for confrontation.

The future of North-South relations thus depends on two elements. One is pragmatism on the part of the LDCs themselves—and this seems to be emerging. The other is U.S. policy. American initiatives aimed at generating wealth now could help assure that the developing nations continue to absorb U.S. exports and that the U.S. will not be whipsawed politically by European and Japanese rhetorical strategies in North-South negotiations.

If the stage could thus be set for more down-to-earth discussions with the LDCs, where should such bargaining take place? The chief implications of this analysis are that efforts to achieve greater industrialized-country control over the present mechanisms of the North-South dialogue (e.g., UNCTAD, the UN "overview mechanism," and the General Assembly itself) will only further enshrine the myths described above. This would, in turn, virtually assure the tendency on the part of most LDCs to continue to support a bloc politics approach, and protract the search for less-politicized ways to negotiate with the industrialized countries. Hence, what is most needed now in North-South relations are initiatives, by industrialized and developing countries alike, to change the venues in which LDC demands are surfaced and negotiated.

Promising starts have already been made toward transforming the North-South dialogue from a confrontation into a meaningful discussion of complex economic and political issues. Among these, the following stand out in terms of the pragmatic directions taken: the creation of the International Fund for Agricultural Development and the Association for Southeast Asian Nations (ASEAN); consultations with the United States, Japan, and the European Economic Community; the expansion of the soft-loan windows of the regional development banks; and the individual commodity negotiations taking place at Geneva. But these efforts are hampered, in part, by the currency given to the myths described in this chapter, and by the tendency among some LDCs to equate compromise and accommodation with industrialized countries at this level with selling out G–77 interests as a whole. Tactically, the industrialized countries should divest these myths and presumptions of their self-fulfilling character. However, the future of North-South negotiations will depend to a large extent on what the LDCs do themselves to establish priorities. Only in part will it depend on the willingness of the industrialized countries to take policy initiatives to create a new international and economic order—and those initiatives must be based on the realities of the need for an effective dialogue with countries whose outlook and development prospects are vastly different from ours.

II

Social and Economic
Realities

4

DENNIS AUSTIN

Prospero's Island

Belief in the existence of a "Third World" is now almost an article of faith. Like most beliefs, it is held doctrinally under one form, but in practice under quite another. There are not three worlds but two, a developed world and an under-developed world—a world of those who have and those who have not. The haves not only possess more goods; they have a richer life, enjoying political stability, old age, full stomachs, freedom from anarchy, warm houses in winter, cool homes in summer, the advantage of travel, and the marvels of tech-nology. Such are the attributes of the developed world, whether under capitalist or Communist rule, whereas those categorized as "Third World countries" suffer fearfully by comparison.

As with most faiths, there have been definitional amendments; there are now a number of subdivisions within the circle of description of the first United Nations Conference on Trade and Development (UNCTAD).[1] Yet despite the qualifications, the dogma persists that a sharp line divides the powerful and dependent, rich and poor, bad and good. What began as economics has widened into political economy, politics , and morality, but still the shadow line between the developed and underdeveloped worlds is maintained in conference declarations and popular reference.

So widespread a conviction must reflect more than the obvious difference between, say, California and Papua New Guinea. It seeks to divide the world between light and dark. Any myth of that nature has great power, although (like all myths) it has grown and changed in the making. More than twenty years ago, the French scholar Manoni noted that this division is marvelously represented by the characters in Shakespeare's *The Tempest*.[2] Prospero, the exiled noble, takes flight to an island state where he encounters Caliban and Ariel, who represent, respectively, the materialistic or appetitive and the spiritualistic or virtuous sides of human nature. This presents a problem to Prospero, who wishes to use his time on the island to refine his skills at governing so as to return to his native Milan. Caliban will serve any master who exercises a strong will and satisfies his material desires. Ariel, on the other hand, is unmoved by threat of reprisal or material reward; he seeks the less easily supplied reward of freedom. Prospero's dilemma—resolved only through magic—is to rule over both men in a coherent fashion. The dilemma is ultimately resolved only when Prospero returns to Milan, Ariel goes free, and Caliban once again rules his small island, his own king and his only subject.

But within the tormented pattern of relationships among twentieth-century governments there is no such easy end to the problem of dependency between the rich and the poor, the powerful and the vulnerable. Prospero's island has become the world. And the myths, too, have been enlarged. As the colonial world dissolved in the 1950s, a dualistic view of the new international order reappeared in the United States and the Soviet Union. It was as if the old Ariel-Caliban division within the colonial territories had been internationalized and indeed made worse by rival Prosperos trying to weave their spells from Washington and Moscow. There was the same neurotic projection onto the weak of the fears and dreams of the powerful.

By the 1960s, however, the doctrine had put out new forms. The configuration of good and bad had changed again. Caliban and Ariel (however defined) had begun to join forces. Or so, at least, it was assumed. And it is true that a number of Asian, African, Caribbean, and Latin American governments, dispirited by lack of success in controlling their own societies, moved bad-temperedly towards the assertion that the rich and powerful were all culpable. A continued interdependence between the money and markets of the wealthy and the resources of the poor added to that exasperation, and the effect is now plain to see. We are regularly presented internationally with what is loosely described as a North/South, or a non–Third World/Third World, or a haves/have-nots division.

The distinction is confirmed among the generous-hearted young by a kind of paper radicalism that, crudely expressed, states: the Third World is poor because it is dependent, helpless because it is poor, and blameless because it cannot help itself. The belief rests comfortably on a number of related dogmas—for example, that although African and Asian governments buy arms to fight local wars and to maintain internal control, they are enticed to purchase them by the governments of the industrial nations, among whom the dynamics of growth and surplus wealth are predicated on the dependence of others. It is also recognized that Third World societies are often governed corruptly; but that too, it is said, comes from the dislocation inflicted by colonial rule or from the intrusion of foreign capital. Even the bloody tyrants among their leaders—Amin, Bokassa, the archetypal Papa Doc (and more recently his son, Baby Doc), or the more brutal of the Latin American dictators—can be explained away as atavistic reactions to the need for a national self-assertion against the past, quite apart from the fact that many of them are propped up from outside: by the United States, the Soviet Union, the French, the International Monetary Fund (IMF).

It is easy to understand why such a dualism is endorsed. It projects a simple picture of the whole globe, including the moral helplessness of the poor—an easier view than that of a changing, multiple, uncertain world of the not quite good and the not very bad, or the more or less wealthy and the more or less poor. Moreover, dependency is not only exculpatory. It *transfers* the blame, and it ties in neatly with the allied belief that all would be well if only this or that particular obstacle, beyond one's immediate grasp, were to be removed. Those who lack power can actually take comfort, therefore, from their impotence. Since it is beyond their capacity to change the world, they need only demand action by others. At their most romantic, such arguments reflect a deep sentiment of longing, a longing for Prospero's island without Prospero and the computations of wealth and power. The world, it is said, must be remade until a new international order emerges, transformed by a radical restructuring of its society and economy, within which there will be neither wealth nor poverty, neither power nor dependence. Then, and only then, will Prospero and Caliban, and even Ariel, be changed into self-reliant creatures, and man will cease to be a capitalist wolf to his fellow men.

So runs the creed. And even the industrial rich have been half-persuaded in public declarations, if not of their guilt, at least of their need to respond to such assertions—in marked contrast, one might note, from earlier, more robust beliefs. It has not been very long since it was argued that the world could be put right politically—and enabled to grow economically—not by expiation, but by imitation. The formulae varied, but the confidence was there. Newly independent countries had only to adopt the Westminster Constitution, or accept La République Francaise, or turn Communist, or listen to Washington or the IMF, in order to follow in the wake of the successful. That kind of optimism is gone but for a few of the party faithful in Moscow and the more devout partisans of the Carter administration. To each, then, today, his own political culture. But it is still possible, it seems, to believe that all poor are one poor, and all the rich are culpable.

The actual effect of such a belief has been very bad. It has produced a crude, distorted picture of the world of sovereign governments. It ignores the diversity of states even within those that pass for the founding members of the Third World. Its rigid fixity also leaves out the politics not of dependency but of morality, avoiding the awkward fact that the desperately poor and extravagantly rich are as likely to be found within a single state as in the division between states, and that the crude and the tolerant are at opposite ends of a broad spectrum of new and old states alike. And it posits a loose kind of international morality that a number of uneasily based governments have used as cover for their own deficiencies at home. Underlying the distortion, there is a disregard of the capacity for ameliorative change among non-European societies—perhaps a residual belief still in Prospero's magic? In short, there has been an old-fashioned and an ill-fashioned look to such arguments.

The distortion also lacks substance. Even without such subcategories as the oil-rich and oil-poor countries, there was always something very odd about a dualism that omitted the huge fact of China—powerful, poor, nondependent, and immensely distinct by its long history and self-contained culture, yet no longer able to be left out of any full view of an international order. Nor have the imprecise boundaries of a

Third World, however modified, been able to take proper account, in or out, of a number of intermediate countries such
as Turkey or Israel or South Korea or Iran and the poorer
Communist states. (By 1977 Cuba, for example, was numbered among the members of a New International Economic
Order, Albania was not.) *Exceptiones probant regulas?*
Perhaps. Yet even among the central core of the Third
World, the former colonies that have been independent only
since World War II (though Latin America is a huge exception to *that*), the range of political experience and economic
attainment has been very wide. The difficulty of attaching a
single label to whatever is meant by such a category can be
seen by examining the indices generally adopted.

Colonial Rule

Only a generation or so ago colonial governments were internationally recognized as sovereign and legally administered;
but as colonial control was surrendered in the 1950s and
1960s, the postcolonial differences became marked. It was
hardly surprising. Colonialism had been diverse, different in
its British or French, Belgian, Dutch, or Portuguese settings;
distinct also from one part of the globe to another, even within the same empire. It was molded to—and by—the pattern
of local culture. French rule in Algeria was not only unlike
that of Belgium in the Congo, but also unlike French control
of Indochina; British rule in Barbados was different from its
administration of Kenya or Sri Lanka or Cyprus. Only from
the commanding heights of Marxist theory, or a simple
American morality, could colonialism be seen as an undifferentiated phenomenon. The distinctions have widened
into sharp contrasts now that European empires (and the
shorter-lived Japanese and American possessions) have
come to an end. A good deal has happened since independence to accentuate the differences, including civil wars,
coups d' etat, the rise and fall of particular leaders, changes
in commodity prices, and the change from old to new patrons.

It is a mistake to put too much stress on continuity in history. Politically, before-independence was unlike after-independence in one critical aspect: namely, that rule by foreigners is always different from government from within one's own society. Form, too, is different from content. Whatever the similarities, there has frequently been a sharp political contrast between a colonial administration and its nationalist successors. The former was an intrusion, however locally devoted its officers might have been to those over whom they ruled. They were always a foreign elite, banded together under the governor as much by a code of colonial behavior as by instructions, and although there might have been some backsliding—"going native"—they were, as Kipling portrayed them in India, always a disciplined hierarchy. It was not the lawlessness but the *law* of the jungle that ruled their conduct as a set of guardians whose strength lay in the pack.

> Now these are the Laws of the Jungle, and many and mighty are they;
> But the head and the hoof of the Law and the haunch and the hump is—Obey.

Their nationalist successors have no such code of ethics or surety of racial solidarity. They are party or military leaders who retain control by exercising power over their own kind. The difference can be sharply expressed at its extreme by noting that no governor ever hanged one of his colonial officers, whereas Nkrumah in Ghana imprisoned his own party colleagues, and Idi Amin in Uganda beat to death civil servants, judges, university teachers, and his fellow army officers alike. One needs to be careful when looking at the persistence of colonial characteristics to note also the interruption of the legacy or, more truly, the new departures as well as the old continuities.

Colonial rule, therefore, is a "variable" in the experience of many new states. On the one hand, the effect is now a diminishing force. On the other, it has bequeathed different legacies. For there must be some carry-over from the past, however attenuated. The long history of British rule in Barbados has preserved an unbroken structure of parliamentary government since 1626. The gruesome quality of Leopold's misrule in the Congo, though redeemed by government from Brussels, pointed the way forward to Mobutu's Zaire, where it frequently seems as if time has not simply stopped but turned back, its local forces in rebellion, and large tracts of the eastern and southern provinces

> . . . a darkling plain
> Swept with confused alarms of struggle and fight
> Where ignorant armies clash by night.

Artificiality

At a more abstract level of expression, it is sometimes argued that an overriding characteristic of Third World states is that they are flawed by communal division. They bear the stamp of artificiality. They lack, it is said, identity. The result is that national loyalties are weak and without any strong center of allegiance. They may include old societies, but for the most part they are new states. No wonder, therefore, that the location of political authority is uncertain and that, in consequence, institutions and procedures fail to command respect.

There is a good deal of truth in such descriptions. Yet even among countries generally singled out as "Third World," variations in the degree of heterogeneity, whether of an ethnic, religious, racial, or linguistic nature, and in the relative strength of national loyalties, are also notable. Nor can it easily be said that diversity breeds instability and/or political coercion. If that were so, Sri Lanka would be less liberal and less steady than, say, Turkey or Libya. And that is certainly not the case. Malaysia, too, is plural and relatively noncoercive; Uganda is plural and murderous. Of course, at the extremes, as in Lebanon or Cyprus, where local conflicts are reinforced from outside, communal division and political collapse are clearly linked.

But the growing literature on pluralism does not point easily in any direction, nor can it isolate a category of states even nominally "Third World" in character. One might argue that India, for example, has a sufficient historical identity, both colonially rooted and precolonially derived, and is sufficiently self-aware as a political community, to maintain free institutions; at least it has kept the military at bay and has changed its politics without massive violence. Yet Egypt—a very ancient state—is constantly and precariously poised between order and breakdown. Nor is there any clear demarcation between industrial and nonindustrial states in this respect. The politics of ethnicity have plagued states that might be thought to have the resources to cope with the problem: Belgium, Canada, the United Kingdom (of which Ulster is still a part), France, and substantial urban areas of the United States.

Resources

Between Prospero and the Calibans and Ariels, it is assumed, there lies not only power, but the wealth on which power is based and from which the comfortable life of the industrialized nations is derived. It is certainly true that many Asian and African states are poor, particularly those affected by drought and famine. But the economic range between extreme poverty and quite substantial wealth among nonindustrial states is very striking: Gabon is oil-rich beyond the dreams of Lesotho; Jamaica and Kenya are far wealthier than Rwanda and Upper Volta. Even within the literature of dependence, there are MDCs and LDCs—more- and less-developed countries. Even the dependent poor have weaker and poorer states dependent on them, just as the rich have the not-so-rich dependent on *them*. The bland assertion

that there is a Third World unable to break the bonds of a
world economy that holds it in thrall—in the grip of growth
without development, or within an enclave economy of
benefit only to a parasitical state bourgeoisie—makes little
allowance for the relatively well off (Venezuela, the Ivory
Coast, Malaysia), and no allowance at all for the very successful (Singapore, South Korea, Hong Kong, the ex-colonies
of New Zealand and Australia, or the once politically stunted
and feudal Japan).

The Japanese are, indeed, a remarkable example of those
who convert feudal rags into industrial riches. In 1847 an official of the emperor informed a persistent Dutch envoy that
"His Majesty charges us to inform you that it is of but slight
importance to the Empire of Japan whether foreigners come
or do not come to trade." By 1853 Commodore Perry had
forced upon a reluctant shogunate the market economy of
the West. But still the British shook their heads in sorrow,
because "for nearly two centuries and a half Japan had been
cut off from the atmosphere of competition, and had never
had the opportunity of warming her intelligence at the fire of
international rivalry." Who is getting scorched today? By
the 1970s British ministers were flying to Tokyo to ask for a
curtailment of exports into Western Europe. A reversal
of dependencies?

It has been argued that it was easier in the nineteenth century for the non-Western world to catch up and overtake. But
there are late twentieth-century states, particularly in the
Pacific Basin, that are both dependent and becoming dominant. They, too, are busily "indigenizing," in the sense of
bringing into one national economy the duality of domestic
and foreign sectors. Japan is ceasing to be singular. Other
Asian countries, notably South Korea, Singapore, Taiwan,
and Hong Kong, have begun to frighten the life out of older
industrial nations. South Korea has even managed to alarm
the Japanese by its combination of low wage costs and
modern technology in texiles, shipbuilding, electronics, steel,

and petrochemicals.³ It is hardly a question of Caliban and Ariel distancing themselves from Prospero, but of their capturing and using his skills against him.

There is, to be sure, a distinction between totally managed economies and those in which private wealth is allowed to have its say. When the state is all-powerful, one may fear that the cruel and strong will seek not wealth but power; where mixed economies sustain the state, it may be, as Keynes observed, that "dangerous human proclivities can be canalised into comparatively harmless channels by the existence of opportunities for money-making and private wealth. . . . It is better that a man should tyrannise over his bank balance than over his fellow citizens."⁴ But that has nothing to do with contrasts between Third World and industrial countries. Between the worship of power, leading to tyranny, and the worship of riches within a privileged elite, lies the entire spectrum of states that comprise the present international system—not a dualistic world of those with, and those without, resources.

What should be done, then, about the many desperately poor who lack resources, power, and skills? No one seems to know. El Salvador and Tanzania are unlikely to reach the level of the Ivory Coast or Kenya, neither of which can as yet hope to rival Trinidad, nor can Trinidad equal Singapore and Taiwan. Within the present century, it is inconceivable that the huge disparities between the poorest of the poor and the very prosperous can be diminished more than just a little by an intelligent and generous use of the power of the latter. Whether that small amount of progress is best done by market access, un-tied aid, commodity agreements, or a different pricing mechanism in petroleum products is a matter for argument in each instance. But simply to divide the world between an apocryphal Third World and the non–Third World is no help at all. It is likely to conceal the plight of the worst. Hence the subdivision into the "less developed," although even that is a crude categorization, since the very poor are often more dependent on the poor than on the rich.⁵

Political Order

It is easy enough to conjure up a Third World of tormented
states and an industrial world of steady societies under firm
political control, although such an image ignores a whole
area of recent argument concerning the ungovernability of
industrial and postindustrial states, and there must be few
who see Italy in the 1970s and 1980s as under firm control.
Still, it is true enough that many of the recently independent
states and most Latin American societies are badly governed. It is certainly a singular fact that no independent
government, in all the fifty or more states of the African continent, has been removed from office by an election alone; it
is rather by the army or an assassin that such change occurs.

Yet the picture is not quite so unrelieved. Such general
phrases as "the instability of the Third World" may give too
permanent a title to what may be a passing phenomenon. If a
single explanation of the present unsettled pattern of military coups and successful governments were needed, I would
not emphasize the paucity of resources, or the effect of dependency on multinational companies and distant agencies
of control. After all, a society or state may be held in a steady
subservience, as one might say of Liberia under former president Tubman. Poverty, too, may immobilize a society and
confirm one or another section of its rulers in power by
passivity, as might be said of Upper Volta.

No, I would argue that the breakdown of authority in many
new states, and its broken-backed misrule, are due primarily
to novelty—the novelty of elites and their nervous in-
capacity in office.

In the broadest sense possible, the effect of the dissolution
of a major empire is invariably calamitous. It leaves behind
an uncertainty about successors and the institutions they in-
herit. The "proof," so to speak, may be seen by the avoidance
of breakdown when the last-hour efforts of the imperial
power have been more successful than elsewhere, as in the

Ivory Coast under French rule, or Ceylon under the British. But time may repair the omission even among the most unsuccessful, as leaders become established as ruling elites or even as classes, some tolerant, some brutal. To put the matter crudely: if Africa and Asia cannot settle down to their inheritance of colonial procedures and institutions, they may yet settle down to tyranny. Stability is an ambiguous virtue. The regime of Papa Doc at one extreme, and that of Stalin at another, were both, in a sense, "stable." But that, too, is oversimple. The variety of political experience is bound to be as complicated politically throughout the former colonial states as it is likely to be in relation to economic performance. Already, a number of such governments, including those commonly seen as controlling Third World countries, have preserved a relatively peaceful continuity under changes of regime: India, Malaysia, Jamaica, Costa Rica, Colombia, Fiji, Sri Lanka.

Nor is it at all certain that the world of industrialized states will remain politically steady. They may take any loss of wealth harder than others. He that is down need fear no fall. It is perhaps the rich, not the poor, who are at risk. The little state of The Gambia is dependent, without resources, ex-colonial, ethnically divided, and overshadowed by its neighbors; yet its half-million citizens have a freedom of political expression, a steady government, and civil liberties very different from the history of many richer, more tormented states. Naturally, it would be helpful if across the world — Third, Fourth, First, and Second alike — there were ancient traditions harmoniously related to the present, a benign period of political history, adequate resources, a clear location of power, skillful leaders of clear moral perception, and a close identity between citizens and state. The world unfortunately is not like that at all, and, even if it were, the sinfulness of civic man might still corrupt it. The future is much more likely to reflect the past — an unsure pattern of confident as well as sickly governments, strong as well as feeble regimes. All history in this sense is the history of uncertainty.

It is in respect of morality—political morality—that one can actually bring back a division of the good and the bad, not in relation to dependency and power, or wealth and poverty, or old and new states, but between liberty and oppression. If a dualistic picture of the world were needed, I would take what might be called "the view from Amnesty," and the sight of that political landscape would soon put to rest the assertions that the wealthy are democratic because they are rich, or that the dependent are brutal because they are poor, as if political freedom were a commodity that went only to the highest bidder.

The View from Amnesty

One does not have to be so simple as to believe in the totality of darkness on one side and the purity of light on the other. There are no unreservedly good governments, though there may be unredeemably bad ones. The moral yardstick that can be used is plain enough: the number of political prisoners and the use of torture; freedom from imprisonment without trial (of rich and poor, political and nonpolitical alike); and the right to own and freely use a passport.

Very few states, indeed, grant such rights today. How many are being tortured in the prisons of the Soviet Union or Cambodia, South Africa, Uganda, South Yemen, Chile, Vietnam? It does not matter whether the jailer and the prisoner, or the torturer and the tortured, are rich or poor, or white or black or piebald. The greatest evil of this century occurred in an industrial country of Western Europe, that same country from which the most passionate expression of freedom had been heard a century earlier. Nor would it be difficult to group together those states where there are no political prisoners, no dark cellars or closed rooms where men and women scream out in pain. A single postage stamp would bring a list of the not-too-bad and the atrocious from the headquarters of Amnesty International.

Its *Annual Reports* make grim reading. They tell of man's political cruelty, and no distinction is drawn between one part of the world and another. The picture is too bleak to be divided into North and South, or between "the rich and the bad" and "the poor who can't help it." The introduction to the 1977 report states quite simply: "As many as 117 countries are mentioned in this publication. In most of them serious violations of human rights have been reported. . . . Government-sanctioned torture is still practised in a horrifying number of states in spite of the newly adopted U.N. Declaration against all forms of torture."

Torture is the vilest crime, under practices of medieval barbarity. But there are other cruelties, including the policy adopted by some Latin American governments of destroying all traces of their victims—"disappearance"; or long periods of solitary imprisonment without trial in a number of Asian countries; or the legal base of state victimization in the Soviet Union. As the same report states: "Human rights are violated in a majority of countries all over the world. All major regions, all political or ideological blocs are involved—in spite of the Universal Declaration of Human Rights." Countries are described one by one, from which it appears that

the techniques of repression and the impact of these techniques vary. There are differences not only in number of victims, but also in methodology, objectives, duration and both short-term and long-term consequences. In some countries, regimes allow para-military groups to kidnap, torture and assassinate political activists; in others prisoners are kept in detention for years without trial. In some police stations torture is carried out with electric shocks; in others with psychological methods. In some prisons the inmates are refused all communication with their families; in others they are starved. There is absolutely no point in trying to judge which measures are categorically "better" or "worse" than others. Similarly it would be a misleading exercise to grade or rank regimes. In the end, what matters is the pain and suffering the individual endures in the police station or in the cell.

There is also no point in defining the worst, if only because the view from Amnesty is incomplete. Some countries are cleverer than others at concealing their crimes. "Amnesty International has carefully monitored all available information from North Korea and can only report that it contains no detailed evidence whatsoever regarding arrests, trials and imprisonment. . . . There appears to be a complete censorship of news relating to human rights."

The descriptions, country by country, are calm and precise, and—as if it were not so grim a catalogue of horrors—almost schoolmasterly in tone, in the fashion of end-of-term reports. "Generally, Burundi appears to have settled down to a period of relative stability and reconciliation after the massacre and huge exodus of Hutu refugees during 1972." Tanzania, it is interesting to note, does not appear at all favorably. The level of coercion has risen, and there are "reports of torture still being carried out," in marked contrast with Kenya where, at the time of the 1977 report, the "total number of detainees is probably less than 10." Even so, there are much worse countries: Ethiopia, Cambodia, Guatemala, Chile, and South Africa.[6]

Interestingly enough, such lists can be seen as constantly changing over time, although some countries remain steadily at the freer end of the scale, others no less steadily at the oppressive end. There is a broad middle band along which there is a good deal of movement, oppressive regimes becoming less oppressive (India, Greece, Venezuela, Sri Lanka), and others moving up the scale of oppression (Sierra Leone, Tanzania, Burma, Bangladesh). Some have state-controlled economies; others, a mixed economy. But the bad and the not-so-bad are to be found in both camps. Size is not important; Nigeria is politically free to an extent unknown in South Africa or China. Barbados is a small free island a whole world apart from Haiti, or even Grenada.

Nor is wealth, or poverty of resources, a conclusive factor. That *is* a little surprising, perhaps, since a general belief in the freedom bestowed by wealth is commonly expressed. Get rid, it is often said, of unemployment, or ghetto housing, or famine, or disease, and you will enable not only citizens to trust their governments, but rulers to elicit support without coercion. In other words, if all the world were as rich as Scandinavia, humanity would be as free from torture and arbitrary rule as Sweden. Well, perhaps. Yet I would not swear to it. Over the past century, the industrial states have been murderously cruel to each other: war, gas chambers, and concentration camps have destroyed far more human beings than have the feeble attempts of many non-Western, non-Communist states.

Nor does there seem to be any direct correspondence between wealth on one side and freedom from internal oppression on the other. The Soviet Union is comparatively wealthy; India is relatively unoppressive, and the poverty of India did not prevent a move back in 1977 towards a less authoritarian regime. Of course, poverty itself is oppressive. But who is to say that political oppression is a counterweight to the burden of poverty? It is very often not a remedy for economic distress but an added trial, and not infrequently an additional source of economic misery.

It was neither poverty, nor dependence, but inflation that moved the politics of Latin America further toward dictatorship and toward the would-be populist dictators who raised the level of inflation. Nor, in this respect, have all the Latin American countries moved in the same direction. Nicaragua and Costa Rica might be thought to be in much the same category of "Third World dependence"; yet the former is brutally governed by a coalition at war with itself, and the latter is an open society free from prisoners and torture. From the lofty height of theory, the difference may not be very important. But it must matter a good deal to Costa Ricans and Nicaraguans.

There is, to be sure, an authoritarian argument, used by radical and conservative critics alike, that defends the need to place order above justice, based on the belief that disorder may be worse than injustice. Left-wing critics use the argument to "defend the revolution"; conservative writers uphold the belief in order to avoid anarchy. If states without justice are robbers, are not societies without obedience murderous? But there is an extremism about such aphorisms that is often the ground for more injustice, more enforced obedience, and more authority than are needed. *Sub specie aeternitatis,* as saints and poets have told us, good and evil may be the opposite sides of the same coin of a divine order imperfectly understood by men. Dante could place above the Gates of Hell the inscription:

> FECEMI LA DIVINA POTESTATE
> LA SOMMA SAPIENZA E IL PRIMO AMORE.*

But, brought to earth, the divinity of love is all too quickly corrupted to a state religion of necessity, and a placing of party slogans above the labor correction camps. In this temporal world of political uncertainties on Prospero's island, we have to choose, and the "view from Amnesty" may help us to see a little more closely the not-so-good and the very bad.

Exactly why the view of the world should be as it is— frightening in one direction, often comforting in another— is a great puzzle. Why should Botswana be very poor and politically tolerant, the Soviet Union technically advanced and politically brutal? Why is Taiwan dependent and prosperous, Burma much poorer and less dependent? In many ways, such questions are so wide as to be meaningless. Even if one is talking only the economics of trade access and debt cancellations, the boundaries of the Third World are stretched beyond definition. When S. Rajaratnam, foreign minister of Singapore, could say, "We the poorer countries [must be] willing to practice the old-fashioned virtues of hard work, thrift and sacrifice,"[7] he was a long way from Niger or the

---

Sacred justice moved my architect
I was raised here by divine love.

Solomon Islands. There are too many differences to sustain the comparison.

But that is precisely the difficulty of talking loosely about the Third World or a New International Economic Order (NIEO). Nor can it be sensible for the 77 or 99 or 106 countries to go on acting as if the world were a dyad or triad. The effort to achieve a collective will defeats its purpose. Only when there are relatively clear common interests, as among the oil-producing states, is there likely to be the strength of joint action—and even those states have had to struggle to preserve a common policy. The recent and abortive meeting of what were once said to be "nonaligned countries" is a good illustration of the worn-out inutility of beliefs that try to separate the world into divided camps. But it is primarily on grounds of misconception that it is surely time to discard outworn arguments about a Third World and its subdivisions, or a North-South division of the globe.

Prospero's island is now too crowded and too complicated to bring all its difficulties under a pseudodoctrine based on a belief that, since it no longer carries conviction, dangerously darkens counsel.

5

S. E. FINER

The Military and Politics in the Third World

Armed force is the single most important political actor in the Third World. Nearly half of the countries in the developing world are ruled by military nominees, and in most of the remaining states, only the military stands between the regime and its downfall.

So much for today: but what of the future? Over the last twenty years one military coup has followed another at the average rate of some eight per annum. This rhythm, remarkably steady from year to year, shows no sign of slackening. Indeed, 1981 showed a record figure of no fewer than eleven military coups.

Yet, on the other hand, we find some individual countries where after decades of military intervention there has come a long period of calm. Mexico witnessed one thousand *pronunciamentos* in its first century, but it experienced its last — and unsuccessful — uprising in 1938. Venezuela, which suffered fifty armed revolts in the first century and a half of its history, has been a civilian state for the last twenty years. And even Syria, which experienced fourteen military coups between its independence in 1946 and 1970, has seen no more of them since. May these isolated instances soon come to apply to all developing countries? If the armed forces return to the barracks, what kinds of regimes will they bequeath? And, again, does it matter whether they stay or return to the barracks? Will it make a substantial difference to the material and moral circumstances of their peoples?

To explore these questions, first we shall lay out the bare facts. Secondly, we will examine the claims made in favor of military regimes, whether by sympathetic academics or by the regimes themselves. Only then shall we be able to address ourselves to the questions stated above and turn to the prospects for the future.

Military Intervention in the Third World

Almost all the Third World states are ex-colonies of European powers. There are indeed a handful of very old states like Iran, Thailand, or Yemen that were never formally colonized by the Europeans but that, in the age of imperialism, were either dominated or controlled by them. There are also the 20 Latin American republics that, although certainly ex-colonies of Spain or Portugal or France, became independent about 150 years ago: they are "old" states by today's standards. The great majority of Third World states are, however, the fallout of the European empires after 1945. As of January 1982, there are 127 states in the Third World (including China), and 20 of these are the Latin American ones. Of the 106 states (excluding China) that remain, 86 attained their independence after 1945. Sixteen became independent in 1945—55; 38 in 1956—65; 23 in 1966—75; and 9 new states arose in the 1976—81 period.

If a first striking characteristic of the Third World is that it is overwhelmingly ex-colonial, and a second is that it is predominantly a post-1945 creation, the third is that politically, most of its component states started their independent lives under some variant of the Western-style, party-competitive, representative government system. The exceptions are few and, paradoxically, lie at opposite ends of the scale: the revolutionary regimes (North Korea, North Vietnam, Guinea, Burma, Algeria, followed by Cuba [1959] and then, in the 1970s, Vietnam, Laos, Cambodia, Angola, São Tomé, Mozambique, and Guinea-Bissau) on the one hand; and on the other the traditional monarchies (Saudi Arabia, which has been joined in the late 1960s and early 1970s by the monarchies, sultanates, and emirates of the Persian Gulf). The remainder, some 100 states, started off with the Western constitutional and party-competitive model. (This includes Morocco and Jordan, which are supposedly "constitutional" monarchies.) The traditional monarchies and the revolutionary regimes are unashamedly authoritarian in theory and in practice. In contrast, the remainder began as democratic, representative, and constitutional states. So we come to the fourth striking characteristic of the Third World: in perhaps three-quarters of its component states, the liberal democratic order has been swept away and, in one form or another, a tyranny has been installed in its stead.

This has come about by three main channels. In a few cases the duly elected authorities have declared a state of emergency and under cover of this have suspended political activity and individual freedoms. Whereas in the cases of India and Sri Lanka such constitutional emergencies were of limited duration (and these two states have reverted to constitutional rule), the Philippines provides a striking example of a country in which a constitutionally elected civilian ruler has suspended the constitution and has maintained himself in office through martial law. President Marcos is a civilian and has surrounded himself with civilians, and his repression is carried out chiefly through the paramilitary constabulary rather than the regular army. But apart from this, for all practical purposes his rule is not dissimilar from that of the most autocratic of the military regimes.

More numerous, but still limited in number, are the states where the competition of parties has been suppressed in favor of a single official party, as in the Ivory Coast, Senegal, Zambia, Malawi, Kenya, or Tanzania. The first characteristic of these regimes is that they are unquestionably civilian, but the second—the operative role of the single party—is much more problematical. In Tanzania the party has a real rather than a token significance; in the Ivory Coast it has long ossified, to become a mere dues-collecting and legitimizing device for the president and his chosen advisors.

The principal way in which liberal democracy has been subverted in the Third World, however, is by military intervention.

Here we must beware. Military intervention in politics is not necessarily illegal or violent; it can and does take place at a number of levels. Even in the best-ordered civilian polities the military will have a view to express, and they may move into the gray area where "advice" becomes "pressure": the "advice" will be backed by some kind of sanction, e.g., threats of resignation by the heads of the armed services if their opinion is not followed. Clearly, the more the regime is dependent on civil military support for its survival, the more influential the advice of the military is likely to be. Beyond "pressure" lies *blackmail*—the threat to withhold armed support for a government that is being pressed out of office by dissident forces in the country, for instance. Beyond such blackmail lies the overt *threat:* unless the military's advice is followed, it will use violence against the government. And beyond threat lies the *coup:* by a show of violence the military removes the government and installs another—which may be another civilian government but is much more likely to be a military junta. This last is the military *take-over*.

The military coup, then, is in itself a very conservative indicator of the weight of the military presence on government: much more pressure—but we have no means of knowing how much—is almost certainly being applied behind the scenes. Nevertheless, the number, sequence, and distribution of military coups offer an astounding indicator of the military presence in Third World politics.

Military coups, 1958–1982. We have selected the last quarter-century as the time period for the analysis of military coups in the Third World, in preference to going back to 1945, because it is more representative of world trends. The great proliferation of newly independent states occurred from 1960 onward, not in the 1945–1960 period. Until about 1960, coups that did occur took place almost exclusively in Latin America and in the Arab world, the former (like the two coups that occurred in Thailand during this period) being a continuation of the pre-war trend. From 1958 onward, the spread of coups became much more diversified as the number of independent states rose from 95 in 1958 to 170 at the end of 1981 (almost all of them in Asia and Africa, though recent years have witnessed the multiplication of island mini-states in the Caribbean and South Pacific). From a full list of coups we can derive the following conclusions:

1. The total number of coups (successful and unsuccessful) amounted to 195, or over 8 per year. Of these, only 8 occurred in Europe (including Cyprus as part of Europe), which is in itself a signal proof of the immensely greater vulnerability of the Third World as compared to European and European-type industrialized countries in North America and Australasia. Of the remaining 187 Third World coups, 124 were successful and 63 failed.

2. Analyzed by region, there were 8 coups in Europe, 60 in

Asia (including the Middle East), 45 in Central and South America, and 82 in Africa (including the North African states).

3. However, although the number of coups has continued at a fairly even rate and shows no sign of abating, the number of countries affected by them is much smaller, because some countries have suffered many more than one coup during this period. In all, 8 European states have been affected as opposed to 61 Third World States — 16 in Asia, 31 in Africa, and 14 in Central and South America. Starting from 0 in 1958, the number affected had risen to 19 by the beginning of 1963, 36 by 1968, 45 by 1973, and to the present figure of 61 by January 1982. This last number represents 48 percent of all Third World states.

4. Further, two additional features are worth noting. First, the number of states suffering repeated coups shows a continuous rise (see tables 1 and 2). (This is not simply an artifact of the way the tables are composed; obviously, for example, if the time period is set to begin at 1958, then all the states struck by coups in the 1958−1962 period will appear as "first-timers.") The proportion of the "first-time" states to the total number of military coups launched during a given period is indicated in table 1.

Table 1

Third World States Struck by Coups for the First Time as Percentage of Total Coups, 1958−1981

Period	"First-time" states	Coups	Percentage states to coups
1958−62	19	27	70%
1963−67	18	48	37
1968−72	10	35	29
1973−78	9	41	22
1979−81	5	36	14
Totals	61	187	

Table 2

Third World States Struck by Coups for the First Time Compared with Total Coups, 1973–1981

Year	"First-time" states	Coups
1973	3	6
1974	1	7
1975	2	11
1976	0	7
1977	2	10
1978	1	10
1979	1	8
1980	3	9
1981	1	9

This trend is particularly striking over the past eight years, as indicated in table 2.

The second noteworthy feature is correlated to the first: the distribution of coups to affected states is disproportionate indeed; some states have suffered very large numbers of coups, while others have suffered one or two at most (see table 3).

Table 3

Distribution of Coups per State, 1958–1981

Coups suffered	States affected	Total coups
1	15	15
2	16	32
3	12	36
4	6	24
5	4	20
6	3	18
7	2	14
8	1	8
9	1	9
11	1	11
Totals	61	187

Thus 18 states account for 104 of the coups or 55 percent of the entire total; and there are 8 states that between themselves have accounted for 60 coups, nearly one-third of the total. These extremely coup-prone states are: Bolivia (at 11); Iraq (9); Syria (8); the Sudan and Ghana (7 apiece); and Ecuador, Benin, and Thailand (6 apiece).

One final point is worth remarking. Whether one examines the earlier 1963–1967 period or the latest 1973–1981 period, approximately half the military coups were launched not against a civilian regime, but against one that had already been taken over by the military. This is not surprising: military coups almost always generate military regimes, and by the most conservative estimate, these constitute one-third of all Third World states at present. Before turning to examine them, however, it is necessary to ask why the military intervenes.

The causes and motivations of military intervention. A military coup is, obviously, an act of will. Soldiers must *want* to launch one. In principle, therefore, military coups ought to occur randomly throughout every type of state in the world. But as we have seen, only 8 European states have been affected since 1958 compared with 61 Third World states. This suggests that the explanation for military intervention must be sought as much in the nature of a society as in the outlook and organization of its armed forces. Conditions in some societies are conducive to military intervention, while in others they offer impediments. In the latter, a rational soldiery will not take lightly the chance of intervening, or at least of intervening overtly by a military coup. Sometimes the military is irrational or misjudges the conditions, and in such cases we do indeed find putsches like the Kapp Putsch in Germany in 1920, the Four Generals Revolt in Algeria in 1961, and the abortive coup in Spain in February 1981. On the whole, the conditions for successful takeover do not exist in the industrialized, well-organized, and civically conscious societies of Europe, North America, and Australasia. Nor, in most cases, do the armed forces entertain a wish to take over. For a very long time they have internalized the doctrine of civilian supremacy, and experience shows that a society would have to undergo enormous social convulsions and polarization (as in France during the Algerian crisis of 1958, and more recently in Poland) before affecting the military's view that politics should be left to the politicians. The German High Command did not take over between 1918 and 1933 despite social upheavals, nor did the French military between 1958 and 1961; and these exceptions illustrate the rule. As for Poland, the army's conduct was altogether exceptional, for it was motivated at least as much (I would say, predominantly) by fear of Russian invasion as by concern over the internal situation.

In the first group of societies (those possessing features conducive to military intervention), the probability of coups depends on the motivation and mood of the armed forces; for it must not always be supposed that they are eager to play an active political role. In many Third World countries, where only the support of the military stands between the regime and internal anarchy, the military is politically disengaged; Morocco, Jordan, Colombia, and Nigeria provide examples. But these countries bear a constant risk. The Libyan coup of 1969, for example, may serve as a paradigm. For decades the organized social base of the monarchy—the Senussi Tribe, of which King Idris was the ancient and venerable head—had decayed, leaving no other solid basis of public support. Only the small army stood between the monarchy and its overthrow. Once the army decided to act, which it did in 1969, it took power with a single bold stroke. It is therefore in those states where the societal conditions are conducive, and the military has the motive and capacity to act, that the military coups occur. These two conditions are far more likely to occur in Third World countries than in the industrialized states. What we must ask now is first, what these "conducive" societal conditions comprise, and then, what constitutes the military's motive and capability.

The societal factor. Abstractly (the concrete issues will be introduced shortly, below), what is conducive to military intervention may be summed up as the "absence of organized and public opinion." Where "opinion" does not exist at all or is confined to a tiny and unrepresentative minority, the military—which possesses an advantage over other bodies by virtue of its organization, hierarchy, discipline, intercommunication system, and corporate pride—will be able to impose its will without hindrance; whether it acts or not depends upon its own discretion. This is true even in more advanced political cultures where although an "opinion" may be said to exist, it is unorganized or its organization is very fragile. Moreover, the thesis holds even if such opinion is highly "public," i.e., consensual. But it is still more valid where, on the contrary, this opinion is fragmented and, even worse, polarized; in these conditions the lawlessness and disorder that ensue are likely to tax a civilian government to its limits and induce the military to take over in the name of "law and order."

A vast majority of Third World states are in the former condition (e.g., Equatorial Guinea, Haiti, and the Central African Republic); but there are others that suffer from the opposite form of malady. These are countries where there is indeed an opinion as well as organized political parties, trade unions, agrarian leagues, and the like—but the opinion is bitterly polarized into two uncompromisingly inimical factions. In such circumstances no civilian government, even with the best civic tradition, could hope to survive, because it could support one faction only by drawing on itself the enmity of the other.

The examples of Chile (1973), Pakistan (1977), and Turkey (1980) spring to mind. In these circumstances the military may intervene to support the faction it favors

(Chile), or simply to try to guarantee public order (the original and now abandoned motive of General Zia's intervention in Pakistani politics), or to try to rearrange the political order (Turkey). The second of these roles, that of the neutral arbiter, is well illustrated by the British army in Northern Ireland. In the polarization of Catholic and Protestant extremists in that unhappy country, no civil government can live without being either pro-Catholic or pro-Protestant. Hence the suspension of representative government by the British government and the establishment of a peace-keeping role for the British army. But here, the British civic tradition of civilian supremacy operates and it is to the central cabinet that the army chiefs respond. By contrast, in Third World countries the military itself is both player and referee.

In short, the greater the consensus in a society, and the stronger the width and the organization of that consensus, the less the likelihood that a rational military will contemplate intervention. To find out whether or to what degree the societal conditions are conducive to intervention, or to what extent a state is at risk from its own armed forces, we need to answer two questions:

First, is there a widespread public approbation of the procedures for transferring power, with the corresponding belief that no exercise of power in breach of these procedures is legitimate; and, further, is there a similarly widespread public recognition of who or what organ constitutes the sovereign authority, with the corresponding belief that no other person or organ is legitimate?

Second, is there a political public and how well organized is it into communities or secondary associations such as trade unions, churches, corporations, and political parties?

Note that a positive answer to one question does not necessarily entail a similarly positive answer to the other. In Chile (1973), Pakistan (1977), and Turkey (1980), the political public was strongly organized but sharply polarized. This is true of Argentina today. In such countries the political crisis is *overt*. On the other hand, opinion may be consensual but so weakly organized that the military can move in without hindrance. Opinion that is not merely weak but also self-divided *a fortiori* creates the political preconditions for the coup (i.e., public disorder) as well as potential partisan support from civilians that both legitimates the coup and affords useful allies.

Now most, though not all, of the Third World countries are societies that generate precisely these conditions. On the whole—and we must stress this qualification because we are generalizing about 127 countries ranging from the Comoros and Seychelles to India—political opinion is compartmentalized by the persistence of clans, localism, the hermetic villages, immemorial tradition, the inadequacy of postal road and rail communication, and feeble mass media. Even where opinion does exist, it tends to be weakly organized. The secondary associations, whose integration with the processes of government is an organic feature of the industrialized states, are fluid in the Third World, where the primary group of association, such as family, clan, and regional, religious, or linguistic community, is tough and durable. And these, unlike the secondary associations, are *divisive*. Thus, even where opinion is organized strongly, class, communalism, micronationalism, or some other stratified compartment serves to divide it. Furthermore, most of these states were for centuries ruled by traditional headmen, chiefs, sheiks, or absolute monarchs. This rule was either harnessed to or supplanted by the colonial interlude of rule by an alien bureaucracy. The Western institutions with which the imperialist states endowed them were—except in interestingly rare cases such as India—utterly novel. Thus in such countries popular views about legitimacy, even supposing sophistication enough to make such a distinction, are fragmented; and even where legitimacy is not fragmented, it is too weakly mobilized to support a regime or government against an insurgent soldiery.

The military factor. It is still customary for students of these problems to print tables of the size of the armed forces of the Third World countries. There is absolutely no reason for them to do so. Size bears no relationship whatsoever to the likelihood of a military coup—though the number of soldiers and, more importantly, of officers may have a great deal to do with the style of government the military adopts if it has taken power. Fewer than 150 paratroopers subverted the government in Gabon in 1963; 600 troops, out of an army of 10,000, destroyed Nkrumah in 1966; the Northern Region of Nigeria (with some 30 million inhabitants) was subverted in January 1966 by a mere 500 men and 30 officers; the entire government of Liberia (1.8 million inhabitants) passed into the hands of a tiny group of noncommissioned officers, led by Master Sergeant Samuel Doe, when they broke into the executive mansion and murdered the president (April 1980). The reason for this apparently paradoxical fact is really quite simple: the very last thing intervention-minded officers wish to embark on is protracted civil war, especially if it is likely to force them to fire on brother soldiers. The interventionist officers are not interested in civil war but in a coup, and a coup is to civil war what a judo match is to a prizefight.[1]

It has been shown in study after study that in the majority of Third World countries the social mobilization of the public is so poor that the military, with its fivefold advantage in organization, hierarchy of discipline, intracommunication, corporate spirit, and, most importantly, armaments, becomes overwhelmingly the most powerful organized corporation in society. However, this unity, discipline, etc., is consistent with considerable latent divisions inside the armed forces. Where the military is large and modernized, as for instance in countries as dissimilar as Brazil and Argentina on the one side or Egypt and Syria on the other, there are divisions that may be reflected in political differences between the three services (in Argentina, these divisions were nakedly exposed in the aftermath of the Falklands debacle—the fall of

General Galtieri, the quarrel over his successor, and ultimately the exit of both navy and air force from the military junta).

Further, the military, whether by services or as a whole, may be divided into ethnic or regional components like the Nigerian army in 1966 or—to take a recent example—the Lebanese army in 1976, which simply disintegrated under the influence of the society's intercommunal vendettas. Similarly, the forces may be split by political allegiances; up to the 1970s, the highly politicized armies of Syria and Iraq offered striking examples of this. And it has been noticeable of late that the officer corps (which in almost every case is what we mean when we talk of "military" intervention) may be divided by rank or age. Sometimes senior generals speak for the entire armed forces as an entity. In many cases, however, the coups are led as much against these generals as against the regime by the younger members—brigadiers at the most, but on the whole those ranking from colonel downwards.

It is oversimplified to talk of "the" military, and very misleading for two important reasons. The first is that it is uncommon (although it does happen from time to time) for a military coup to be staged by a consensus of the officer corps. On the contrary, most are staged by quite small groups of officers, who have neutralized their expected rivals in the forces on the one hand, and acted without any complicity or even knowledge of the remainder on the other. In short, the great majority of military coups are made by a faction that relies on surprise to capture the government and believes that the doubters, and even the outright opponents of the coup in the armed forces, will decline to react against it—partly on the ground that it is more prudent to wait and see, partly on the "solidarity" ground that "brother does not fire on brother." The second reason that the generalization is misleading is borne out by the data cited earlier that demonstrated the increased frequency with which coups tend to come about in countries that have experienced them at least once before. One of the most significant causes of counter-coups is the existence of feeble military governments established by military forces that are internally divided to begin with.

The military—or rather (in view of the caution expressed above), the military faction that intervenes—does so for any one or combination of five major motives. (It should be noted that this permits no fewer than *thirty-two* different combinations of motives.)

The first is the one that is always proclaimed by the coup-makers: namely, the national interest. Here, two points must be noted. First, a plea from a group of officials, constitutionally subject to the government of the day, that it was compelled by the national interest to act illegally and seize power by force (or the threat of it) is in itself a remarkable phenomenon. It implies and is meant to imply that the armed forces have a special obligation to the nation (viewed as a continuing corporation in terms that Edmund Burke might have expressed),[2] and that this entails a special protective role, overriding constitutional obligations to obey the rulers of the day. This special relationship and the moral obligation to defend the nation even against its own rulers have always been the self-perceptions of the Latin American armed forces, since it was from their hands that most, if not all, the Latin American republics received their independence (Brazil being a notable exception). Similar examples include a number of states created since 1945: Burma, Indonesia, and Algeria, for instance. In other places—e.g., in the Muslim and particularly the Arab states—a superior and special status for the armed forces is traditional. Such a view was not shared by the armies of the African states at their dates of independence; but, as they got rid of their European officers, they very rapidly adopted it. Moreover, it is not unknown in the West. Even in the United States, General MacArthur defended his defiance of President Truman in 1952 by asserting: "I find in existence a new and heretofore unknown and dangerous concept that members of our armed forces owe primary allegiance or loyalty to those who temporarily exercise the authority of the Executive Branch of Government rather than to the country and its constitution which they are sworn to defend. . . ." However, this view was and is decisively rejected not only by the civil authorities in the West but also by the vast majority of officers whose dogma is, rather, the doctrine of civilian supremacy.

The second point follows from this. Given such a perception of their role, it is unsurprising that "the defense of the nation" should always be the justification soldiers put forward for their intervention in politics. Most often it is a simple rationalization, a political formula, and will not survive empirical investigation. But in certain cases this claim that the intervention was motivated by a concern for the nation is indeed valid. When the Ethiopian army intervened in 1974, it was on the valid ground that the imperial government had failed to tackle the terrible drought that had killed off tens of thousands of the population. When General Spinola led the Portuguese revolt in 1974, he was certainly motivated by the belief that the colonial wars were bleeding Portugal white and had to be stopped. When General Zia intervened in Pakistani politics in 1977, it was to stand between two armed civilian camps that threatened to plunge the country into civil war. The Turkish intervened in 1980 to impose its own mailed fist on the extremist factions of right and left who between them were murdering 200 people a week.

However, there are four other motivations that can and do run concurrently with concern for the national interest and that stand as sufficient motives for intervention independently of—arguably, often in direct opposition to—that claim. These are (1) corporate interest, (2) regional ethnic or communal interest (in polyethnic armies), (3) class interest, and (4) personal interest. In the 1960s and early 1970s scholars were mostly concerned about the *reasons* for the military take-over of civilian regimes, and much dispute took place over the respective weight to be assigned to these four motivations. It was not made better by the deep-rooted and pervasive belief that, at the end of the road, there is always a *single* cause for a major political phenomenon; this belief, apart from any scholar's genuine pleasure in believing that he has found the key to the universe, derives its rationale from an absurd belief among some political scientists that they not only can, but must, develop their discipline to make it as exact as the natural sciences—or, even more absurdly, as exactly predictive as celestial mechanics. Today, however, interest has rightly shifted from the causes of military coups to their consequences: what kinds of regimes they establish and with what social and economic consequences. For the most part, then, scholars in this field have abandoned the quest for a single motivation to explain the decision of the military to intervene. The greatest remaining dispute centers upon the relative importance of class motivation versus corporate self-interest.

Corporate self-interest is a summary term for three particular concerns, which, incidentally, are in no way mutually exclusive. The armed forces react against cuts in the military budget or they demand increases; they react against political interference in promotions and conditions of service, i.e., they demand a high degree of internal autonomy or, as it were, self-regulation; and finally, they oppose any paramilitary forces not under their own control—popular militias, constabularies, and the like. There is strong empirical support for the salience of this particular motivation for intervening: a study made of 229 military coups in order to identify soldiers' grievances reports that 23 percent were motivated by "corporate positional grievances" (e.g., autonomy, the absence of rival militias, etc.), 33 percent were due to "resource grievances," and 31 percent were preemptive strikes against governments expected to restrict corporate

privileges. Unfortunately, these categories overlap so that it
is not practicable to determine from them the exact proportion of coups motivated by corporate self-interest as against
these other motivations.

As for *class* interest—or if you will, the perception of a national interest in (perhaps subconscious) class terms—there
is no reason to doubt its importance as a motive in certain
regions. It is hardly visible in sub-Sahara Africa, where
classes in the Western sense hardly exist. Yet it can be witnessed in the course of events in Ethiopia (1974 onwards)
where groups of army officers from a middle-sector background intervened harshly against the landowning oligarchy
that made up the governing elite. The same can be said of the
Middle Eastern Arab states and also those of North Africa. It
is preeminently in some of the Latin American countries,
where a large and often organized working-class movement
exists, that one begins to approximate Western class
analysis. In many of the coups (Brazil from 1974 onwards,
Argentina from the Peronista post-1945 era, and Chile in
1973, for instance) this motivation is clearly very powerful.
In most countries today, officers no longer come from the traditional "upper class" of rural landowners or captains of industry and neither do they come from manual laborers.
Rather, they are from the multitude of occupational classes
intermediate between these two. Insofar as they are governed
by class perceptions, officers can be led into overthrowing
governments of predominantly oligarchic-landowner elites
(Egypt, 1952; Syria and Iraq, post-1963 and post-1958, respectively; and Ethiopia, 1974 and subsequently, for instance)
and also into overthrowing governments that favored mass
expectations in a populist style, as in the Latin American examples just given. This is why it is not possible any longer to
view military coups as being always "reactionary," as was
the case when only the Latin American coups were considered. Nowadays it is obviously possible for military coups
to be regarded as "progressive": hence liberal or leftist ad-

miration for the Peruvian or Ethiopian juntas as well as for the Portuguese armed forces in the first flush of their revolutionary enthusiasm. Indeed, in certain Communist quarters it has been seriously asked whether the forces might not be able to substitute in the "historic role" of the peasantry or proletariat by establishing a so-called "revolutionary democratic dictatorship" under their own hegemony.

The view that class interest is paramount has, however, been strongly expressed by a group of Western scholars who have drawn from it very wide *a priori* conclusions about the necessarily modernizing role of military rule. We shall deal with this claim in the second part of the chapter.

There remain to discuss only the communal/ethnic/ regional motivation on the one side and the personal on the other. The latter has been strongly argued for by Samuel Decalo in his study of military intervention in Africa.[3] He points out that "systemic tensions" are the "*backdrop* of all political life in the continent," and that often the prime reason for a military's intervening is the internal dynamics of its officer corps, which he then narrows to the personal self-interest of a small group of plotters within such a corps. This is unquestionably true of some cases: Idi Amin's coup against Obote in 1971, Captain Micombero's seizure of power in Burundi in 1965, let alone the cases Decalo has studied in detail, namely the Congo Republic and Benin. But this does not detract from the *primary* importance of class or corporate self-interest.

The importance of communal/ethnic/regional motivations was dramatically illustrated by the first and second military coups in Nigeria in 1966, with the Ibos pitted against Hausa-Fulani and ultimately with the secession of the Ibos to form their own independent state of Biafra. It is also illustrated by the fate of the multicommunity Lebanese army when civil warfare erupted in 1976. Under the stress of the surrounding communal tensions, that army simply melted away. Africa is preeminently a region where such motivations are important. One scholar who has made a systematic study of the grievances of coup-makers concludes that between 1946 and 1970 the percentage of coups related to these motivations stood at 12 in Asia (without the Middle East), 19 in the Middle East, and no fewer than 27 in Africa.[4]

To summarize: Military intervention in politics is to be seen as the outcome of two variables: the *societal* factors that conduce to military intervention, and the *capacity* of the military to intervene, allied with its motivations for doing so. Without conducive societal factors there is unlikely to be intervention, and if it occurs it will not succeed. Without the motivation and will to intervene, there will be no intervention. Societal factors are conducive to such activity in almost all the states of the Third World, and the military has the motivation to intervene in about half the states—although it could, in fact, develop such a motivation in all of them.

The Military Regimes

The different kinds of military regimes. After what has been said, it might appear easy to define a military regime: one that is the outcome of a military coup. But, in that case, what about regimes that take their shape and many of their orders from a military that does not use the coup or any threat of violence against a civilian regime, but simply exercises a pressure sustained by the knowledge that the military is the first as well as the last resort of the regime against domestic violence or insurrection? And what would we say about a situation like that of France after 1958, in which a military man (General de Gaulle) was brought to power as the result of military intervention but operated under constitutional restraints and sent the army back to the barracks?

The fact is that the class of "military regimes" embraces a number of distinct sub-types that merge, gradually, into civilian regimes. It is a semantic matter where we choose to draw the line. At the "most civilian" end of the spectrum there are, for instance, regimes that are constitutional and party-competitive, but where the constitutional guarantees are suspended from time to time, often for long periods. Consider, for example, Sri Lanka, where a state of emergency under which 18,000 persons were imprisoned lasted from 1971 to 1977. Next, there is a sizeable group of countries with a constitutionally appointed chief executive or head of state who is, however, ultimately reliant on the active support of his military forces. A large number of such states are supposedly "constitutional monarchies"; some are absolute monarchies like the Sultanate of Oman, or the Emirate of Bahrain; and then there is the remarkable example of the Philippine Republic, where President Marcos, duly reelected in 1969, introduced martial law in 1972 and—using its provisions to suspend Congress, arrest opponents, and censor the press—has governed as a personal dictator ever since, using referenda from time to time to validate his actions.

These are indubitably *civilian* regimes. To stress the military presence, however, we might call them *military-supportive* regimes.

We now come across another subclass of civilian regimes, with powerful and self-confident armed forces that have intervened in the past and will intervene again, only temporarily and from time to time, when they feel it their duty or interest to "correct" the course the civilian political forces are steering. A classic illustration is the 1971 demand of the Turkish army (which had already made a coup in 1960 and was to launch another in 1980) that forced the cabinet to quit and martial law to be imposed. But this was also the way (intermittent, in-and-out) that the Argentine military behaved throughout the 1960s. Again, these regimes are civilian, but if we wished to draw attention to the influence of their military component we could call them *intermittently indirect* military regimes.

The next class of regimes is much more arguably "mili-

tary." It comprises countries that are headed by civilians or
military men no longer on the active list, as a result of
behind-the-scenes military muscle and pressure. Guatemala,
El Salvador, and Panama provide examples of this kind of
regime, which with some justice we might call the *indirect
military* regime.

It is only at this point that we reach *military regimes*
proper. At the moment of writing, these number 36 (Algeria,
Argentina, Bangladesh, Benin, Bolivia, Brazil, Burma,
Burundi, Central African Republic, Chad, Chile, Congo Republic, Egypt, Equatorial Guinea, Ethiopia, Ghana, Honduras, Indonesia, Iraq, Korea, Libya, Madagascar, Mali,
Mauritania, Niger, Pakistan, Paraguay, Rwanda, Somalia,
Sudan, Syria, Thailand, Togo, Uruguay, Yemen Arab Republic, and Zaire). As we shall see, there is some reason to question whether Egypt or Algeria really belong to this set any
longer.

The format of military regimes. There are three questions to be answered in connection with these military
regimes: what is the role of the armed forces as such (as opposed, for instance, to the ruler they have installed); what is
the relationship of the government to the rest of the political
system; and to what depth does the government penetrate
the life of the country?

The role of the military in a military government. The first major characteristic of these 36 governments, and the one that
distinguishes them from the indirect military or purely
civilian governments, is that the head of state has been installed by virtue of a military coup. This is true for 32 of these
states; for the remaining 4 it must be modified to read that
the heads of state are latter-day selections by the military,
after the original coup. Thus, General Figueiredo is the
military's fifth successor to General Castelo Branco
(1964–1967) in Brazil. Similarly, in Egypt, Vice-President

Hosni Mubarak succeeded President Sadat, a member of the original coup of 1952, who himself had succeeded Nasser; in Iraq, Saddam Hussein succeeded General Bakr, successor to President Arif in 1965; and Dr. Mendez was put into power by the Uruguayan military to replace President Bordigerry in 1976. Also, of the heads of state in all these countries, Messrs. Hussein and Mendez are the sole civilians. All the rest are military men.

However, the installation of a military man in the presidential office by means of a military coup does not necessarily imply that the armed forces as a whole, or their senior ranks, or even that group of the senior ranks that made the coup, will continue to play a creative part in governing the country afterwards. It is doubtful that the Zaire military plays any significant part in shaping policy under General Mobutu, and a similar caution might well be raised about the Egyptian army under Hosni Mubarak. We can go on, therefore, to distinguish two major groups of military regimes. The first group, numbering 24 countries, installs a group of officers next to the president in what is sometimes called a Revolutionary Command Council, High Security Council, National Political Bureau, Supreme Military Council, Supreme Revolutionary Council, or, as is most common in Latin America, a Junta Militar. These bodies are very small, rarely having more than twelve members and sometimes consisting of only three. It is they who exercise sovereign power. To carry on the day-to-day work of government, these councils appoint cabinets that may be military in composition, mixed civilian-military, or wholly civilian. From the point of view of the armed forces control position, it does not make much difference how the (subordinate) cabinet is composed; in practice we may note that only one such cabinet (in Benin) is wholly military, thirteen are mixed, and ten are civilian.

The remaining states, numbering 12, do not possess command councils. In one of them (Burma), the cabinet is almost

entirely military, so that the armed forces are as securely
entrenched here as in the former group. Of the remaining 11,
the (military) head of state governs through a mixed civilian-
military cabinet. In these states, one might surmise that it is
the president who makes policy, with the advice and the support of the military, certainly, but by no means at their initiative. A glance at the countries in this group (Brazil,
Egypt, Indonesia, Iraq, Togo, Madagascar, Paraguay, South
Korea, the Sudan, Syria, and Zaire) suggests that this is correct. In none is the military installed in a command council,
nor has it any place in a cabinet that is exclusively civilian.
These states, we may well surmise, are governed by the head
of state with the military in a supportive rather than a creative role. We shall take up their case a little later when we
have examined the rest of the political systems in these 36
countries.

The political system in military regimes. So far we have examined the executive power in these states to see how far the
military or the heads of state control them. We have seen that
in at least 25 states the military is in control of the executive
branch, and that it plays an important part in another 11.
The next question is: how far does the executive branch control the rest of the political system? This is indicated by the
status of the political parties, of legislatures, and of civil
liberties in military regimes. It may be stated right away
that, except in a handful of marginal cases, military regimes
either disband parties, install their own official single-party
system, or control parties by way of licensing. For the most
part, they suppress legislatures. Also, they suspend those
parts of the constitution that guarantee individual freedoms,
and in many cases carry out mass arrests, practice preven-
tive detention without charges, and establish military or
"kangaroo" courts to "try" their political opponents. Military
governments are all authoritarian, and the only question is
the degree to which their authoritarianism is pushed.

Turning first to the 24 command council–type regimes and the additional state with a wholly military cabinet, we may remark that of these 25 states where the military forms the supreme executive, political parties have been banned in 15. Ten have single-party systems, and 4 of these latter states have legislatures. In these military governments, strictly speaking, the military forces rule without any civilian institutions, or via a party and a legislature that they themselves have fashioned for their own ends and that is an emanation of their power.

But the 11 remaining regimes — 2 with mixed cabinets and 9 with civil — raise the engaging problem as to where, precisely, the military fits in. Regimes with a mixed civilian-military cabinet still provide, *prima facie,* an institutionalized niche for the military as such. The best discriminators between the different types of regimes are two conjoint factors: licensed parties plus a legislature. Included in this group are Brazil (already noted as exceptional), Iraq, Indonesia, Paraguay, Syria, Honduras, Egypt, and Korea. The arrangement in each one of these countries is idiosyncratic, and they can well be said to represent those on the margin of "military regimes." In each, the relationship between popular political forces, the civil bureaucracy, and the armed forces is complex; in each, the balance has been struck in a different way. In all of them it can be said that the effective ruler is the individual head of state — Suharto, Mubarak, Park, Assad, Saddam, and so forth — who maintains the closest ties with the armed forces, listens carefully to their grievances, balances these against other claims on his attention, and certainly regards them as the first and last source of his power. But — and this is the decisive point as far as the military are concerned — their members play a part in policymaking that is advisory and supportive. They are no longer prime movers. If these are to be regarded as military regimes, it can be only on the grounds that they have provided the head of state and can remove him, and that, as a consequence, their interests become the first charge upon the state.

The penetration of the military in the sociopolitical system. There remain two things to be understood about the role of the military in a military regime. These are the extent to which the armed forces move their military-professional personnel into other structures, notably the political parties and the bureaucracy; and how far, as corporate body, they manage national affairs. The first may be styled military *colonization* of other institutions, where the military acts as a reservoir or core of personnel for the sensitive institutions of the state; it means the expansion of military personnel into the political parties, the industrial enterprises, the unions, and the bureaucracy. The military establishments in the military regimes also differ, often very sharply, in the degree to which they press their control of social and, particularly, of economic activities. Some simply superintend the processes of society, correcting their course as seems necessary to them, while others go further and assume the direction of affairs. At least one—Burma—goes much further and even *administers* the major services.

When we consider the extent to which the military colonizes institutions on the one hand and the degree to which it interferes with society and economy on the other, it will be clear that, combining the one variable with the other, military regimes are likely to differ among themselves, sometimes sharply, as to their style of government. And unless we can differentiate between them in this way, it seems, frankly, rather silly to try to estimate the social and political performance of military as compared with civilian regimes. Consider, for instance, the cases of Thailand and Burma. In the first, the Thai military, which has been in power off and on since 1932, (1) rules, (2) does not act as a core, and (3) superintends—rather than directs, let alone administers— the economy. In the Burmese case, the military has been in power since 1962, and it (1) rules, (2) acts as a core, and (3) administers the economy. The Thais have achieved a high growth rate; the Burmese military, on the other hand, has achieved a negative growth rate. One conclusion that may be drawn—and, indeed, frequently is drawn—is that military regimes have a fifty-fifty chance of success in managing the economy. But this is to equate the two regimes simply by virtue of one characteristic—the corporate rulership of the military in each—failing to distinguish what the military does and how it does it. From this standpoint, it might be possible to conclude that the degree of economic success one might expect from the military regime depends on what kind of regime we are talking about. This matter will be taken up shortly. It is mentioned here to show that the distinctions made above are not unnecessarily pedantic, but, on the contrary, are essential to adjudging the claim that military regimes are more successful than their civilian counterparts.

In Nigeria, Ghana, and, as far as we can see, in most of the West African regimes if not all of them, the military as ruler has made use of the preexisting civil administration; indeed, this military-bureaucratic symbiosis is one of the most striking features in this area. Furthermore, there is evidence to suggest that the military as rulers, while definitionally possessing and exercising a veto power, are often very much in the hands of their top civil servants. It has been reported that the Ghanaian military, for instance,

relied heavily on information, advice, execution, and supervision provided by top civil servants, even in areas where the junta members reserved and retained a monopoly on ultimate decisions . . . [and that, in fact,] regardless of the formal organization of power, the real impact of military rule on state administration seems to have been an increase in its autonomy. The military removed or minimized party and "political" pressures on the bureaucrats without bringing in their own system of effective control.[5]

However, the military rulers of these countries did aspire to direct and plan the nation's affairs. The Thai style is somewhat different. The military elite is almost a "connexion" in

the eighteenth-century sense, and has intermarried with the
Chinese business community that is central to the economy,
and with the traditional bureaucracy; indeed, it is common
for leading families to place one son in the army and the
other in the civil service. Political parties have intermittently been permitted, and some of these, too, have effectively been instruments of the military leadership. So
organized, this group has supervised the flow of Thai business and agriculture, and has kept a close watch over political activities.

We can now turn to the 3 countries in the *ruler core* tradition. Burma is the most striking of these. It forms almost the
mirror image of the Thai free-wheeling style. The military is
a politicized army, trained in and professing Burmese socialism. Since 1962, its leading group has carried on a bitter feud
with the civil service, which it regards as a relic of colonialism, and has stuffed the ministries and development agencies and nationalized sectors with its own junior officers. It
has organized and staffed a monopolistic political party (the
Lanzin party), which is hierarchically organized down to the
rural district committee level where the local chairman is,
effectively, the district commissar. It has nationalized industry, transport, internal and external trade, communications,
and finance.

Brazil comes nowhere near Burma in any of these
respects, but it follows the same configuration, albeit at a
considerable remove. Here, the military government has carried out two five-year development plans, involving massive
investment in industry, energy, education, and health. This
is a private enterprise economy, but it is "planned"—or, if
one wishes, subsidized—by the national exchequer. It is far
from the socialist economy of Burma, and the military, as a
core, is a small one. For all that, it is noticeable that there
has been, according to an acute and well-informed observer,
"extensive, direct penetration . . . by military officers."

Indonesia illustrates the military in the role of *support*

core, which is very substantial indeed. The military forces have expanded their administrative functions both centrally and in the rural regions. They have created and staffed the higher echelons of their own "official" political party (Sekber Golka), which has found no difficulty in winning elections to the House of Representatives, and they have permeated and become the major power in economic entrepreneurship and management. The military's economic empire includes large holding companies, industrial and commercial conglomerates, and trading syndicates, as well as individual firms engaged in banking, petroleum, timber, and transport.

We can end our survey by looking at a state where the style of the regime has shifted markedly over time: Egypt. In June 1954, the supreme rulership was exercised by the Revolutionary Command Council (RCC), consisting of eleven officers. Under this was the cabinet, with nineteen ministers, eight of them from the RCC, who obviously dominated the remaining eleven civilian ministers. At the same time, more than one thousand officers were made ambassadors, provincial governors, managers, directors of economic agencies, and the like. By June 1974, however, the RCC no longer existed. There was then a president (an ex-officer), a vice-president (also an officer), and thirty other cabinet ministers, of whom only one—the minister of war—was an officer. Furthermore, of this cabinet, fifteen members bore the title "doctor," and another seven that of "engineer." At the same time, the flow of officers outside their service had dried up. Thus, in twenty years the Egyptian military had moved from the role of a ruler-core directorate to that of simple support.

With remarkable smugness, the Left and Far Left repeatedly assure us that "power grows out of the barrel of a gun," but they do not add that it will return there again unless it acquires mass popular support. The military are acutely aware of this, since they occupy hot seats, not comfortable armchairs.

A junta that is acclaimed when it comes to power (and

many are) will call elections or referenda to prove it. If it is unpopular, then it will *fix* elections and referenda to "prove" how popular it is. If neither avail, then it can either oppress its public with whips rather than scorpions or, alternatively, decide to hand power back to the civilians.

This exit from power is fraught with difficulties. The causes for which the soldiers made their coup are likely to be abandoned or destroyed. Even worse, the returning civilian politicians may wreak revenge on the soldiers who turned them out. Hence, most military establishments that decide to turn power back to the civilians seek certain built-in guarantees against either of these gloomy possibilities. Sometimes this takes the form of a special constitutional status for the military; thus, when the Turkish army returned power to the political parties in 1962, it made sure that its own nominee and leader occupied the presidency, and that it was represented, as military, in the upper house of the Turkish parliament. More usually, the military withdraws but keeps a watchful eye on the antics of the politicians. In this way, the original command council type turns into the indirect type, where the military monitors the government, pressuring it on an intermittent—but sometimes continual—basis. But such monitoring, after a time, seems inadequate, even dangerous, if the civilian government seeks to curb the military's power; and so, usually, this spell of indirect rule is terminated by yet another coup and another command council regime. The process is vividly illustrated by the entire course of Argentinian politics since 1930, when the armed forces intervened for the first time in this century and have not ceased since.

Genuine legitimation is very hard to come by. Few military establishments willingly turn their backs on power; those that do, carefully monitor their civilian successors, and very few, indeed, find these sufficiently worthy over a period of years to accept a role of political neutrality. Venezuela and Colombia are interesting examples of countries where this has apparently occurred.

For the most part, the military establishments that eschew the retreat to the barracks react in one of two typical ways— more severe repression, or fake legitimation. This can be illustrated by the *va-et-vient* in the military regimes that occurred from the end of 1976 to the beginning of 1978.

First, let us note instances of genuine—if modest—relaxation and institutionalization of the regimes. Nigeria proceeded towards the election of a constituent assembly, with a view to a return to civilian rule. Paraguay likewise convened a constitutional convention. President Sadat of Egypt permitted the appearance of three political parties—one of which is "official" (and always wins, of course)—but he later suppressed two of them. In Indonesia, elections took place for the House of Representatives, although, as already noted, the military's official party (Sekber Golka) was assured of a majority.

Now we can see the instances of fake legitimation, or "quasi-civilianization," for what they are. In Burma, where the military junta led by Ne Win had already put off their tunics and affected the civilian title of "U" (The Honorable), General (now U) Ne Win was reelected as chairman of the ruling Lanzin party (still retaining full powers as before). In the Central African Republic, the former President Bokassa (now deposed) proclaimed himself Emperor Bokassa and introduced a new constitution, which, however, vested full executive power in himself (status quo ante December 1976). The Council of the Revolution was dissolved, and the emperor presided over a civilian cabinet. In Libya, President Qadhafi introduced a new constitution in March 1977. The command council has been replaced by a "General Secretariat" in which Colonel Qadhafi and the other four former members of the RCC sit, retaining their power as before. In Bangladesh, General Zia, having persuaded President Ahmed to step down for him, had his assumption of the presidency confirmed in a referendum (May 1977).

So much for fake legitimation. But this can go only so far.

The alternative is heightened repression, and this is much frequented. We can pass rapidly over the states of terror unleashed by the Dergue in Ethiopia and the now deposed President Amin in Uganda, since these are matters of every-day knowledge, and note the Argentine military's postpone-ment of civil rule, imposition of further penalties on trade unions, and dissolution of still more political parties in the last two years. In Chile, in March 1977, President Pinochet imposed a total ban on parties and extended the state of siege for another six months, although at the very moment of writ-ing he has announced a complete amnesty on political prisoners.

The performance of military regimes. It was the 1960s that saw the most extravagant claims made for government by the military, perhaps because the data were so scarce. This was due to the liberal academics' perennial triumph of hope over experience. Even to this day, African military rulers are almost never referred to as "dictators"; this term is reserved for Latin Americans. The heads of state in coun-tries like Nigeria or Pakistan are politely referred to as "the military rulers" of such and such a country.

Three claims were made for military government. The first was that the military were the most prominent—or perhaps the only—"modernizing" force in the Third World. The second was that the military were perennially middle class, and acted as spearheads to enable the middle class to take over. The third was that the military alone could bring stable political conditions to their strife-torn countries. Not a single one of these claims has turned out to be unequivocally true; in general, it can even be said that each has proved false.

The military as modernizers. Two *a priori* assumptions were made here. The first was that all military regimes were alike; the second, that all military were also alike in that they and they alone were technologically specialized, were competitive with other military (and thus sensitized to the need to build up their own country's economy), and, finally, had an admiration of advanced societies to which they went overseas for training. Even as it stands, these arguments ring false in most countries of the Third World. Take the claim for "technological skills" and the like: almost all of the African armies are tiny infantry armies hardly running to more specialized units than a couple of signal platoons or a company of engineers. Also, if the claim were true, we should expect the navies to be more innovative and even more revolutionary than the armies, for their hardware is far more technically advanced. Instead, the navies nearly everywhere have proved conservative.

However, it is unnecessary to pursue this *a priori*, since there are enough regimes in existence to permit empirical inquiry into whether military regimes are economically more successful than civilian ones. And indeed, since 1970 there have been three inquiries of this kind on a global basis. The first, by Eric Nordlinger, took 74 countries and tested the military against the civilian regimes with respect to their performance in seven fields amenable to governmental manipulation. Aggregating all these indicators to form a summary index, and making no distinction for region, Nordlinger concluded that the political strength of the military in a country's polity was correlated to success in all seven fields by a factor of only 0.04. This is statistically negligible, and the only implication is that the performance of a country was statistically the same whether the military were in charge or not. Finally, these correlations change when the 74 states are broken into their component regions. It then turns out that only in Africa was military rule positively correlated to the growth of GNP (0.45), to industrial growth (0.42), to agricultural growth (0.60), and to educational expansion (0.34). As for the other regions— Latin America, the Middle East and North Africa, and

Asia—with 3 statistically insignificant exceptions, there
was a negative correlation between military rule and each
single field of endeavor. In short, the military made matters
worse, not better. And when we turn back to the exception
noted in Africa, it turns out that the basis of the calculation
is a mere 6 military regimes in which the military are said to
have been "influential," and only 1 in which they were actually in office.[6]

A second inquiry using aggregate data was mounted by
McKinley and Cohan. This drew on a more ambitious universe—all the independent states in the world over the decade of the 1960s, excluding only the Communist states, for
which data were not available. They summarized their major
finding thus: "While the civilian regimes have a higher export
growth rate and a lower cost of living rate than either military
regimes or regimes that have previously experienced military
rule, none of these differences is significant."[7]

This result clearly differs from that of Nordlinger, who
asserted that in four regions—Africa being the exception—
the military actually made things worse. However, in 1976
Nordlinger's results were reanalyzed by R. W. Jackman. His
method was significantly different from Nordlinger's; in addition, he introduced new and more reliable data concerning
60 independent states of the Third World in the 1960s. His
results contradict Nordlinger's and, in their general conclusions, bear out the rather agnostic conclusions of McKinley
and Cohan: "Military governments have no unique effects
on social change, regardless of level of economic development. . . . Blanket statements portraying military governments in the Third World as either progressive or reactionary are without empirical foundation."[8]

This very important finding receives powerful support
from a splendidly conceived piece of analysis of Latin
America by Philippe Schmitter. He reports:

In summary, no regime-type seems to be exclusively responsible for
"developmental success" in Latin America. Competition, and with

it, less coercion and more participation and voluntary compliance, seems in the long run to have promoted a greater "publicization" of the development process and greater equality in the distribution of its benefits, but with certain "overhead" costs in terms of wider and more rapid policy fluctuations and higher rates of inflation and budgetary imbalance. Military regimes have occasionally been more spectacularly successful in altering the established, and usually stagnant pattern of policy, but their longer-term effect has often been ephemeral—with a marked propensity for systems to return to some pre-established level after "demagogic" excesses. More often than not the military themselves have promoted this return to normality.[9]

We shall conclude: so far no evidence has been deployed to show that, as a class, military regimes modernize or develop their countries better than civilian regimes as a class. But we ought also to add that this is what we might well have expected to be shown, in view of the analysis of military regimes presented earlier. For we have argued that the class of military regimes is not homogeneous and, in particular, that even in its subclasses—as, for example, in the ruler-type subclass—the extent of military penetration and control of society differs very sharply. To a Burma we can juxtapose a Thailand; to an Argentina, a Brazil. Therefore, *prima facie,* there is no reason to suppose that the military class of regimes will substantively differ from the civilian type in economic performance, even if, as a final assumption, we altogether discount the importance of the natural resources of the countries in question. Finally, it must be seen that these closely argued statistical conclusions correspond to one's impression. Brazil and South Korea have achieved spectacular growth under military rule; Burma and Argentina have done spectacularly badly.

The military as spearheads of a modernizing middle class. This argument has taken three forms. José Nun, basing himself on the Latin American experience, propounds the view that since officers are drawn from the middle class, the Latin American coup is a device "for protecting the middle class."[10]

Manfred Halpern, basing himself on the Arab states, draws
the opposite conclusion, waxing lyrical over the middle-class
Arab officers as spearheading the arrival in politics of an
Arab middle class viewed by him as impelled, "out of self-
concern, to establish modern integrating institutions which
can mobilize the spirit and resources of the entire nation."[11]
Finally, Huntington has synthesized these opposite viewpoints by maintaining that, since the officer corps of all armies is nowadays middle class in origin, it will react against
mass politics in Latin America and so play a reactionary role
there; at the same time, it will open the way for radical
middle-class and anti-latifundist regimes in the Middle East
as well as promoting middle-class values in advance of the
traditionalism of the masses in the African states.[12] All three
standpoints are vulnerable, in that the middle class of which
they speak is a vast conglomerate consisting of all who are
not ranchers or great landowners on the one side, or manual
workers and peasants on the other. But the hypothesis has
been empirically confounded by the statistical exercises discussed in the preceding section.

The military as stabilizers. One of the most immediate
causes of the military's intervention is political disorder —
as, for instance, in Turkey in 1971 or in Pakistan in 1977 —
and its accession to power is usually followed by a period of
iron reaction in which constitutional guarantees are suppressed and order is restored. For this reason, one of the
most commonplace claims for military intervention is that it
is a stabilizing force. Once one moves beyond the acknowledged successful bout of repression that follows the coup,
however, military intervention appears in the medium term
to be a powerful *de*-stabilizer. In the first place, the suspension or abrogation of the previous constitution and the imposition of a stern authoritarianism invite countercoups or
civilian insurgency. As Edmund Burke said, "A constitution
without the means of change is a constitution without the

means of self-preservation." It was Nasser who argued that in Egypt, constitutional change by the people was an impossibility in 1952; if the army did not bring it about, therefore, who would? What he said is perfectly correct, but *a fortiori* it applies to the military regimes themselves. Hence, the duration of military regimes is considerably shorter than that of most civilian ones. Nearly half last only two years, 31 percent last between two and five years, and only 21 percent last longer than five years. Nearly half are terminated by violence—in 30 percent of the cases by a countercoup, in another 18 percent by some kind of rising.

The third reason for rejecting the military's claim to act as stabilizers has so far attracted no attention, but is perhaps the most significant of all. The case rests on supposing that society is pulverized into hostile factions whereas the military are united. But suppose that the military are themselves disunited? In that case, the fractionalization of society is paralleled by a fractionalization of the military; both interact. One military faction reaches outside its ranks to pick up civilian allies against its rivals, who also turn to civilian factions to meet this challenge—so the factions of this society find themselves spearheaded by rival gangs of armed men, and their struggle becomes more murderous than before. This is no imaginary scenario. It aptly describes the sequence of events in Nigeria between the two coups of 1966 and the final crushing of Biafra, the course of events in Argentina ever since the overthrow of Perón, and, even more vividly, the anarchy, bloodshed, and confusion in Bangladesh and Ethiopia.

The Future of Military Intervention

Let us pull together some of the trends discussed in the earlier pages. First, the average number of coups—successful and unsuccessful—per annum shows no signs of abating. Next, the number of "first-time" states has decreased in the last decade compared with the previous one, but is still very positive. Third, the number of military regimes—according to our highly conservative definition, which excludes "indirect" and "military-supportive" regimes—is almost double that of a decade ago, and four times the number existing twenty years ago. Taken as a whole, these indicators suggest that the trend is still towards more coups and more military regimes in the Third World.

On the other hand, certain civilian regimes whose socioeconomic divisions would suggest *prima facie* that they were candidates for military intervention have survived, even if by the imposition of emergency regulations—notably, India, Sri Lanka, and the Philippine Republic—while other states whose past history has been a chronicle of nothing but military intervention, like Mexico and Venezuela, have reverted to civilian regimes that have persisted. Such facts must make us more than ordinarily wary of simply extrapolating the trends mentioned in the preceding paragraph.

For all that, it is our view that in the foreseeable future there will be more of the same, much of it in the states that have experienced military intervention already, but with significant extensions to states hitherto unaffected. Most military regimes are handed back to civilians by the decision of the military themselves. The reason that the military so often leave the barracks and seize power again is that such forces continue to nurture the same motivations and to be possessed by the same corporate self-interest that originally compelled them to intervene. They have not become politically neutral after quitting government; they are simply *disengaged.* Yet to ensure that they will no longer intervene requires that they be the former; and this is far harder to bring about than the usually temporary disengagement that is the condition in most of the ex-military regimes—and a large number of civilian but military-supportive states—in the Third World.

For the military to become neutral requires two conditions: in the first place, that they do not fear their civilian successors; and in the second, that these civilian successors do not need the military to keep themselves in power. The first is much easier to meet than the second. The civilian successors will have to be careful to respect the corporate autonomy of the armed forces, spend perhaps exorbitant sums on salaries and materiel, and take active and persuasive measures to ensure broad agreement between their priorities and those of the leaders of the armed forces. Given enough money (and states like Venezuela, Libya, Nigeria, and Algeria have become oil-rich), this is not impossible. It certainly implies a powerful—and perhaps a major—role for the armed forces, as such, in the counsels of state; but this is merely to respect a role that is already traditional in Latin America and the Middle East and much of Asia, and is novel, perhaps, only in sub-Saharan Africa. In any case, these military have come to stay, and to treat them in this way is to face a fact of life.

It is the second condition that is problematical. For, as argued earlier, a very high proportion of the Third World states are in latent but chronic crisis: opinion is feebly organized, often self-divided, and a sense of legitimacy is correspondingly weak or even negative. Precisely because of this, all such states require a strong executive—a requirement that the single party was reputedly designed to meet, though it has not done so, and that accounts for the frequent use of emergency powers and the suspension of constitutional guarantees in the civilian governments of the Third World. To this extent, then, all such states are those with governments that are abnormally dependent on their armed forces. And, indeed, this is precisely why they have experienced military intervention; for the more dependent it is on the military, the more a government must comply with their demands.

Until and unless these conditions alter, as has happened in

Mexico, the most a state can hope for is the contingent disengagement of its armed forces, which is as much as to say that they are likely, given the necessary motivations, to reenter the political arena.

But the creation of political community is a long and extremely delicate process. The history of the European states shows what a mixture of diplomacy and coercion—sustained over decades and, in most cases, centuries—was required to create the firm-rooted national communities of today. In the Third World, quick returns should not be looked for. Some exceptional states may, over a quarter of a decade, lay the foundations for political community on the one hand and military neutrality on the other; but, for the most part, the outlook for a majority of the states is the gloomy one of a first military regime to be succeeded by a second, with the interval filled by alternative bouts of indirect rule, monopartism, or feebly functioning party-competitive systems backed up by martial law or states of siege.

6

PETER T. BAUER

BASIL S. YAMEY

Foreign Aid:
What Is at Stake?

Mr. Hollis B. Chenery, vice-president of the World Bank in charge of economic research, said last year that "foreign aid is the central component of world development." How can this be so? Large-scale development occurs in many places without foreign aid, and did so long before foreign aid was invented.*

Reprinted with permission of the authors from *The Public Interest*, no. 68 (Summer 1982), pp. 53–69; © 1982 by National Affairs, Inc. Some parts of this essay appeared in "The Political Economy of Foreign Aid," *Lloyds Bank Review*, October 1981, and are used here with the editor's permission.

*Throughout this essay, "foreign aid" refers to official economic aid. It thus excludes military aid, private investment, and the efforts of private Western charities.

Official Western aid has now gone to the Third World for about thirty years, more than a human generation. Over this period major deficiencies, even startling anomalies, have become apparent. These untoward results might not matter much if the policy had served to promote the well-being of the peoples of the Third World, but it has not done so. Only exceptionally and in the most propitious circumstances can aid promote or accelerate economic advance, and then merely to a minor extent.

The effects of foreign aid have been quite different. It is foreign aid that has brought into existence the Third World (also called the South). It thus underlies the so-called North-South dialogue or confrontation. *Foreign aid is the source of the North-South conflict, not its solution.* The paramount significance of aid lies in this very important, perhaps momentous, political result.

A further pervasive consequence of aid has been to promote or exacerbate the politicization of life in aid-receiving countries. This major result has gravely damaged the interests of the West and the well-being and prospects of the peoples of Third World countries.

The money spent by the West in no way measures these crucial sequelae of aid. Whatever percentage of their national incomes aid represents, the donor governments cannot wash their hands of the consequences of their so-called caring.

The Creation of "North" and "South"

What is there in common between, say, Thailand and Mozambique, Nepal and Argentina, India and Chad, Tuvalu and Brazil, Mayotte and Mexico? Current public and political discussion envisages the world as one-third rich—the West —and two-thirds poor or even hungry—the "Third World" or "South." In this picture, extreme poverty is the common feature of the Third World.

This is altogether misleading. There is a continuous range of incomes in the world, both between countries and within them, making the line of division between rich and poor countries quite arbitrary. One could say that the world is two-thirds rich and one-third poor, or one-tenth rich and nine-tenths poor, or choose any other two fractions that add up to one. The size of the celebrated gap between rich countries and poor countries (i.e., the difference in their average incomes) depends on the placement of the arbitrary line of division. The picture is also misleading in that many groups or societies in the Third World—especially in the Far East, the Middle East, Southeast Asia, and Latin America—are richer than large groups in the West.

Nor is the Third World stagnant. In recent decades many Third World countries have grown rapidly, as for instance have South Korea, Taiwan, Thailand, Malaysia, Singapore, Jordan, Guatemala, Venezuela, Colombia, Brazil, Kenya, and the Ivory Coast. Indeed, insofar as global aggregation and averaging of incomes and growth rates make any sense at all, both total and *per capita* incomes in the Third World as a whole have, since 1950, grown no less fast than in the West, and probably have grown faster.

It is, of course, hardly sensible to lump together and average incomes of the very different societies of the Third World or South, which comprise some two-thirds of mankind. These societies live in widely different physical and social environments, displaying radically different attitudes and modes of conduct, and their governments pursue very different policies.

But the diverse components of the Third World do indeed share one characteristic. This is not poverty, stagnation, exploitation, brotherhood, or skin color; it is the receipt of foreign aid. *The concept of the Third World and the policy of official aid are inseparable. Without foreign aid there is no Third World.* Official aid provides the only bond joining together its diverse and often antagonistic constituents. This has been so ever since practically all of Asia, Africa, and Latin America came to be lumped together in the late 1940s as the underdeveloped world, and thereafter known successively as the less-developed world, the nonaligned world, the developing world, the Third World, and now the South. These expressions never made any sense except in that they denoted a collectivity of aid recipients.

The creation of the Third World has been the most important and far-reaching result of foreign aid. The Third World is moreover a progeny of the West; the foreign aid that created it did not originate in pressure from the Third World, but rather was introduced and organized by the West. It began with President Truman's Point Four program of 1949. He urged bold measures to help the underdeveloped countries, in which he said that over half of mankind was living in sickness and wretchedness.

Thus by foreign aid the West created a Third World, and one hostile to itself. Individual Third World countries are often neutral or even friendly to the West, but the organized and articulate Third World is invariably hostile. Its purpose as a collectivity is to coax or extract money from the West. In view of the loss of poise, widespread internal dissension, and feelings of guilt in the West, a hostile stance is appropriate to this purpose.

Foreign aid also gave birth to the notion of the West (or North) as a single economic decision-making entity, as a homogeneous aggregate with identical interests, and as an aggregate capable of imposing its collective will on the Third World. In fact, Western governments do not collude over selling or buying prices. Numerous foreign suppliers compete freely and often fiercely for business in Third World markets. Obvious competitors include, for example, construction companies, engineering consultants, and suppliers of manufactured products such as motor cars, trucks, and chemical products. Manufacturers and commodity traders also compete in the purchase of exports from the Third World.

Thus it is foreign aid that has created two fictions: first, that of the Third World as a substantially uniform collectivity with common interests; and second, that of the West as another substantially uniform collectivity, a powerful decision-making unit or homogeneous aggregate manipulating the world economy to the common advantage of its constituents. These fictions have in turn resulted in the reality of the "North-South" dialogue, confrontation, or conflict. References to the modest proportion of the donors' national income that foreign aid represents obscure these far-reaching political results.

Anomalies of Aid

Foreign aid is the transfer of taxpayers' money to distant governments and to official international organizations. The use of the term "aid" to describe these transfers preempts criticism, obscures issues, and prejudges results.

Who could be against aid to the less fortunate? Aid is good, more aid is better. When aid advocates talk of the disappointing record of aid, they mean not that aid has been ineffective or damaging, but that the amounts of aid have been insufficient. The term aid has enabled supporters of intergovernmental transfers to claim a monopoly on compassion, and to dismiss critics as bigoted or lacking in humanity.

The prevailing uncritical—indeed axiomatic—approach to these official wealth transfers has allowed startling and often bizarre anomalies to flourish.

According to the latest available official information (April 1981), Saudi Arabia, Kuwait, Libya, Iran, Iraq, Bahrain, Vietnam, Cuba, and South Yemen all received official Western aid each year from 1977 to 1979. This was at a time when the surpluses of the OPEC countries were widely regarded as embarrassing or as damaging to Western economies, when the government of Vietnam openly persecuted millions of people, and when Cuba dispatched troops to Africa, again to the embarrassment of the West. The survivors among the large numbers of refugees from the Vietnamese government during this period descended on other aid-recipient countries such as the Philippines, Thailand, Indonesia, and Malaysia. Their arrival inflicted substantial costs on these governments and produced much political tension and conflict. Again, in April 1981, the secretary-general of the United Nations announced special aid of $560 million for African refugees, when almost all of these people had fled from governments that continue to receive Western aid.

Substantial Western aid has gone and still goes to governments at war with each other; to governments severely restricting the inflow of capital, the shortage of which is said to be the ground for aid; to governments spending lavishly on obvious prestige projects; and to governments pursuing other policies that retard economic advance and harm the interests of their poorest citizens.

Another anomaly occurs when aid provides for the expansion of output of a product in the recipient country at a time when the donor government is grappling with excess capacity at home, with the resulting unemployment in the industry affected (U.K. aid to expand steel production in Morocco is a current example).

Aid and Economic Growth

Although the case for official transfers is largely taken for granted, various arguments or rationalizations are often advanced. These are addressed primarily to audiences not yet firmly committed.

The central argument for foreign aid has remained that without it Third World countries cannot progress at a reasonable rate, or cannot progress at all. But not only is foreign aid patently not required for development, it is, in actual fact, much more likely to obstruct it than to promote it.

It diminishes the people of the Third World to suggest that, although they crave material progress, unlike the West they cannot achieve it without external doles. Of course, large parts of the Third World made rapid progress long before foreign aid—witness Southeast Asia, West Africa, and Latin America. The emergence of hundreds of millions of people, both in the South and in the West, from poverty to prosperity has not depended on external gifts. Economic achievement has depended, as it still does depend, on people's own faculties, motivations, and ways of life, on their institutions and on the policies of their rulers. In short, economic achievement depends on the conduct of people, including governments. External donations have never been necessary for the development of any country, anywhere. There are, of course, a number of Third World countries or societies that have not progressed much in the postwar period. This lack of progress reflects factors that cannot be overcome by aid, and are indeed likely to be reinforced by it.

Governments or businesses in the Third World that can use capital productively may borrow at home and abroad.[1] This is also true for governments borrowing to spend on the so-called infrastructure, i.e., on facilities that do not yield a directly appropriable return. If spending on infrastructure is productive, it increases taxable capacity so that the governments can readily service the borrowed capital. It follows that the absolute maximum contribution of foreign aid to development, in the sense of the growth of the national income, is the avoided cost of borrowing, i.e., interest and amortization. As a percentage of the national income for large Third World countries, this maximum contribution is at best minute, and is far too small to register in the national income statistics. For India in recent years, the contribution of aid would have been at most on the order of one-quarter to one-half of 1 percent of recorded gross domestic product.

The maximum benefit from foreign aid is thus a modest reduction in the cost of investible funds—a resource that is *not* a major independent factor in economic development. It is evident on reflection that the volume of investible funds is not a critical determinant of economic progress, for if it were, countless poor individuals and societies could not have advanced rapidly in a very short period, as they have done both in the West and in the Third World. The relative unimportance to material progress of the volume of investible funds has been confirmed by much recent research, including that of Simon Kuznets, Edward Denison, Moses Abramovitz, and Sir Alec Cairncross.[2] It is economic achievement that produces assets and money; it is not assets and money that produce economic achievement.

However, suppose that, contrary to the results of reflection and observation, the volume of investible funds were a critical determinant of economic advance. If it were, then those actions of many Third World governments that restrict the inflow of foreign private capital—a course of action made easier by receipts of aid—would be evidence that these governments gave a low priority to economic development. The same applies also to the practice of several governments, including those of India and Nigeria, of in effect passing on to other governments part of the aid they themselves receive.

Any benefit from the reduction of the cost of investible funds is likely to be small. It is also likely to be more than offset by the adverse repercussions of official aid. And these repercussions are brought about by amounts of aid that, while small in relation to the national income of recipient countries, are nevertheless often a *significant* part of their government revenues and of foreign exchange receipts. These are the relevant magnitudes in assessing the principal repercussions of these transfers, because aid goes to governments and it increases both the revenues and the external balances at their direct disposal. In India, for instance, the latest official statistics available show that aid receipts in 1978 were of the order of 1.25 percent of officially calculated gross national product—but were about one-fifth of the country's export earnings. The figure of the government's tax receipts in 1978 is not available to us, but in the mid-1970s aid was of the order of one-fifth of its tax revenues. Thus, according to the latest official statistics, foreign aid to India as a proportion both of export earnings and of tax revenues was about thirteen times as significant as it was as a percentage of recorded gross domestic product.

How Aid Can Inhibit Development

The adverse repercussions of official aid operate precisely on the personal, social, and political factors that determine economic development.

Most importantly, aid increases the money, patronage, and power of the recipient governments, and thereby their grip over the rest of society. It thus promotes the disastrous politicization of life in the Third World (a subject to which we shall return). When social and economic life is extensively politicized, people's livelihood or even their economic and physical survival come to depend on political and administrative decisions. This result promotes conflict, especially in the multiracial societies of most Third World countries. Such a sequence diverts energy and attention from productive activity to the political arena; and the direction of people's activities is necessarily a crucial determinant of economic performance.

There are further untoward implications and repercussions of foreign aid that are far from trivial. Aid enables governments to pursue policies that patently retard growth and exacerbate poverty, and there is a long list of such policies. These include: persecution of the most productive groups, especially minorities, and sometimes also their expulsion; restraints on the activities of traders and even the destruction of the trading system; restriction on the inflow of foreign capital, enterprise, and skills; voluntary or compulsory purchase of foreign enterprises (which deprives the country of skills very helpful to development, besides absorbing scarce capital); forced collectivization; price policies that discourage food production; and, generally, the imposition of economic controls that restrict external contacts and domestic mobility, and so retard the spread of new ideas and methods.

Aid also is apt to bias development policy towards unsuitable external models. Familiar examples include steel and petrochemical complexes and official airlines. Moreover, in some instances the adoption of external prototypes has gone hand in hand with attempts at more comprehensive modernization, including attempted transformation of people's mores, values, and institutions. Such policies can have dangerous, even explosive, consequences (as in Iran).

Foreign aid further impairs the international competitiveness of economic activities in the recipient countries by helping to create or maintain overvalued exchange rates or to increase the domestic money supply.[3] (These adverse effects could be offset if the transfers greatly enhanced the productivity of resources, but this is extremely improbable.) It also makes it easier for governments to pursue imprudent financial policies. Unless aid is increasingly forthcoming, these policies lead to disruptive domestic inflation and to balance-of-payments difficulties, which in turn are apt to engender a crisis atmosphere and a flight of capital. This sequence encourages the imposition of specific controls, with adverse economic, social, and political results.

It would be naive to suppose that adverse policies would cease in the absence of aid. What is pertinent is that aid makes it easier to pursue and continue these policies. This is the case because, while it does little or nothing to promote development, aid can relieve immediate shortages, especially of consumer goods and of imports. It is then easier for governments to conceal temporarily from their populations the worst effects of the damaging policies.

Between Aid and the Poor: Third World Rulers

Foreign aid does not go to the pitiable figures we see on aid posters or in aid advertisements —it goes to their rulers. The policies of these rulers who receive aid are sometimes directly responsible for conditions such as those depicted. This is notably so in parts of Africa and Southeast Asia. But even where this is not so, the policies of the rulers, including their patterns of public spending, are determined by their own personal and political interests, among which the position of the poorest has very low priority.[4] Indeed, to support rulers on the basis of the poverty of their subjects does nothing to discourage policies that lead to impoverishment. Many Third World governments have persecuted and even expelled the most productive groups, such as the Chinese in Vietnam and Indonesia, or the Asians in East Africa. On the criterion of poverty, such governments then qualify for more aid, because incomes in their countries have been reduced.

These anomalies or paradoxes are obscured when it is suggested that giving money to the rulers of poor countries is the same as giving it to poor, even destitute people. Giving money to governments is certainly not the same thing as helping the poor. On the contrary: Western aid to Third World governments, especially in Asia and Africa, has extensively supported disastrous economic policies that have greatly aggravated the lot of the poorest. Dr. Nyerere of Tanzania has for many years been a much-favored aid recipient. Apart from large-scale collectivization of farming, his government has forcibly moved millions of people into so-called socialist villages, often far from their homes. These policies have had devastating effects on food production. President Mobutu of Zaire, another recipient of extensive aid, has expelled large numbers of traders. This had led to enforced reversion to subsistence production over large areas, causing much hardship and deprivation. As is well

known, the economic performance of these two countries
compares dismally with that of Kenya and the Ivory Coast,
where such extreme policies have been avoided.[5]

We may also note some less-extreme instances. Lavish
spending on show projects by aid-receiving governments is
familiar throughout the Third World. How do the poorest
benefit from the creation at vast expense of brand-new
capitals such as Brasilia, Islamabad, Abuja in Nigeria,[6]
Lilongwe in Malawi, or Dodoma in Tanzania?[7] Or from international airlines established throughout the Third World, in
countries including those such as Burundi and Laos, where
the vast majority of people do not use the airlines and local
people cannot operate them? It does not help the poorest in
Tanzania or Ghana that their countries have international
airlines with elegant offices in the West End of London and
midtown Manhattan. Many of these projects and enterprises,
facilitated by the flow of foreign aid, represent a drain on
domestic resources and have to be subsidized by local taxpayers. These are but a few examples of the radical
differences between foreign aid rhetoric and Third World
reality.

Would it be possible for the donor countries to help the
poor either by influencing the policies of the recipient
governments or by giving aid directly to the poorest instead
of to their rulers? Neither course is practicable, as such attempts would be resisted and sabotaged by the governments.
Both Western charities and official aid organizations already
encounter difficulties in some countries. But in situations
where it might be practicable to give official aid directly to
the poorest, other problems would arise, many of them well-
nigh intractable.

The most obvious of these problems is the pauperization
and de-skilling of the recipients. In the Third World very
large numbers of the poorest are materially unambitious. Official donations from abroad might serve to turn these poor
into paupers, so that the handouts would have to be con-

tinued indefinitely. Whole societies could thus be pauperized. A recent example, which is informative although extreme, is the large-scale pauperization in the U.S. trust territory of Micronesia. Large numbers of people there have abandoned productive activity, such as agriculture and fishing, because they can live not too uncomfortably on the handouts of the U.S. administration. The results have amounted to a form of dis-development, the de-skilling of people. The outcome of pauperization is persistent poverty, which in turn serves as a rationalization for further aid.

Many people think that worldwide redistribution from rich to poor through foreign aid is a natural extension of domestic redistribution through progressive taxation. But international transfers effected by foreign aid differ radically from internal transfers effected by progressive taxation (whatever the case for the latter). Aid goes from government to government. Unlike progressive taxation, aid transfers are in no way adjusted to the personal circumstances of taxpayers and recipients. Many taxpayers in donor countries are far poorer than many people in recipient countries, in which aid largely benefits the powerful and the relatively well off rather than the poor.

Redistributive taxation postulates basic similarities of conditions, and therefore of requirements, within its area of operation. Globally, these requirements differ widely. The meaning of riches and poverty depends crucially on people's requirements, and thus on physical and social living conditions. This is obvious for physical conditions, notably climate. But it applies also to social conditions, including customs and values.

Unlike progressive taxation within a country, global redistribution relies on international income comparisons. These are subject to very large biases and errors. They greatly understate the relative incomes of large Asian and African countries compared to the West. According to World Bank estimates, the official figure of the national income of

India has to be raised by a factor of more than three to make it comparable to that of the United States. Other scholarly studies have found much larger biases and errors. These arise for such reasons as the use in these comparisons of official exchange rates instead of purchasing power parities; the underestimation (or complete disregard) of much subsistence production; and the neglect of differences in age composition between the West and the Third World. (Such considerations, incidentally, also help to put into perspective statistics on Third World incomes and changes in incomes that purport to be accurate to within fractions of 1 percent.)

Failed Analogies and Justifications

The success of the Marshall Plan in the early postwar years is frequently invoked in support of wealth transfers to the Third World. This analogy fails completely. In postwar Europe the task was not development but reconstruction. The European peoples' faculties, institutions, and political arrangements were appropriate to sustained prosperity, as was evident from pre-war experience. That is why Marshall aid could be terminated in four years and why West Germany could become an exporter of capital soon afterwards. It should be contrasted with suggestions that official aid to the Third World will have to continue for a long time, at least into the twenty-first century.

That suggestion—that aid will have to be continued as far ahead as the twenty-first century—is paradoxical. Aid for development has been canvassed on the grounds that it is necessary to make Third World countries less dependent on the West. As aid cannot contribute substantially to development, the matter is misconceived. Worse still, aid has made it possible for governments to pursue policies such as subsidized import substitution, forced collectivization, inappropriate agricultural price policies, and inflationary financial policies, all of which have not only damaged the interests of the local people but have also increased the demand for imports and simultaneously decreased the ability to pay for them. Thus a number of these countries—such as, for instance, Tanzania—have become more, rather than less, dependent on the West and its largesse.

There are several further defenses of extensive aid, each of which is highly questionable. Foreign aid is often advocated as helpful or even necessary for Western prosperity. It is claimed that aid increases purchasing power and advances growth in the Third World, and thereby promotes exports and employment in the West. This is an argument most often addressed to businessmen and trade unionists.

The claim is invalid. It would be invalid even if the transfers significantly promoted development in the Third World (which, however, they cannot do). Exports bought with the proceeds of foreign aid are given away. It is sophistry to say that people who give away part of their wealth must be better off because those whom they have helped are better off or will be better off. A shopkeeper does not prosper by giving away his cash to people, some of whom may later spend part of it in his shop.

It is sophistry also to say that large-scale aid to the Third World will alleviate unemployment, recession, and deindustrialization in the West. If it were really possible to cure or relieve unemployment or recession by more government spending, it could be done more effectively by Western countries at home, for example, by spending on the modernization of industry and the improvement of the infrastructure, or on industrial or regional subsidies, defense, social services, or personal subsidies. In short, the idea that aid helps the economies of the donors simply ignores the cost of the resources given away.

A political argument favored especially in the United States is that without large-scale aid the Third World will drift into the Soviet camp. This argument is again insubstantial.

To begin with, about one-third of all Western aid is chan-

neled through official international agencies. In the allocation of aid they are not permitted to take into account the political interests of donors. Moreover, the Soviet Union is
represented in the United Nations. It can thus affect the
direction of substantial multilateral transfers under the
United Nations programs, though its own financial contribution is negligible. Indeed, practically all Soviet nonmilitary
aid is channeled to client states, notably Cuba, North Korea,
Vietnam, South Yemen, Ethiopia, and Afghanistan, most of
which have also received aid from the West.

Western political interests are also largely ignored in
direct government-to-government aid (oddly and mislead-
ingly termed bilateral aid). Aid administrators are qualified
neither by training nor, often, by inclination to act as pro-
moters of Western political interests. Much aid is given
regardless of the political conduct of the recipients or of their
political and military significance. Official transfers have
also often helped to bring to the fore governments hostile to
the market system and sympathetic to Soviet ideology. This
is so because aid goes to governments and, as already noted,
tends to politicize life in the Third World. The effect is reinforced by the preference of many influential aid advocates
and aid administrators for governments that claim to run
"planned economies."

Since the earliest days of aid, many of its recipients have
been vocal in their opposition to the Western donors,
denigrating and thwarting them as best they could. Examples range from Nkrumah in the 1950s to Qaddafi,
Nyerere, and Mengistu at present. Many governments that
derive their aid from the West derive their ideology from the
East. Moreover, as noted already, the Third World acting as
an articulate collectivity is hostile to the West.

Aid and Restitution

Many people, especially in the Third World but also in the West, think of aid as restitution or partial restitution for past wrongs. But what are these supposed wrongs? Contact with the West has been the prime agent of material progress in the Third World. Material achievement in the less-developed world diminishes as one moves away from the foci of Western impact. The poorest and most backward are the populations with few or no external contacts, the aborigines being the limiting case. To say that commercial contacts damage the Third World is to suggest that people in the Third World do not know what they are doing or what is good for them when they buy from the West, or when they produce for export.

The widely canvassed notion that the prosperity of the West has been achieved at the expense of the Third World is a variant of the familiar misconception that incomes of prosperous people have been extracted from the less well off. In fact, normally incomes are earned—that is, produced by the recipients. Moreover, the notion spills over into domestic discussion in the Third World. It inspires sentiments and policies directed against economically productive but politically unpopular and ineffective groups. The resulting policies inflict hardship on the immediate victims and also harm the economic position and prospects of the population at large, including the poorest people.

The most familiar specific arguments in support of aid as compensation or restitution are unfounded.

Those who think that the West manipulates prices to the detriment of the Third World misconceive market operations. Prices in international markets are the outcome of numerous individual transactions and decisions. They are not set by an organization called "the West." (If they are imposed by the West, why are Third World export prices ever allowed to rise in real terms?) In any case, even if the terms of trade with the South were unfavorable according to some criterion or other, this would mean only that the South had not benefited as much from the contacts with the West as it would have had prices been more favorable. The peoples of the South are certainly better off than if they had no trade to have terms about. As it happens, the terms of trade with the West of most Third World countries in recent decades have been unusually favorable. The overall external purchasing power of these countries' exports over Western goods has been far greater than ever before.

And what about colonialism? The majority of Western aid donors—including the United States, which is by far the largest—never had colonies of any significance. Some of them, including the U.S., Canada, Australia, and New Zealand, were themselves British colonies. And whatever its objectionable features, nineteenth- and twentieth-century colonialism—which is what is meant by colonialism in this context—was of great economic benefit to the peoples of these countries. For instance, Ethiopia and Liberia, which were not colonies, are among the most backward countries in Africa. Much the same is true in Asia—witness Bhutan, Sikkim, Tibet, and Nepal. Incidentally, multinational corporations, the alleged instruments of neocolonialism, do not operate in the most backward countries nor in the most backward areas of better-off Third World countries.

According to United Nations Conference on Trade and Development (UNCTAD) General Principle XIV, passed by an overwhelming majority of UNCTAD in 1964, colonialism is incompatible with material progress. This was declaimed at a time when Hong Kong, the last remaining sizeable Western colony in the Far East, was progressing so rapidly that Western countries were imposing controls on imports from it to protect their domestic industries. The idea that colonial status precludes material progress is refuted by obvious evidence from all over the world.

What about the Atlantic slave trade? Most Western countries were not involved in it at all. Asian countries, the
largest foreign aid recipients, were unaffected. And, horrible
and destructive as this trade was, it was not a cause of
African backwardness. The region most affected by it,
namely West Africa, is the most advanced part of black
Africa. (Incidentally, the Arab slave trade, which began
before Atlantic slavery and far outlasted it, was even more
horrible and was stopped by Western efforts. But the Arab
slave trade is practically never mentioned in this context.)

The claim that aid is a form of restitution for alleged
wrongs opens the door to unlimited blackmail and unlimited
transfers. Transfers motivated by guilt feelings are likely to
be undiscriminating. People afflicted with guilt feelings are
concerned with their own emotional state and perhaps with
that of their fellow citizens, rather than with what happens
to people at the receiving end of the policies inspired by this
sentiment. They are apt to be altogether insensitive or indifferent to the consequences of aid.

Reshaping Aid Policy

Foreign aid cannot achieve its declared objectives and has
far-reaching, damaging political and economic results. Yet it
will not be terminated promptly because of existing commitments and because of the vested interests behind it both in
the government and the market sectors, in the donor as well
as in the recipient countries. Can the worst effects of aid be
mitigated by changes in its methods of operation?

To begin with, it may help a little if aid were to take forms
that made it possible to identify its costs and possibly its
benefits. This rules out indirect methods of aid, such as commodity agreements. Not only are their results perverse, but
their overall impact cannot be assessed. And such schemes
are not subject to any form of public budgetary control.

There may be some advantage in avoiding soft loans in

favor of outright grants. The latter avoid problems of mea-
surement and the confusion between gifts and loans.[8] Aid
should also take the form of direct grants from donor government to recipient government, rather than of payments to
multilateral organizations to be allocated by them to the ultimate recipients. Such direct grants permit a modicum of control by the elected representatives of the taxpayers in the
donor countries, i.e., the real donors. The more distant the relationship between the supplier of funds and their user, the
more likely that they will be used ineffectively. Attempts to
extend the multilateral component of aid should be resisted;
so also should attempts be resisted to make aid more automatic by the introduction of international taxation, as proposed, for instance, in the recent *Brandt Report.*[9]

But these proposed reforms would make little difference in
practice unless the granting of aid were made deliberately
discriminating. Aid would have to be concentrated carefully
on governments whose domestic and external policies were
most likely to promote the general welfare of their peoples,
and notably their economic progress. Aid would have to go to
governments that tried to achieve this end by effective administration, the performance of the essential tasks of
government, and the pursuit of liberal economic policies. At
present, many aid-recipient governments neglect even such
basic tasks as maintaining public security, while nevertheless trying to run closely controlled economies. Selective
allocation of aid along these lines would reduce its propensity
to politicize life, and thereby it would reduce the extent and
intensity of political conflict. It would also promote prosperity in the recipient countries, to the limited extent that
external donations can do so.

Relief of need, especially humanitarian relief of poverty in
the Third World, should be left to voluntary agencies, notably
to nonpoliticized charities. They are already active in this
field. They could do much more if it were recognized that
relief of need belongs to their sphere. In this realm the inter-

national comity among countries calls for official aid only to meet unforeseeable and exceptional disasters.

As for economic development, the West can best promote this by reduction of its often severe barriers to imports from poor countries. External commerce is an effective stimulus to economic progress. It is commercial intercourse with the West that has transformed economic life in the Far East, Southeast Asia, part of Africa, and Latin America.

However, even removal of trade restrictions may well do little for the economic advance of some Third World countries and groups. Where the enlargement of external opportunities would not bring about the economic advance of particular societies, external donations to their governments would be even less likely to do so.

The Central Question

We have had to examine a variety of issues in this essay, including many that are staples in the public and academic discussion of foreign aid. The extended nature of this examination should not be allowed to obscure what we regard as the central and most significant result of foreign aid. This result has been the establishment of the Third World as a collectivity, and one that as a collectivity is generally hostile to the West.

III

International Affairs

7

KENNETH L. ADELMAN
MARC F. PLATTNER

Third World Voting Patterns at the United Nations

With two notable exceptions—one already revealed, the other to be unveiled here—the "Third World" does not exist. What does exist is a veritable hodgepodge of disparate countries ranging from Cuba to Singapore. Indeed, this viewpoint was nicely expressed by former Secretary of State Alexander Haig in the opening statement of his Senate confirmation hearings:

> Much of the fragmentation of power [in the contemporary world] has occurred in the so-called "Third World," a misleading term if

ever there was one. If one thing has become abundantly clear in the last decade or so, it is that the community of condition, purpose—and by extension, U.S. foreign policy—implied by the term "Third World" is a myth, and a dangerous one at that.

Recent American foreign policy has suffered from the misperception which lumps together nations as diverse as Brazil and Libya, Indonesia and South Yemen, Cuba and Kuwait, and which has too frequently produced attempts to cut the national pattern to fit the foreign policy cloth.[1]

Events since the advent of the Reagan administration provide abundant evidence of the raging conflicts that divide so-called "Third World" states. Open warfare pits nations against each other in Southeast Asia, the Persian Gulf, the Horn of Africa, and the Western Sahara, to name but a few regions. Moreover, the headquarters of the Third World—those centralized organizations of developing countries around the world—are quite simply disintegrating. In 1981, an Arab League summit broke up over Prince Fahd's peace plan in Morocco. In 1982, the scheduled Tripoli summit of the Organization of African Unity (OAU) foundered twice on the overt issues of the Western Sahara and Chad and on the prospect of Libyan President Qadhafi's becoming the current OAU chairman; the summit was scrubbed both times for want of a quorum. The nations of Latin America and the Caribbean were thrown into disarray by the Anglo-Argentine war over the Falklands. The Non-Aligned Movement (NAM) has been wracked by a political version of guerrilla warfare between its radical and more moderate factions. This split, combined with the Iran-Iraq war, led to the cancellation of the supreme Non-Aligned event, the Heads of Government summit, scheduled in Baghdad for September 1982. Finally, the Group of 77 (G–77) has been subjected to increasing friction between radical OPEC states and the majority of its members.

With such divisiveness rampant in Third World organizations, there remain only two ways in which the Third World may be identified. The first was given by British economist

P. T. Bauer, who claimed with as much truth as wit that the Third World gained identity as those states bound by an expectation or even a demand of foreign aid. Naturally, this demand is made upon the First World or industrialized democracies because the socialistic totalitarians of the Second World are notoriously stingy. The second and more original way of identifying the Third World comes out of an examination of the voting record at the United Nations General Assembly. The large number of states that share the same concerns and causes in that forum can be classified as the "Third World."

The World of the United Nations

In large part, the Third World is more genuinely a creation of the United Nations than of foreign aid. Without the United Nations, there would in fact be no Third World—at least no Non-Aligned Movement or Group of 77. For without the United Nations, there would be no central place to gather regularly to coordinate views, to disseminate position papers, and to duplicate reports. The scrapping of the OAU and Non-Aligned summits in 1982—previously the high points of Third World solidarity—reinforces the indispensability of the United Nations to Third World identity.

Besides constituting an assembly point where Brazil can meet Swaziland, the Lao People's Republic can greet Jamaica, and Vanuatu can caucus with Bhutan, the United Nations furnishes the administrative apparatus for the NAM to function at all. The UN furnishes free use of its conference halls, simultaneous interpretation, subsequent translation, and printing and distribution of NAM and Group of 77 documents.[2]

Just as the United Nations in many ways creates the Third World, so does the Third World dominate the United Nations. Theirs is a symbiotic relationship; neither may live without feeding off the other. The United Nations General Assembly (along with its many subsidiary organs) is a body whose agenda mirrors Third World priorities, preoccupations, even obsessions. The vast preponderance of resolutions passed and of rhetoric delivered there bears the unmistakable Third World imprint. Hence the "automatic majority" of Third World nations in a body organized on the principle of one nation, one vote.

The magnitude of such a majority is considerable. With the addition of three new members (Vanuatu, Belize, and Antigua and Barbuda) in 1981, the United Nations now comprises 157 nations. Of these, 23 can formally be considered members of the West (i.e., of the Organization for Economic Cooperation and Development [OECD]).[3] Two additional states, Israel and the Republic of South Africa (which has been illegally denied voting privileges in the General Assembly and in specialized agencies), are often associated with the West. Ten member states (two of which, the Ukraine and Byelorussia, are no more nation-states than are Delaware and Nevada) can clearly be regarded as charter members of the Soviet bloc. Two other communist nations, China and Albania, though plainly not part of the Soviet bloc, have declined to join Third World organizations; they stand in splendid isolation in the bloc-obsessed world of the United Nations. If these 37 states are subtracted from the total United Nations membership, there remains a Third World contingent of 120 countries, more than three-quarters of the entire body.

Theory and Practice in the United Nations

In theory, of course, identifying these 120 countries as being unaffiliated with East or West need not mean that they constitute a coherent bloc. They are often at each other's throats. Moreover, many have vital security relations with a superpower (e.g., Cuba and Vietnam with the USSR, and El Salvador and Thailand with the U.S.).

But the divisive issues within the NAM are those shunted aside. The Iran-Iraq war—which has extracted a staggering human toll and which has grave consequences for one of the world's most important regions—did not become the subject of a single General Assembly resolution until the war was more than two years old. The Non-Aligned Movement moves together because of widespread agreement on the Middle East (viciously anti-Israel), Southern Africa (ferociously anti—South Africa), disarmament (ardently pro-disarmament, or more properly, pro-disarmament by the West), and economic development (passionately pro—foreign aid, or more properly again, pro—foreign aid from the West). The Middle East alone was the subject of over one-third of all General Assembly resolutions in 1981; Southern Africa about one-fifth; and disarmament, economics, and administrative housekeeping (such as United Nations budget or appointments) the bulk of the rest.

Because of this selectivity of agenda items, the Third World keeps its cohesion and constitutes an impressive voting bloc in the United Nations. In fact, it is far more cohesive than the Western group and almost as cohesive as the Eastern bloc. The Warsaw Pact countries always vote as the Soviet Union wishes them to vote. Consequently, in the 1981 General Assembly, they had a bloc solidarity of 99.2 percent.[4] NATO countries voted with the U.S. some 74 percent of the time. The NAM—so much larger than either major Eastern or Western blocs and so much more diverse—voted with Yugoslavia 98 percent of the time, with India 97 percent, and with Singapore and Cuba 92 percent. (It tells something about the United Nations that diametrically opposed states there can have nearly the same percentage of agreement with the NAM.)

While everyone knows that the United Nations treats Israel and South Africa as humanity's pariahs—indeed, as the main threats to peace in the world today—fewer know of the United Nations litany on economic issues. Economic development commands broad consensus in the United Nations in rhetoric, though not in practice nor in results. For NAM members exhibit great variations in their levels of prosperity, their specific economic interests, and their domestic economic policies. The Third World includes the richest nations, measured by per capita GNP—the Persian Gulf sheikdoms—as well as the poorest nations of the globe. It embraces countries with centrally planned economies that wholly exclude foreign private investment, as well as market-oriented economies that avidly seek the presence of Western multinational corporations.

Nonetheless, the Third World approach to economic issues at the United Nations is carefully tailored to minimize disagreements that otherwise would spring from their discordant domestic economic arrangements. Hence a cardinal principle of the New International Economic Order—the Third World's holy writ on matters of this kind—affirms the "right of every country to adopt the economic and social system that it deems the most appropriate for its own development."

In regard to development, the Third World countries focus their attention and their energies in the United Nations almost wholly on the international economic system. This nicely deflects blame from their own leaders to ours. The Third World seeks to maximize the amount of assistance flowing there from the developed countries (i.e., from the West). The NAM seeks various sorts of special, nonreciprocal preferences for these states with respect to trade and other international economic relations. And it seeks to increase its own influence over the institutions most critical to the workings of the world economy (above all, the International Monetary Fund). These efforts all pit the Third World nations as a group against the West. Thus, even those Third World countries that have relatively market-oriented economies find themselves in an adversary relationship with the U.S. on economic matters at the United Nations.

This unity on economic issues at the United Nations has given rise to the most comprehensive institutional embodiment of the Third World—the Group of 77. This organization, which derived its name from the 77 nations that joined together at the first UNCTAD (United Nations Conference on Trade and Development) conference in 1964, has now expanded (largely due to the emergence of newly independent nations) to embrace 123 countries.[5] The *political* diversity of the nations within this grouping is truly awesome. The G−77 is not only latitudinarian enough to include both Koreas; it has successively embraced Allende's Chile and Pinochet's Chile, the Shah's Iran and Khomeini's Iran, Somoza's Nicaragua and the Sandinistas' Nicaragua.

In all United Nations economic negotiations, the G−77 functions as a true party caucus. A group position acceptable to all members is laboriously hammered out and then presented by a group spokesman. Although it often is subject to intense internal struggles, the G−77 rarely drops its public facade of unity.

Nonetheless, the cohesion of the G−77 on economic questions does not much affect the overall pattern of General Assembly voting, since most economic issues in the United Nations are traditionally negotiated until a frail consensus is achieved (often with reservations by many states), rather than brought to a formal vote. Thus UN economics, like too many UN diplomats, tend toward abstraction, reflecting little of and contributing little to real life.

Not all economic issues are, however, so whittled down. Some come up for vote, where they contribute to the overall voting pattern in the United Nations, pitting the U.S. (in particular) and the West (in general) against the Third World−Soviet blocs. On all resolutions in the 1981 General Assembly, NAM countries' voting with the U.S. ran from a high of 47 percent (Malawi) to a low of 9 percent (Seychelles), with a NAM median of 25 percent. The NAM's voting the same way as the USSR ran from a high of 99 per-

cent to a low of 65 percent with a median of 85 percent.[6]
There were 74 United Nations General Assembly votes that
the U.S. considered "most important" in 1981. On these
"critical votes," the nonaligned voted the same way as the
U.S. an average of 11 percent of the time, and the same as
the Soviet Union 88 percent of the time.

The Top Ten

For the sake of clarity, we identified 10 votes, out of the some
300 cast, that were of greatest importance to American national interests and to principles of freedom, nonaggression,
and fair play. These by no means constitute a typical sample
of General Assembly votes. All 10 were the subject of extensive U.S. lobbying; and by design, the list excludes any
resolutions on which the vote was overwhelmingly one-sided.
This means that on all 10 of these votes, developing countries
knew both that they were voting on an issue about which the
U.S. deeply cared, and that they would not be isolated by
refusing to oppose us. Under such conditions, many developing countries proved willing to vote with us, or at least to ab-
stain or remain absent. Within the general context of Third
World opposition to the U.S. in the General Assembly, these
10 votes provide the most discriminating and reliable
measure of any country's friendliness toward both the U.S.
and the principles upon which our country was founded:

1. *Kampuchea.* This resolution called for the withdrawal of
   the Vietnamese from Kampuchea and for free elections
   for the Kampuchean people. It passed by a vote of 100
   (U.S.) affirmative—25 negative—19 abstained.

2. *Afghanistan.* This resolution called for the immediate
   withdrawal of foreign (i.e., Soviet) troops from Afghanistan and reaffirmed the right of the Afghans to self-
   determination. It passed by a vote of 116 (U.S.) affirmative—23 negative—12 abstained.

3. *Chemical Weapons.* This resolution extended the mandate of the Special United Nations Chemical Weapons Experts Group so that it could continue its investigations of the alleged use of chemical weapons (yellow rain) by the Soviet Union and Vietnam. It passed by a vote of 86 (U.S.) affirmative—20 negative—34 abstained.

4. *El Salvador.* This resolution placed the entire blame for human rights violations on the provisional Salvadoran government and called for negotiations with the guerillas, rather than elections, to resolve the situation. It passed by a vote of 69 affirmative—22 (U.S.) negative—53 abstained.

5. *Abu Eain.* This resolution deplored the action of the U.S. in extraditing to Israel Ziad Abu Eain, a Palestinian accused of a terrorist bombing attack, and termed "illegal" Abu Eain's prior detention in the U.S. for over two years though he was given the full benefit of our legal system. It passed by a vote of 75 affirmative—21 (U.S.) negative—43 abstained.

6. *Nuclear Collaboration with South Africa.* This separately voted-upon paragraph in a larger resolution strongly condemned the U.S. (and other Western states) for (falsely) alleged collusion with South Africa in the nuclear field. It passed by a vote of 56 affirmative—24 (U.S.) negative—51 abstained.

7. *Nuclear Neutron Weapons.* This resolution asked the Disarmament Committee to start negotiations on a convention prohibiting the production, stockpiling, deployment, and use of neutron weapons. It passed by a vote of 68 affirmative—14 (U.S.) negative—57 abstained.

8. *Guam.* This amendment to a draft resolution in Fourth Committee on foreign military bases eliminated reference to earlier resolutions hostile to U.S. interests. It passed by a vote of 66 (U.S.) affirmative—41 negative—16 abstained.

9. *Appointments to the International Civil Service Commission (ICSC).* This was a U.S.–sponsored motion asking the secretary-general to draw up a new list of candidates for appointment to the ICSC. The U.S. candidate for this important body had been defeated when candidates from other countries were entered in the voting in an illegal manner. This motion was defeated by a vote of 35 (U.S.) affirmative—46 negative—49 abstained.

10. *Israel in the Occupied Golan Heights.* This resolution at an Emergency Special Session of the General Assembly in February 1982 declared that Israel is not a peace-loving state and has not carried out its United Nations Charter obligations, called on United Nations members to apply various sanctions against Israel, and strongly deplored the U.S. veto of a Security Council resolution on this issue. It passed by a vote of 86 affirmative—21 (U.S.) negative—34 abstained.

There are several ways to score such votes, but the most effective way is to add one point for each vote in agreement with the U.S.; subtract one point for each vote opposed to the U.S.; and not count abstentions or absences. Thus, perfect agreement with the U.S. yields a score of +10. Total opposition to the U.S. yields a score of −10. A country that voted with the U.S. five times, against us twice, and abstained or was absent three times, would have a score of +3.

There are also several ways to compare such scores to other measures of importance, but surely one popular way is to compare voting scores to the amount of U.S. foreign aid a country receives. American taxpayers do not give aid to gain United Nations votes, nor do NAM states vote in the United Nations so as to increase the aid they receive. Nonetheless, one would expect the U.S. government to give the most foreign aid to those developing states with whom we most share values and positions on the greatest number of critical world issues, as expressed in United Nations voting behavior.

However, this is not true—as seen in table 1, which ranks U.S. aid recipients according to the +10, −10 voting scores. In addition, column 2 presents for each country listed the percentage of agreement of its votes with those of the U.S. on a larger sample of 74 relatively important General Assembly votes. Columns 3, 4, and 5 present the proposed levels (as of February 1982) of U.S. economic assistance, military assistance, and total assistance that each of these countries is to receive in fiscal year 1983.

The Need for Awareness

In certain ways, knowledge is power. To know that certain countries to whom the American taxpayers give enormous amounts of funds either do not share our principles and world outlook or do not possess the courage of their convictions is to know something important. Unfortunately, the amount of poverty in the developing world far exceeds the magnitude of any conceivable U.S. foreign assistance program. Thus our entire aid budget could easily be absorbed by relatively friendly countries, without any need for our helping to support governments that are unremittingly hostile to our policies and values. Greater public awareness along these lines may help to promote more sensible policies in the future and, perhaps, even to raise the level of discourse and behavior in the United Nations. One can always hope.

Table 1

Pro−U.S. Voting in the UN Correlated with U.S. Foreign Aid

U.S. aid recipients ranked by scores on 10 key votes	Percentage of agreement with U.S. on 74 important votes	U.S. assistance for FY 1983 (in thousands of dollars)		
		Economic	Military	Total
+9				
Israel	100.0	785,000	1,700,000	2,485,000
Portugal	61.1	20,000	93,600	113,600
+8				
Turkey	38.1	351,040	469,100	820,140
+6				
Austria	56.1	—	45	45
Colombia	34.1	3,600	12,860	16,460
Guatemala	83.3	13,009	251	13,260
+5				
Bolivia	50.0	30,125	100	30,225
Chile	52.6	—	50	50
Costa Rica	42.9	85,000	150	85,150
Dominican Republic	37.9	47,783	10,250	58,033
El Salvador	35.0	164,921	61,300	226,221
Fiji	31.6	[a]	55	55[a]
Iceland	62.7	—	20	20
Papua−New Guinea	40.6	[a]	20	20[a]
Paraguay	66.7	—	50	50
Philippines	27.1	103,093	52,050	155,143
Samoa	34.4	[a]	—	[a]
Singapore	30.0	—	50	50
Uruguay	39.2	—	50	50
+4				
Argentina	28.6	—	50	50
Bahamas	29.0	—	60	60
Barbados	18.4	[b]	—	[b]
Honduras	43.6	63,064	15,301	78,365
Jamaica	34.3	112,014	6,700	118,714

Table 1 (continued)

U.S. aid recipients ranked by scores on 10 key votes	Percentage of agreement with U.S. on 74 important votes	U.S. assistance for FY 1983 (in thousands of dollars)		
		Economic	Military	Total
Liberia	28.3	55,430	15,800	71,230
Morocco	28.1	52,713	101,600	154,313
Niger	18.3	20,854	5,450	26,304
Solomons	41.2	a	——	a
Spain	37.0	12,000	403,500	415,500
Thailand	25.0	40,400	93,250	133,650
Zaire	23.4	37,142	21,300	58,442
+3				
Antigua (Brit.)	62.5	b	——	b
Belize	18.7	b	100	100[a]
Brazil	20.8	450	50	500
Central African Repub.	31.4	1,000	——	1,000
Comoros	21.1	352	——	352
Egypt	19.6	1,021,344	1,302,000	2,323,344
Eq. Guinea	36.4	1,307	50	1,357
Gabon	28.6	——	3,100	3,100
Greece	37.0	——	282,568	282,568
Haiti	41.2	34,725	715	35,440
+2				
Bangladesh	17.9	160,611	225	160,836
Malawi	55.6	7,577	60	7,637
Malaysia	19.3	——	13,350	13,350
Mauritius	16.7	6,183	——	6,183
Nepal	18.2	14,479	75	14,554
Pakistan	21.5	256,381	275,800	532,181
Senegal	21.0	43,762	5,450	49,212
Somalia	22.4	60,714	30,550	91,264
Suriname	16.1	1,000	75	1,075
Swaziland	22.6	7,183	——	7,183
Togo	15.8	4,503	75	4,578
Upper Volta	20.9	17,459	135	17,594
Venezuela	14.5	——	50	50

(continued)

Table 1 (continued)

U.S. aid recipients ranked by scores on 10 key votes	Percentage of agreement with U.S. on 74 important votes	U.S. assistance for FY 1983 (in thousands of dollars)		
		Economic	Military	Total
+1				
Burma	12.1	17,500	200	17,700
Djibouti	11.8	4,599	1,600	6,199
Ecuador	14.5	12,288	6,700	18,988
Finland	47.6	——	40	40
Ivory Coast	25.0	——	50	50
Lesotho	16.3	19,611	——	19,611
Peru	13.5	67,638	6,700	74,338
St. Lucia	13.3	b	——	b
St. Vincent	10.0	b	——	b
Sudan	15.8	128,388	101,675	230,063
Tunisia	19.0	141,703	11,907	153,610
0				
Botswana	19.5	11,130	5,125	16,255
Cameroon	7.7	18,016	10,150	28,166
Dominica	c	b	——	b
Indonesia	19.7	92,269	52,725	144,994
Kenya	10.8	75,985	36,500	112,485
Oman	12.7	15,000	40,100	55,100
Rwanda	13.3	8,783	1,575	10,358
Sri Lanka	13.6	71,155	150	71,305
−1				
Bhutan	10.4	956	——	956
Burundi	8.3	8,030	30	8,060
Guyana	9.5	2,672	50	2,722
Lebanon	8.7	8,000	15,750	23,750
Panama	6.1	12,344	5,501	17,845
Mauritania	9.0	10,983	50	11,033
Vanuatu	13.0	a	——	a
−2				
Gambia	14.6	5,922	——	5,922
Ghana	11.7	17,854	450	18,304
Zimbabwe	6.8	75,000	3,150	78,150

Table 1 (continued)

U.S. aid recipients ranked by scores on 10 key votes	Percentage of agreement with U.S. on 74 important votes	U.S. assistance for FY 1983 (in thousands of dollars)		
		Economic	Military	Total
−3				
Chad	4.8	216	——	216
Jordan	6.6	20,256	77,900	98,156
Yugoslavia	7.5	——	130	130
Zambia	9.1	27,000	150	27,150
−4				
Cape Verde	1.7	2,988	35	3,023
Cyprus	1.9	9,000	——	9,000
Guinea−Bissau	2.2	2,396	35	2,431
Mexico	4.6	7,700	245	7,945
Sierra Leone	6.2	5,344	25	5,369
−5				
Guinea	4.7	4,770	35	4,805
Mali	3.6	9,650	125	9,775
Tanzania	1.8	17,715	75	17,790
Yemen (North)	3.3	27,998	16,500	44,498
−6				
India	3.2	210,433	200	210,633
−7				
Benin	3.3	517	——	517
Uganda	3.1	5,500	50	5,550
−8				
Congo	1.5	2,258	35	2,293
Madagascar	2.8	1,031	20	1,051
São Tomé	2.9	61	——	61
−9				
Angola	3.3	362	——	362

(continued)

Table 1 (continued)

U.S. aid recipients ranked by scores on 10 key votes	Percentage of agreement with U.S. on 74 important votes	U.S. assistance for FY 1983 (in thousands of dollars)		
		Economic	Military	Total
−10				
Ethiopia	1.4	1,867	——	1,867
Mozambique	2.9	600	——	600
Seychelles	2.0	2,376	——	2,376

[a]Likely to receive some portion of $5.1 million in South Pacific Regional economic aid.

[b]Likely to receive some portion of $60 million in Caribbean Regional economic aid.

[c]Dominica was absent on all General Assembly votes.

8

DANIEL PIPES

The Third World Peoples of Soviet Central Asia

Most of the fifty million Third World peoples of the Soviet Union live in Central Asia, a large area north of Iran and east of the Caspian Sea.* These are Muslims (Turks and Iranians) who fell under Russian rule over a century ago. In striking contrast to other Third World peoples, who have been ruled by Europeans and who by now enjoy independence, the Central Asians are still governed from Moscow. The fact that so many Third World peoples are in the Soviet

---

*If, strictly speaking, the Third World is defined as those developing areas under the aegis of neither the United States nor the Soviet Union, then all peoples of the Soviet Union are in the Second World. We might say, however, that they are potentially Third World peoples.

Union under Russian dominion raises many questions about
their relation to the Soviet Union and their potential rest-
lessness for independence. Central Asia being very little
known, we shall begin with some introductory facts.

Historical Background

During the past several centuries, as West Europeans sailed
around the world conquering territories and establishing colonies, the Russians followed a similar pattern by a different
process. They, too, conquered territories and established colonies, but rather than sail, they marched.

Russians expanded into Asia in three stages.* In the first,
beginning in the 1580s, they crossed the Ural Mountains
and continued east through Siberia all the way to the Pacific.
Although they traversed immense distances, they encountered only sparse populations of primitive peoples and
reached the Pacific in 1638 without serious opposition. The
non-Russian peoples of this vast area concern us little,
because they are still few and primitive.

The second wave took about 150 years, from 1711 until
1855. During this period the Russians conquered the
Caucasus region and present-day Kazakhstan. Although
both of these areas had larger and more developed populations than Siberia, they, too, included few centers of power or
culture.

The third and final wave went more rapidly. Between 1864
and 1884, the Russians took control of all the important
cities of Central Asia—Bukhara, Samarqand, Khiva, Kho-
kand, and Merv—all of which, surprisingly, fell almost without a struggle. And thus the Russians found themselves sud-

---

*In order to concentrate on Third World peoples, this chapter ignores the equally im-
portant Russian expansion westwards into Europe. Central Asians do not constitute all
the Third World peoples in the Soviet Union by any means, but they are the largest in
number and the most important of them.

denly wielding power over some 5 million persons of an alien civilization.

The vast majority of Central Asians were Muslims. For a millennium they had actively participated in Islamic civilization, producing many of its great dynasties and cultural achievements. Accordingly, the population was heavily oriented to Muslim areas of the south and east. Most of the population spoke Turkic, but some spoke Iranian, and Iran had a predominant cultural influence; in important ways, Central Asia was virtually a part of Iran.

The Central Asians did not constitute national groups in the Western fashion. Divided politically and linguistically, they had almost no sense of territorial loyalty. Rather, they primarily considered themselves to be Muslims. The area had had only fleeting and antagonistic contacts with a distant but expanding Russia, so when the Russians appeared as conquerors, they were completely alien to the indigenous peoples.

Although the Russians had reached Central Asia by land, they acquired and ruled the region as a colony, their land empire closely resembling the sea empires of the British, French, Dutch, Spanish, Portuguese, Italians, Germans, and Belgians of the time. The Tsarist government was unabashedly imperialistic in its expansion. Like other colonial masters, it believed in the overwhelming superiority of its own culture. The Russians insisted on using their own language, despised local customs and culture, especially Islam, and held attitudes characteristic of all European colonizers in the Third World. Russian settlement in Central Asia resembled that of the French in Algeria, the British in Rhodesia, or the Portuguese in Angola.

The Tsarist government also exploited its colonies for strategic and economic benefit, much as did the other European powers. Central Asia served the Russians in stopping a British advance north from India. The government built a railroad connection to Russia, encouraged the planting of cash crops such as cotton, and set high tariff levels for foreign goods in order to keep Central Asia as a captive market for Russian industrial products. Russians settled Central Asia not only in towns but also on farms, especially to grow grain in the Kazakh plain.*

Before 1917, Russian Communists unambiguously condemned every instance of European imperialism, including the Tsarist presence in Central Asia. On coming to power, the Bolsheviks promised a new era, and spoke of the cultural—and even political—autonomy of the old colonies. Yet despite such intentions, those areas are still part of the Soviet Union almost seventy years later. Why were these promises not met?

The Communists found it much easier to give away the Tsar's possessions than their own. Once in power, they resisted every effort to break up the empire—indeed, they reconquered a number of non-Russian regions that had set up local rule. Finally, in 1924, with the turmoil of the revolution and the subsequent civil war behind them, the Soviet government began implementing a "nationalities policy." Rather than release the non-Russian peoples from Soviet rule, this policy provided them with national republics within the Soviet Union. In Central Asia, this meant dividing the region into five republics that, with minor adjustments, survive to the present: Kazakhstan, Kirghizia, Tajikistan, Turkmenistan, and Uzbekistan.

The boundaries of these republics were drawn with scrupulous attention to the minor linguistic variations in Turkic dialects (which explains the extremely odd shape of Uzbekistan). The republics did not reflect national groups, however, for there was no national consciousness along linguistic or any other lines in Central Asia. (This is as artificial as dividing the United States along the lines of

---

*The term "Russian" in reference to settlers in Central Asia also includes other Slavic speakers, primarily Ukrainians.

regional accents.) The creation of national republics introduced a new political concept: suddenly, on orders from Moscow, the Central Asians became five distinct peoples.

Imposing national republics on the Central Asians served the Soviet government in two important ways. First, it broke the unity of the region and thus reduced the likelihood of all Central Asians acting together in concert against the Russians. Secondly, by providing the Central Asians with their own power structures, if only in form, the Bolsheviks technically ended the colonial nature of their rule in Central Asia without allowing a fundamental shift in power. This latter point had great significance.

The establishment of national republics justified permanent Bolshevik rule over non-Russians through a breathtakingly simple change in ideology. Unlike imperial regimes, which overtly subsumed the interests of the colonies to those of the ruling peoples, the Soviet leaders claimed that the non-Russian peoples voluntarily chose to become part of the Soviet Union and also that fraternal ties made their relationship mutually beneficial. They argued that federation with the progressive forces in Russia brought benefits to all peoples; Moscow's revolutionary government had equal appeal to non-Russians and Russians. If, then, joining the Soviet Union was an enlightened act of benefit to the society as a whole, then breaking away would be counterrevolutionary, merely the selfish response of the bourgeoisie. In short, making the old colonies into nominally independent republics allowed the Bolsheviks to argue that non-Russians had freely chosen to remain under Russian rule. Overnight, the colonized peoples found themselves transformed from oppressed masses into "younger brothers" in the struggle for peace and equality. The doctrine of Marxism-Leninism being by nature anti-imperialistic, the Soviet Union could not—in theory—have colonies. As it would so often in years to come, Marxism-Leninism showed itself flexible enough to buttress any argument.

Colonies or National Republics?

Did Central Asia really cease to be a Russian colony after
1924? Or did the creation of national republics mask a fundamental continuity between Tsarist and Soviet rule? The
USSR claims that Central Asia is no longer a colony, but an
independent republic; a closer look shows that the assertion
does have some basis.

"Colony" here means a region subjugated to an alien
people where the ruling class is not only distinct but has a
home elsewhere. If the experience of Central Asia since 1924
has resembled that of the West European overseas colonies
such as India or Algeria, we may call Central Asia a colony.

The argument against the colonial nature of Central Asia
emphasizes how much better off it has been than a typical
colony. The Central Asian peoples have benefited from their
own political structures, from dramatic economic gains, and
from great advances in education. Most striking is the fact
that, in important ways, they have fared better under Soviet
rule than have the Russians themselves. They have suffered
less terror, dislocation, bureaucracy, religious persecution,
and economic mismanagement. But, the counterargument
goes, prosperity and education have nothing to do with colonialism; the colonial relationship is defined by power. A colony need not be badly off, but it must be ruled by aliens. In
order to analyze these conflicting viewpoints, political, economic, and cultural features deserve closer attention.

Politics. The political situation of Central Asia differs
from that of a typical colony in several ways. Its lack of
power is a consequence of centralized Soviet rule, not of in-
equity between Russians and non-Russians. A totalitarian
government such as that of the Soviet Union requires
centralization; Moscow controls innumerable details in the
lives of all Soviet citizens, including the Russians. Thus, the

absence of power in Central Asia can be explained without reference to its predominantly non-Russian population; it would have little self-rule no matter who lived there.

Given the nature of the Soviet government, the distance of Central Asia from Moscow has benefits, for it slightly relieves the people of the region from the heavy hand of the state. Living far from the center of power, their actions are less subject to the intense scrutiny of the government; of all Soviet peoples, the Central Asians experienced the least terror during Stalin's rule and less interference since. In an important way, then, these Third World peoples enjoy a better quality of life than the Russians.

In two other ways, too, Central Asians do not fit the status of a colonial people. First, they enjoy complete legal equality with the Russians. They do suffer discrimination, but it is illegal. Central Asians are full-fledged citizens of the Soviet Union. Second, the Soviet army conscripts all citizens, without regard to regional or ethnic origin. Central Asians serve just as Russians do. Once in the army, no distinction is paid to origin, and all nationalities are freely mixed. This too contravenes the colonial pattern.

At the same time, Central Asia shares vital characteristics with colonies. It has the trappings of power but not the substance. Like the maharajas of India, who retained formal authority while the British ran their affairs, the republics of Central Asia are independent and sovereign. Indeed, they not only have their own foreign and defense ministries, but even the constitutional right to secede from the Soviet Union. Two Soviet republics (though not Central Asian ones) are full members of the United Nations. All this is a sham, however; the republics neither make their own foreign policy nor influence decisions made in Moscow, their foreign and defense ministries are hollow showpieces, and the UN presence fools no one. All power to deal with the outside world resides in Moscow.

Moscow's power is not limited to foreign policy; in internal affairs, too, it has the last word. While the republics make numerous local decisions, Moscow can always reverse them. There can be no rivalry between Moscow and the republics; the latter have no forces to array against the center. The instruments of power are all in Soviet—not the republics'— hands. The army and the secret police are controlled by Moscow, vital economic matters are directly supervised from there, and so on. The power that republics or local authorities have is delegated by the central government. One need not look far for indications of Moscow's power in running the republics: it can order the outcome of court cases, set censorship guidelines, discipline party members, or reverse any locally made policy.

What little power the republics have is largely for propaganda purposes. The outside world generally, and foreign visitors specifically, must find at least some self-government in Central Asia. Were it not for foreign opinion, the republics would probably have less authority than they do now.

Centralization of power need not imply Russian control over Central Asia; if Central Asians participated in government in proportion to their population, they would no longer be under Russian control and the region would not be a colony. Again, efforts are made to show that they do participate, but a closer look reveals that this, too, is fraudulent, for Russians dominate every decision-making body. The minorities' token representation gives them almost no say in deliberations that decide their fate. A decision from Moscow is a decision by Russians, and all decisions are ultimately made (or affirmed) in Moscow.

Not only do Russians dominate, but the whole Soviet regime is bound inextricably with their nationalism. Far from representing an internationalist ideology, as it originally intended to do, the Soviet government represents Russian interests; it is a linear successor to the Russian empire. This has the important psychological effect of limiting the patriotic feeling of Central Asians for the regime. They generally view it less as their own than as a Russian government.

Russian power extends even within the Central Asian republics, where Russians hold many key positions. Normally, Muslims hold the top positions and ceremonial posts, while Russians fill key second-level jobs to keep a close watch on local developments. Russians also double up with Muslims in many positions. They are appointed directly by Moscow, and they maintain tight control over the local political apparatus. Tashkent will never experience a spring like Prague's.

The presence of many Russian settlers in all the Central Asian republics makes it possible to keep all political positions in local hands and still include many Russians. Moscow need not send Russians out to the provinces, for so many of them are already there. While technically keeping power in the hands of residents, the capital can give real authority to the Russians among them.

In sum, the Russians allow the Soviet Third World peoples little more power than did any colonial masters. But whereas earlier European empires made no efforts to hide this fact, the Russians have elaborated political structures and an ideology to disguise it. Ironically, while the Soviet Union has contributed to making the present an anti-imperialist age by attacking all forms of colonialism, it has done the most to refine the colonial relationship by shedding its overt features. A "fraternal tie" looks better, but in real terms it means the same thing—the control of one people by another. Economic and cultural affairs clearly reflect this power relationship.

Economics. In some ways, again, Central Asia defies classic colonial patterns. Although Central Asia had barely any industry in 1917, it has developed considerably since then. Dramatic improvements in productivity and standards of living have taken place, often greater than those of the Soviet Union as a whole.

The government has made substantial efforts to accelerate growth by investing heavily in Central Asia. Moscow has apparently put more money into the region than it has extracted.[1] If this is true, it defies all colonial precedents, for no metropolitan power ever intentionally invested more in a colony than it derived from it. Close analysis also shows that much of this investment could have brought larger returns elsewhere in the Soviet Union;[2] one may, therefore, conclude that it was put into Central Asia to improve its standard of living. Martin Spechler dubbed this "welfare colonialism."[3]

The Russian connection has thus brought Central Asia economic benefits, lifting the region to a prosperity that the local peoples on their own could not have attained. Comparison between the Central Asians and their nearest kinsmen in independent countries—Afghanistan, Iran, and Turkey—bears this out. Regardless which index one looks at—per capita income, mortality rates, medical services, electric power—in all respects, Soviet Third World peoples are far ahead of their independent neighbors. In part, this may be due to the more stable government in Central Asia; none of its neighbors has had the same government since 1920, and all have witnessed turmoil in recent years.

Central Asia compares favorably not only with the Third World countries to its south, but also with other regions of the Soviet Union. It experienced a smoother development under Soviet rule than most other regions. Aside from the catastrophic collectivization efforts in the 1930s, the Central Asians have almost escaped the economic excesses and reversals that have so severely afflicted the rest of the Soviet Union. In contrast to other regions, Central Asia has received enough money for agricultural investment; as a result, it is the only region in the country with a successful agriculture.[4]

In all, an economic picture emerges that compares favorably with both Central Asia's independent neighbors and other regions of the Soviet Union; this latter point especially turns the usual colonial relationship on its head. Can one yet maintain that Central Asia is economically a colony of Russia's? Yes, because the power relationship implies that Moscow holds nearly total control over Central Asia's economy; whatever Central Asia enjoys, it has at Moscow's pleasure.

To begin with, the centralized policy of the Soviet government implies that Moscow makes economic as well as political decisions, right down to the trivial level. Distant bureaucrats fix factory schedules, farm productivity, and worker payment. Krushchev himself once lectured the Uzbeks on the best type of sheep for them to raise. Thus Moscow exercises a detailed tyranny over Central Asian economic life. Beyond this, it directly controls the most sensitive industries, such as gold and military production, to the exclusion of local authorities.

Along with internal control, Moscow determines foreign trade to and from Central Asia. The people and governments of the area do not dispose of the hard currency they earn. Instead, their profits go directly to Moscow, which usually allows them only a fraction of those funds for their own use.

Central Asia serves the classic colonial purpose of providing Russia with cheap raw materials and then importing its industrial goods. (India, for instance, filled this role for Britain.) All the cotton in the Soviet Union is grown in Central Asia, but in 1964 only 9 percent of it was processed locally, the rest sent out of the region.[5] In return, the Russians cut Central Asia off from direct foreign trade, and exploit it as a captive market for their inferior industrial goods.

Typical colonial relations exist not only between Central Asia and Moscow, but also between the Muslims and Russians living in Central Asia itself. The Russians there tend to have the better land and the better jobs (like the French in Algeria). The region presents a model case of ethnic stratification, wherein one group, the Russians, commonly enjoys economic advantages that few from other groups share.[6] Even if this situation can be explained by differences in skills, motivation, and education, it still reminds the Muslims of who runs things.

Without underestimating the economic advantages that Central Asian Third World peoples have over their independent brethren to the south, it is true that in the present age of nationalism this matters very little. The economic benefits of colonial rule have been apparent in many regions, yet this almost never influences a people (unless its numbers are very small) to prefer remaining a colony. While the blacks in South Africa are richer than their compatriots everywhere else in Africa, this does not make them content; they do not compare themselves with poorer blacks in distant countries, but with the richer whites in their midst. Given the choice, all peoples choose independence, regardless of economic consequences; surely this applies also to the Muslims of Central Asia. Welfare colonialism is still colonialism; "Soviet Russia seeks political domination, even at the price of economic discomfort for its own citizens."[7]

Culture. Here, too, Central Asia differs in some ways from the typical Third World colony. Education has made tremendous strides since 1917. The Tsarist government before then had done nothing to encourage education, so until 1917 the literacy rate in Central Asia was minuscule; currently, nearly everyone can read. This extraordinary change came about as a result of the heavy Soviet emphasis on education, and the willingness of the government to spend on it. All children must attend school; numerous technical programs prepare them for skilled jobs; and there are now several universities in the region. These advances in education distinguish Central Asia from a typical colony, in which the Third World people suffer from the European power's unwillingness to spend money on their education. In many cases, too (including the Tsarist one), the colonial power prefers an uneducated colony, expecting it to cause less trouble.

In an odd way, the Soviet treatment of religion argues again for Central Asia's relatively favorable experience. On principle, the Soviet authorities discourage religion, yet Islam has fared better than Christianity. Having Christian origins themselves, the Communist leaders have persecuted Christianity with particular venom; they care less about Islam. If mosques were turned into post offices, Russian Orthodox churches were used as barns.

Granting the real educational advances in Central Asia and the small advantage of Islam over Christianity in the Soviet Union, Russian attitudes toward Central Asian culture, and Russian control of it, betray a colonial relationship. Both the Russian settlers in Central Asia and the Soviet regime lack respect for the Islamic civilization of Central Asia. Russians are convinced of their own cultural superiority, and they betray an attitude of aversion and suspicion toward the alien culture of the region. This attitude exactly matches that of other European colonial rulers.

In Tsarist times, the Russians viewed Islam as a sinister force; they did not understand it, and they made few efforts to come to terms with it. The Communists added an atheistic ideology to that mistrust. True, their atheism challenges all religions, but it has two special consequences in Central Asia. First, since the atheistic doctrines come from men of Christian origin, Muslims see them as a covert Christian attack on Islam. Russians have always despited Islam—earlier in the name of Christianity, now in the name of atheism. The results are similar, and Muslims respond badly to both types of attack. Second, because Islam is tied to every aspect of a Muslim's life, an attack on the religion also denigrates his whole way of life and his culture. By assailing Islam, the Russians malign much more than the Central Asians' religion.

Soviet policy toward the Turkic and Iranian languages of Central Asia indicates most clearly the power Russians wield in cultural matters. The government played havoc with the

local languages by changing their scripts and word meanings.[8] The Soviet government ordered that the Central Asian
languages drop the Arabic script, starting in 1922, to isolate
the Muslims of the Soviet Union both from their Islamic
heritage and from Turkic and Iranian writing originating
outside the country. Those who learned to read the Latin
script could not easily handle written matter from before
1917; this gave the Soviet authorities greater control over
their reading matter. Also, by abandoning the Arabic script,
the Soviets made it difficult for Muslims in the Soviet Union
to communicate in writing with Turkic and Iranian speakers
elsewhere. The intention to isolate was proved by the Soviet
reaction to Ataturk's reforms. When, in 1928, he required
the Turks in Turkey to adopt the Latin alphabet, the Soviets
ordered a second change in script, from Latin to Cyrillic.
Cyrillic letters remain in use until this day.

The change from Latin to Cyrillic letters involved another
change too. Whereas the Latin alphabets for the many
dialects of Turkic had represented each sound by the same
letter, the Cyrillic alphabets for the many dialects assigned
different letters for the same sound. The intent behind this
needless complication is clear; the different letters placed
obstacles in the way of communication between nationalities. In this manner, alphabet policy reduces the chance of
unified action by Turkic speakers against the Russians.
Again, Russian interests dominate.

The redefinition of words in the Turkic and Iranian
languages also indicates Russian power. While the Soviet
government has eliminated meanings of Russian words related to religion and traditional culture, it is one thing when
Russians tamper with their own language and quite another
when they do so with that of others. Disregarding the sentiments of those who speak these languages, the Russians
have shuffled word meanings around to suit their purposes.[9]
This is blatant cultural imperialism. Russians are convinced
they know the truth, and so impose their ideas on a non-

European people. It matters little whether their truth be Christianity or communism; the Russians have the desire and the means to force their will on other peoples.

In the final analysis, Central Asia does appear to be a colony of Russia. Economic progress and relative well-being notwithstanding, the complete and arbitrary power that Russians exercise argues for this conclusion. Russian control of distant alien lands makes those areas Russian colonies. Shrill anti-colonialist rhetoric to the contrary, the Soviet Union retains the classic relationship of European ruler and Third World colony. Of all European peoples, the Russians alone retain a large colonial empire.[10] The other great empires have been reduced to disjointed bits: Macao, Belize, Gibraltar, Reunion, St. Helena, the Falklands, etc. (South Africa is no longer a colony of Europe, but an independent country.) Only the Russians are left.[11] Why is the world so little aware of the Russian empire? How have the Russians maintained strict colonial control without anyone noticing?

The Russian empire kept out of view thanks to two features: the land connection, and the creation of republics. Regardless how far the Russians went, they stayed on land, so their colonies lacked one obviously colonial quality of a sea empire. Although Central Asia lies much further from Moscow than does Algeria from Paris, the sea constitutes an insurmountable barrier to making Algeria part of France, while the land tie between Russia and Central Asia facilitates their connection, obscuring the alien quality of Russian rule in Central Asia.

The establishment of republics has also served to make the Russian empire invisible. Powerless local governments allow the Russians to maintain control while bestowing the appearance of autonomy. Although Russians rule, this becomes evident only upon closer inspection. Setting up controlled local governments in colonies is the major Russian contribution to the refinement of colonial rule.

Prospects and United States Policy

Central Asia's invisibility is coming to an end with its population explosion and its heightened political awareness. As the region gains importance, the United States needs to formulate a policy, if only because conditions in Central Asia offer a momentous opportunity for checking Soviet aggressiveness and power.

Central Asia has undergone a demographic surge that is transforming its role within the USSR. In the years between the censuses of 1959 and 1970, the major nationalities of Central Asia increased in population by 51 percent, as shown in table 1; increases between the 1970 and 1979 census were still an impressive 32 percent. Russian gains during the same periods were 13 and 6 percent, respectively.

Table 1

**Population Increases of Major Central Asian
Nationality Groups**

Nationality	1959–1970 percentage increase	1970–1979 percentage increase
Kazakh	46	24
Kirghiz	50	31
Tajik	53	36
Turkmen	52	33
Uzbek	53	36

Source: Alexandre Bennigsen and Chantal Lemercier-Quelquejay, "L'Islam dans les Republiques musulmanes sovietiques," in *L'Islam et l'Etat dans le Monde d'aujourd'hui,* ed. Olivier Carre (Paris: Presses Universitaires de France, 1982), pp. 166–67.

On the average, the Central Asian nationalities are increasing by half in each decade; this comes to about 3.8 percent per annum, a figure that approaches the biological maximum. The Muslim population of Central Asia numbered some 13 million in 1959, 20 million in 1970, and 27 million in 1979. Central Asian Muslims constituted 6 percent of the total Soviet population in 1959, 8 percent in 1970, and 17 percent in 1979, and they will make up an ever-larger proportion of the Soviet population in the coming decades. As the region grows in numbers, its concerns must demand more attention from the Russian authorities.

The surge in the Muslim population is already transforming the Soviet work force and army. Young Muslims of Central Asia are coming of working age in large numbers just as the Soviet economy needs additional low-skill manual workers; the timing might be just right. Like the workers from the Mediterranean area who seek work in North Europe, the Muslims of Central Asia can go north to jobs in Siberia and Western Russia. The difficulty lies in matching workers and positions, for Central Asians are reluctant to leave their region, and most of the new jobs cannot be relocated in Central Asia. Will they migrate; will the jobs come to them; both, or neither? Soviet and Western analysts are debating this issue;[12] and it does bear attention, for if Central Asian workers and the jobs are not brought together, the Soviet economy will suffer and Central Asians will be restlessly underemployed.

Central Asians in the army are another worry for the Russians. If universal conscription is continued, Muslims will constitute a third of future recruits by the 1990s. This could have a profound effect on Soviet military policy. Not only are most Central Asians ignorant of Russian, less educated, and less skilled, but their loyalty to the Soviet Union and their motivation to fight for it are open to question.

Politically, too, Central Asia promises to become more troublesome. As its isolation breaks down, the Muslims are beginning to enjoy increased contacts with the outside world. These have made them increasingly aware of the world order and of their own anomalous position. In a world divided into sovereign nations, why are they one of the few peoples still not independent? Why are they yet under the thumb of a distant city?

Until now, Central Asian nationalism has been muted, but in the long run it seems inevitable that these peoples, like all others, will demand independence. Eventually (though when is a matter of great disagreement), the Uzbeks, Tajiks, et al., will become stubbornly nationalistic, and the Soviet regime will face unprecedented internal troubles. The articulated discontent of Central Asian Muslims not only will cause domestic unrest, but could also severely damage the Soviet Union's cultivated anti-imperialist image and sabotage its standing in the Third World. At the same time, however, while both the Islamic revolution in Iran and the Afghan resistance against the Soviet invasion of their country stirred responses among the Muslims of Central Asia, neither of these events appears to have precipitated a major shift in mood.

The potential importance of Central Asia—and of all the non-Russian areas of the USSR—cannot be ignored by the United States government. To date it has done nothing; it has never challenged the right of Russian rule in the region, nor has it formulated a policy regarding future self-determination in the Central Asian republics.

This timidity has been due to an American understanding of the extreme Soviet reaction against any official discussion of Central Asia. The Russians would consider this a precipitate provocation. Raising the issue would sharply antagonize the Soviet Union, and what could we gain by it? Further, we face the danger of raising nationalist hopes in Central Asia without being able or willing to support them. If the United States suddenly made an issue of the colonial situation in Central Asia, peoples there might take it as a signal that this country encourages their efforts to achieve independence. If local movements there rose in response, the United States would have a commitment to stand by them. Fearing both a terrible turn in relations with the Soviet Union and responsibility for developments in Central Asia, the United States government has refrained from meddling.

The sensitivity of the Central Asian question is reason for caution, but not for inaction. Two reasons argue in favor of raising this matter: it is consistent with the U.S. policy since World War I of opposing all colonial rule and favoring self-determination; and it serves our purposes, in that a cautious discussion of Russian rule in Central Asia could cause the Soviet Union great embarrassment in international circles and could possibly contribute to the dismantling of its empire.

How might the topic best be brought up by the U.S. government? By addressing the world at large, not the Russians or the Central Asians. We must avoid any suggestion of encouragement to the Third World peoples of the Soviet Union, for we want no responsibility for fomenting unrest.[13] This would only poison relations with the USSR and force us to be accountable for uncontrollable developments there.

We are not precluded, however, from expanding radio broadcasts to Central Asia. The Voice of America currently programs 2½ hours daily, and Radio Liberty programs 10 hours. While this is about two times more broadcast time than before the Iranian revolution, the potential significance of Central Asia warrants yet greater increases in programming, particularly as this would hasten the autonomist urges described here.

Rather than try directly to influence events in the Soviet Union, we should make the world aware of the situation there. Were the United States, for example, to submit Central Asia as a topic for discussion at the United Nations Committee on Decolonization, this alone would make the matter an international issue. Such discussion would put the Soviet Union on the defensive, and it might have a particular influence on Muslims, who feel strongly for their co-religionists.

The recent American emphasis on human rights met with a cool international response because it embarrassed most of the world. In contrast, a campaign against colonialism would

win wide international support. The United States and its
allies need not wage this campaign on their own against the
USSR. It should be enough to raise the issue and then let the
Third World countries apply pressure on the Soviet Union.
Their displeasure carries far more weight than ours because
they, unlike us, are potential allies.

The U.S. task, then, is to make the Third World aware of
the situation in the Soviet Union. The European colonies,
such as the Ukraine, will concern the Third World very little,
but it will take great interest in Central Asia, an area of
Third World peoples ruled by Europeans. By making known
the situation in Central Asia, not only may we cause the
Soviet Union to lose its prestige as an anti-imperialist power,
but Third World pressure might speed up the formation of
nations within the Soviet Union and lead to the release of its
many colonies. Needless to say, this has enormous implications for the future of the whole USSR.

The more the Third World knows about Soviet Central
Asia, the better both for the Central Asians and for ourselves. As the Central Asians grow in numbers and gain political consciousness, their obscurity and invisibility will end.
Their status as the last major Third World peoples under
European rule will become a vital matter of international
concern in the coming years.

9

ROBERT E. HARKAVY

Military Bases in the Third World

United States–Soviet competition for access to military bases in the Third World has become more globally dispersed in recent years. Likewise, bases—more commonly now referred to as "facilities" to denote shifts in ultimate sovereign control—have become a more visible and complex North-South issue, even as relations between the hitherto strong or relatively independent and the weak or relatively dependent countries have arguably become more symmetrical.

In the broadest sense, the current geopolitical struggle over overseas access can be taken as a culmination of long-developing historical trends. At least three somewhat distinct though telescoped phases may be discerned over the past sixty-odd years. They, in turn, merely reflect broad

shifts in systemic or epochal characteristics of the colonial
(including the interwar), early postwar, and recent postwar
eras.

Changes in Geopolitical Value of Forward Bases

Prior to World War II—extending well back into the nineteenth century—most overseas bases were, quite simply, an
automatic by-product of colonial control. They were owned
outright; the user's full sovereignty applied to a base, as opposed to a facility, in the current sense of that much-
belabored distinction.

Earlier global basing systems, therefore, were a function of
the size of overseas empires. Britain had by far the most extensive network of naval bases, with France following somewhat behind. The United States had a weak forward defense
perimeter in the Pacific Far East and the Caribbean, much of
it acquired after the 1898 war with Spain. The Russians concentrated on developing their huge contiguous continental
land empire, while Germany stewed vengefully in the revi-
sionist aftermath of the 1919 peace settlement that left it
fully bereft of extended points of military access. Finally,
Holland, Spain, Portugal, and Belgium had some scattered
assets. As stated by Mahan[1] and other sea power theorists,
Britain's global basing network was both cause and effect in
relation to its vaunted, undivided sea control; similar
generalizations were proffered for the preceding periods of
Dutch and Portuguese maritime dominance.

In the interwar period, there were instances in which
sovereign states granted long-term basing access to others.
In a period of more rapidly shifting alliances and a less
strictly ideological basis for those alignments, there were no
discernible predecessors to the organized rival security networks that were to emerge after 1945 as NATO and the Warsaw Pact; nor were there precursors to the bilateral pacts
between large and small powers that were to serve as foun-

dations for overseas basing arrangements. Germany's use of Italy's Libyan air bases in the late 1930s and Japan's apparent concurrent naval access to Siam were among the few exceptions. Likewise, the U.S.–U.K. Lend-Lease agreement in 1940, which gave the United States a vast forward basing presence along the entire West Atlantic littoral in exchange for some overage destroyers, was a harbinger of things to come.

After 1945, the early bipolar Cold War period initially saw a lopsided balance of basing assets between the superpowers at a time when the spatial lines of competition so strikingly mirrored the traditional Mackinderian image of heartland and rimland. The Soviets were, up to the late 1950s, constrained within a contiguous continental empire. Their then-weak navy had forward bases only, at times, in China, Finland, and Albania. Extended, long-range military air transport networks were then but a distant hope. The United States, meanwhile, ringed the Soviet-dominated Eurasian landmass with the NATO, CENTO (Central Treaty Organization), and SEATO (Southeast Asia Treaty Organization) alliances, which, supplemented by the extensive remnants of British and other West European–held colonial outposts, provided layers of redundant air and naval access of all sorts. These arrangements were underwritten by huge outlays of military and economic aid, some in the form of World War II surplus weapons stocks. More important, a solid convergence of the political and security aims of the United States, on the one hand, and its various clients among the "forward" states along the containment ring, on the other, went virtually unquestioned on all sides.

As a result, the United States was availed of vast assets usable for strategic nuclear deterrence (bomber recovery bases, tanker facilities, ballistic missile early warning systems, etc.), a variety of technical intelligence-gathering functions, air staging, and forward deployment of combat ships and tactical aircraft. In most if not all cases, the terms of U.S. access were permissive beyond the required *quid pro quo* of aid and protection, so that, among other things, easy interconnected access for fighting or supporting "local" brushfire wars was provided throughout the developing world without the shackles that would later become so familiar.

Beginning in the late 1950s, but accelerating during the 1960s and beyond, vast changes in the superpowers' struggle for overseas assets gradually occurred—changes that were to become a central element in what some would more broadly perceive as a fundamental shift in the global balance of power. Those changes were propelled by the rapid decolonization process that produced numerous new sovereignties in Africa, Asia, and the Pacific, many of which— after brief transitions—turned to radicalism and Soviet arms. The containment ring was leapfrogged—first in Egypt, Syria, Ghana, Guinea, Somalia, Cuba, Indonesia, and Yemen; later in such disparate places as Peru, Grenada, Cape Verde, Libya, Laos, Madagascar, and Mozambique.

The United States suffered a gradual but relentless decline in its once formidable network of basing assets, variously because of Europe's loss of colonial territories, the withering of the U.S. formal alliance system, and shifts in various LDC (less-developed country) political orientations. Bases once nearly taken for granted were lost in Libya, Morocco (partially), Ethiopia, Mauritius, the Maldives, Ceylon, Thailand, Vietnam, Iran, Pakistan, et al. And, after the Vietnam debacle, seemingly solid U.S. basing bailiwicks such as Turkey, Greece, Spain, and even the Philippines became more precarious, contingent, and expensive, as frightened hosts now ambiguous about a U.S. presence began to raise the ante. The provision of security through basing agreements with the U.S. came to be seen as of questionable credibility, if indeed not a provocation to the Soviets and to internal domestic opponents who came to have a propaganda field day with such visible reminders of past humiliations.

In an attempt at reversing what had become a negative long-term tide, the Carter administration—goaded by events in Afghanistan and Iran into central concern over the Persian Gulf—moved to enhance U.S. access to facilities in Southwest Asia and the Horn of Africa in connection with the Rapid Deployment Force. Facilities were aggressively sought in Egypt, Kenya, Somalia, and Oman. Previous inhibitions about buying such access with arms transfers were, for the time being, muted. Such efforts were extended by the Reagan administration, ambitious of a new maritime grand strategy and not visibly hamstrung by inhibitions about human rights, arms control, and other such "global issues" of the late 1970s.

Just as the United States, however, attempted to reverse the decline of its military access, many Third World nations—individually and collectively—were beginning explicitly and loudly to raise the issue of superpower basing presence as an aspect of dependency. More and more, the subject began to appear on the North-South agenda with, as usual, the bulk of the animus asymmetrically directed at the United States. Iraq even floated a "charter" in 1980 in an effort to organize LDCs against the practice of providing access to superpowers. There was some applause, but many states in the Third World were fundamentally ambivalent. Compromised sovereignty was balanced by real security needs that could be fulfilled by arms assistance and/or a superpower's base presence.

It was at this point that the seemingly merely semantic but practically important distinction between "bases" and "facilities" came to public prominence. Egypt's President Sadat, for instance, was insistent that the forward depot at Ras Banas on the Red Sea be merely a contingent *facility* for the United States (available only on an ad hoc basis), and not a *base,* which might revive the memory of the less than fully controlled British and Russian presences. In a better bargaining position, and in no need of aid, Saudi Arabia's leaders spoke haughtily and casually about the remote possibility of providing the United States with facilities under some circumstances. Actually, as the environment for U.S. and other powers' access became less and less permissive, and with European colonialism all but vanished, it was, by 1980, hard to think of anything that might anymore qualify as a real "base."

Even in the teeth of such growing ambivalence in the South, however, the Soviets' determined quest for expanded naval and air access continued. They suffered losses as well as gains (Egypt, Sudan, Somalia, maybe Iraq, defected in line with shifted diplomatic orientations), but more of the latter. Various recent reports noted Soviet use of "permanent" facilities in Vietnam (major submarine facilities astride sealanes of communication [SLOCs] from Japan to the Middle East), Laos (airfields), Cambodia (naval access), Angola and Mozambique (astride SLOCs leading from the Persian Gulf to Western Europe), and Afghanistan (air bases within interdiction range of the Straits of Hormuz), and varying degrees of access in Libya, Algeria, Cape Verde, Tanzania, and India (perhaps also in Grenada and Nicaragua). There were growing Western fears of increasing Soviet long-range power projection capability, potentially applicable, alternatively, for interdiction of raw materials flows, for intervention in or support for "surrogate wars," or for outright warfare with the West in a variety of possible scenarios. At best, as far as the West was concerned, the expanding Soviet access network promised heightened shifts in perceptions throughout the world about a global change in the overall balance of power.

As the balance of overseas assets available to the United States and the USSR has shifted, so too—to some extent—has the geographic location of primary targets of access competition. Strategic value has tended to be ephemeral. The recent focus of resource competition over the Persian Gulf has spotlighted access requirements around the Straits of Hormuz and the Bab El Mandeb. Britain's conduct of its Falkland Island operations spotlighted the irreplaceable value of Ascension Island, if not that of the Falklands themselves in relation to the Panama Canal. The newer geopolitical focus on the Caribbean has prompted U.S. interest in bases in Colombia and Honduras, areas where such interest had, until very recently, been dormant. Various political problems around the Indian Ocean have resulted in greated importance being attached to the ocean's various islands: Diego Garcia, Mauritius, Gan, Mayotte, Socotra, and the Cocos. And the growing precariousness of former U.S. footholds on mainland Asia has placed a higher premium on retention of access to islands in the West Central Pacific now clamoring for various degrees of independence.

Changing Technological Requirements for Basing Access

While the global political basis for the contending U.S.–Soviet access networks seems to have been greatly altered after 1965 (more Soviet access, fewer and more reluctant U.S. basing hosts, more diffuse lines of contention replacing the heartland/rimland model), evolving military technology and associated strategies, tactics, logistics, etc., have altered basing requirements. The numbers, types, and uses of required bases have changed. However, there have been confusing crosscurrents, perhaps requiring a basic division of the subject into strategic/nuclear and conventional levels. On balance, the overall *quantitative* requirements for access appear to have been reduced, as increased requirements for esoteric technical facilities may have been more than compensated for by a reduction in those for "traditional" air and naval facilities.

Over a long time—particularly if one uses the interwar period or late 1940s as a baseline—there is no question that the sheer quantitative requirements for forward naval and air bases and air staging facilities have declined. There are

two basic reasons for this trend, which may have leveled off
in the past decade or so. First, air forces and navies are much
smaller now in terms of discrete units or systems; more combat punch has been packed into a smaller number of larger
and more sophisticated planes and ships. In the 1930s and
1940s, even minor powers had over 1,000 combat aircraft,
and far larger numbers of surface ships than would now be
the norm. Japan, for instance, had some thirty to forty airfields on Formosa and Hainan at the outset of World War II;
Italy had twenty or more main air bases each in Ethiopia and
Libya. Compare, indeed, the vast basing network once used
by Britain to support its global navy with the present dependence by the United States on only Yokosuka, Subic Bay,
Bahrain, Naples, and a few other places.

The other major reason for the decline in the quantitative
requirements for traditional facilities is the enhanced
ranges, particularly of aircraft but also of ships. Improved at-
sea refueling capabilities, aerial refueling, and the advent of
nuclear propulsion have had a very major impact. During
World War II, the United States required lengthy staging
networks across the North Atlantic (Newfoundland, Labra-
dor, Greenland, Iceland, etc.) with which to ferry aircraft to
the U.K. There was also an extended chain (Cuba, Trinidad,
Guyana, Brazil, Liberia, British West Africa, Sudan) with
which to move supplies to British forces in Egypt. Nowadays,
U.S. C–5 and C–141 transports can fly from Delaware to
Israel without any intervening ground stops. One recent
Rand report on overflights and use of overhead airspace indicated that with retention of just two small island bases—
Ascension and Diego Garcia—in conjunction with adequate
air refueling assets, the United States could conduct signif-
icant logistical operations almost anywhere on the globe.[2]

Concerning strategic nuclear deterrence in all of its
ramifications, quantitative access requirements have also
declined. Gone is the need for forward "reflex" bomber bases
(Morocco, notably) as a key element of deterrence, though

recovery bases are still so designated. Going too, gradually, are requirements for "forward" Polaris SSBN basing, though this did not ever involve any LDC; likewise, the declined U.S. need for fighter interceptor and defensive radar picket stations involved only U.S. NATO allies in the North Atlantic area.

But, as the major powers have become *less* dependent on access to LDC bases for *traditional* air and naval requirements (even omitting the importance of the subjective domain of routine port visits and coercive diplomacy), new needs have arisen for a whole host of *technical* functions. Quantitative access requirements for technical functions have risen; the need for integrated, functioning networks in some cases has shifted the geographic priorities for access diplomacy.

The current trend here is a culmination of one long under way, begun near the turn of the century with Britain's extensive use of overseas access for the numerous cable terminals that gave it a huge advantage in communications. During the interwar period, all major powers moved to set up overseas "wireless" networks and countervailing intelligence intercepts; just prior to 1941, forward access for radars came to the fore.

Those trends have now greatly expanded. The United States now requires extensive overseas facilities for, among numerous other things, intelligence gathering, satellite tracking, missile telemetry, land-based submarine and anti-submarine positioning, radiation collection (to monitor nuclear proliferation), communications, radars, and so forth. Most fall under the broad categories of intelligence, communications, and continuous sensing or monitoring.

The specific quantitative requirements here are large. The United States maintains many such facilities all over the globe. And there is more geographic dispersion than with the more traditional facilities ringing the USSR—facilities are needed in or offshore of East Africa to relay data from satellites parked in synchronous orbit over the USSR, and such stations may be required in Africa, Latin America, and Oceania to provide global coverage.

The Soviets, too, have crucial requirements for technical facilities in the Third World, despite the fact that they have relied on mobile seagoing platforms far more than the United States. And, of course, the open nature of U.S. society lends itself to comparatively reduced Soviet requirements in some areas. Cuba in recent years, for obvious geographical reasons, has hosted an elaborate complex of Soviet technical facilities; others have been deployed in such disparate locales as Laos, Equatorial Guinea, Uganda, and Mali.

Further, it should not be forgotten that, particularly in the Soviet case, access is sought throughout the Third World for activities that, while falling into a gray area between the civilian and military, may indeed have purposes less benign than advertised. The global Soviet fishing fleet—administratively as well as substantively an arm of the Soviet navy—is involved in electronic intelligence and "shadowing" operations, and with access to numerous LDC ports has often served as an opening wedge for basing of Soviet warships. Aeroflot, involved in a variety of security operations, similarly makes good use of extensive entree in the Third World. The same holds true for the Soviet "scientific" oceanographic fleet.

As the locus of facilities requirements has shifted, so too have there been corresponding changes in the strategic significance of numerous LDCs. Whereas in the past, some nations (Liberia, Maldives) had special significance as staging bases for (then shorter-ranged) aircraft, some now appear more crucial because of their location along routes used by nuclear submarines (Indonesia), or because they are favorably placed to relay satellite information where more than line-of-sight transmission is not yet developed, or because they can provide a listening post to monitor the telemetry of Soviet missile tests (China, Iran, Turkey, Pakistan). Later technological developments, presumably mostly involving satellites, may yet, however, reduce these presently burgeoning requirements. If so, some political relationships will be altered accordingly, which will also perhaps affect the overall nature of North-South relationships as they relate to basing dependency.

Not to be forgotten as part of the evolving diplomacy of access is the crucial matter of aircraft overflights, involving a range of practices and traditions. Some allied or friendly nations allow others more or less full, unhindered, and continuous overflight rights. In other cases, ad hoc formal applications for permission to overfly must be made well ahead of time; approval may or may not be granted, depending upon the purpose and situation.

These have become important issues, particularly in cases of arms resupply operations by major powers during Third World conflicts, wherein both combatants (and their major power supporters) may become involved in frenetic diplomacy to ensure en route overflights to sustain their forces. The 1973 Middle Eastern war was the classic case. Less well known cases include the Soviet resupply efforts on behalf of Angola, Ethiopia (versus Somalia), and Vietnam (versus China) during the past decade.

Changing Costs of Facilities Acquisitions

We noted that in the past, major powers' access to overseas facilities was based first on outright colonial control and then (telescoping the era of colonial control) on ideologically-linked formal alliances in which security guarantees and gratis military aid compensated the host for, usually, very permissive access for the major power user.

In recent years, numerous contextual political changes have wrought wholesale shifts in the diplomacy of basing, on the whole amounting to a much more symmetrical—if not inverted—calculus of leverage between users and hosts. The former must now bargain hard for access in a much less permissive environment; the costs, economic and otherwise, are now far higher. Preeminently, arms transfers have become the primary coin for facilities acquisitions.

Generally, the following factors have been germane, in varying degrees of applicability, to this change in user-host relationships:

- A systemic shift away from ideologically-based bipolarity, resulting in numerous LDCs purchasing weapons from both major blocs simultaneously or in rapidly shifting phases;

- Greatly increased leverage of some LDCs due to raw materials shortages and accompanying fears of cutoffs, involving mostly oil but other commodities as well;

- Lessened expectations of outright superpower intervention in the developing world (whether ultimately portentous or not is yet to be learned) and, in turn, a general lessening of LDC requirements for protection against and deterrence of same, causing some "decoupling" of security relationships;

- In the United States, at least, decreased availability of funds for military and economic aid, removing the latter as an omnipresent bargaining chip as was earlier the case;

- Developing norms about dependency, involving LDC governments' sensitives to other Third World countries' perceptions of their insistence upon maintaining sovereignty.

There appears to be a significant and growing correlation between arms transfers and strategic access. Actually, given the importance of the former as an instrument of diplomacy, it may really be described as an intervening variable measuring overall political association, usually supported by the facts of alliances and/or obvious ideological affinity.

Most facility arrangements appear to coexist with sole or

predominant supplier acquisition styles—that is, where a recipient acquires all or most of its arms from one supplier. Conversely, the multiple-source acquisition of arms, particularly if across the major power blocs (i.e., the recipient receives both Western and Soviet arms simultaneously), more often than not occurs where no major power has significant strategic access, indicating a degree of neutrality or ideological evenhandedness.

Virtually all of the dependent nations that have granted the Soviet Union major basing facilities have received most of their arms from them: Syria, South Yemen, Somalia (earlier), Angola, Cuba, and Iraq. Iraq, however, even before its war with Iran, had begun to acquire some French weapons (including Mirage F−1 fighters) while still vastly increasing its acquisitions from the USSR. And the Iraqis apparently put fairly strict limits on Soviet access to air and naval facilities. It is also noteworthy that those major Soviet clients that have maintained significantly diversified arms sources *across* the major blocs—Libya, Nigeria, India, Sri Lanka, and Algeria to a lesser extent—have demonstrated visible reluctance to grant the USSR major "permanent" facilities. This may in some cases have had less to do with diluted ideological affinity than with the availability of alternative sources of arms; size, wealth, or both may be other factors. The contrast between Libya and India, on the one hand, and Ethiopia, South Yemen, and Angola, on the other, may be instructive, although the impact of a Soviet presence in deterring external threats may also have played a role in the latter case. But in no case does the Soviet Union have major basing facilities where U.S. or other Western arms supply predominates.

The same generalizations hold for the hosts to major U.S. facilities. There have been only a few cases where U.S. and other Western basing rights have coexisted with some (though not predominant) Soviet arms supplies to the host, most notably Iran, Cyprus, and Morocco.

This is not meant to convey the impression that arms transfers can *always* be a sufficient inducement to bring about the granting of access, and once granted, to retain it. The USSR has not, for instance, acquired major naval bases in either Algeria or India, even with heavy weapons transfers—though that has obviously been one intent. Moreover, arms shipments were not sufficient to maintain Soviet access in Egypt, though it might be argued that denial of more advanced arms was one major reason for Sadat's rupture of what had seemed a solid relationship. Likewise, U.S. arms sales, including the F-15 and AWACs (Airborne Warning and Control) aircraft, have not sufficed to acquire the United States permanent facilities in Saudi Arabia; nor have supplies to Indonesia. These exceptions do not, however, invalidate what is clearly a strong and perhaps growing trend.

Concerning the arms transfer/base nexus, it is apparent that this has been, heretofore, primarily a two-nation game. The arms supply policies of Britain and France, to the contrary, have been characteristically commercial, i.e., devoid of such political purposes as the acquisition of bases. Recent French arms sales and base acquisition policies in West Africa, however, may contradict such assumptions to some extent.

Generally, in an era of increasingly coordinated security and economic policies, spanning a variety of domains or regimes, the growing connection of arms supply to the acquisition of access may be perceived as part of a broader trend toward linked transactions. Hence, France can ensure oil supplies from Iraq not only via arms transfers but also through provision of nuclear technology (a nuclear "sweetener") and a national color TV network. Germany's nuclear deal with Brazil involved not only cash sales of raw uranium but also, apparently, some significant German sales of warships to Brazil. The Soviet-Libya relationship has evidenced similarly linked transactions. And, in many cases, bases have obviously entered such bargains: witness the recent U.S.–Somalia and U.S.–Kenya negotiations, or those involving the USSR with Syria and Vietnam (the precise actual linkages are often left publicly obscure).

It should be further pointed out that whatever correlations exist in the arms transfer/base nexus, they are to be measured not only by quantitative arms data (monetary values or discrete numbers of weapons systems) but also by the qualitative component of the transfers. Between suppliers and recipients, particularly where the latter are not lacking in political clout or alternative arms suppliers, what may be at issue regarding the *quid pro quo* is whether the transfer of a given sophisticated system will be politically tolerable. Very often, this involves not only questions of rapid destabilization of a regional arms balance, but perhaps also the potential jeopardization of technical secrets should the systems later fall into the wrong hands. The U.S. dilemma—and its outcome—regarding sales of AWACs and the Phoenix missiles accompanying the F–14 fighter to Iran were fully illustrative of this problem, as was the later U.S. dilemma regarding AWACs for Saudi Arabia.

Such considerations have affected the basing diplomacies of both the United States and the USSR in recent years. The level of sophistication of arms to be supplied by the United States to Egypt and Saudi Arabia has become closely bound up with the degree of facilities access to be granted the United States. The United States apparently had to agree to the transfer of advanced attack aircraft in order to expedite its base negotiations with the Philippines. The recent Soviet pact with Syria, which clearly increased Soviet air and naval access to the country (perhaps involving permanent billeting of Soviet pilots), appears hinged not only on security assurances, but also on still more advanced weapons sales to a country that does not lack older ones in massive quantity.

New Terms for Old Relationships

Arms transfers are not, of course, the only element of *quid pro quo* for the major powers' overseas facilities, though they appear increasingly central, near ubiquitous. In a related vein, diplomatic and/or military support is often important and useful, as witness the aforementioned Soviet-Syria relationship, or the force demonstrations mounted by the United States on behalf of Kenya in some recent periods of trouble.

Trade concessions have not, apparently, significantly been used as *quid pro quo* for bases, though they have come under discussion. They also run into various collateral considerations—for instance, conflicts with the obligations of GATT (General Agreement on Tariffs and Trade) agreements such as the recent Tokyo Round. Whether the Soviets have explicitly greased basing deals with trade concessions—such as purchasing Egyptian or Sudanese cotton exports—is not known for certain.

Explicit rental agreements may, however, be becoming more frequent as *quid pro quo* in an era witnessing the withering of convergent security perspectives between hosts and users, if not also of formal alliances. Rentals can be a relatively more advantageous form of payment in that they can allow for a clearer picture of cost (an annual unambiguous budget line-item) and hence encourage a more rigorous cost-benefit evaluation of facilities requirements. That has more or less come to characterize the U.S.–Philippines arrangement (though it is more complicated than that), and may well be the wave of the future. More and more—at least for the United States—the matter of basing access may be put on a somewhat bloodless and nonideological business basis, but hence also made subject to questions about how the nonquantifiable price of U.S. protection figures in the bargain.

Of course, the attribution of the term "rent" to many basing agreements, if not explicitly stated as such, would be more or less accurate where economic or military aid is involved. For the United States in recent years, this has involved a confusing mix of instruments: Security Supporting Assistance (SSA), the Military Assistance Program (MAP), and the loans involved in Foreign Military Sales (FMS) financing. The old MAP program, once crucial to the U.S. forward support system, has recently been whittled down to some eight recipients, for most of which—Greece, Portugal, Spain, Turkey, Philippines, Thailand—it has acted in large part as rental payment for facilities. FMS financing has similarly been used in several of the above cases, and in South Korea as well. Other forms of economic assistance— AID (Agency for International Development) loans and grants, Food for Peace, the Peace Corps, etc.—have a less frequent and visible connection to basing access and involve numerous nations with no military ties to the United States. (Still, South Korea, Portugal, Morocco, and other facility hosts were prominent recipients of Food for Peace assistance.) The same could be said for Export-Import Bank loans, as here too, key base hosts such as Spain and the Philippines have been heavy ExIm loan recipients.

For the United States, it is only in recent years, after the collapse of the vaunted Bretton Woods international economic system and the fall of the dollar, that the financing of an overseas basing system has become a serious problem. Thus, by 1970 the United States came to be faced with the inherent disadvantage of its *geographical* position regarding the costs of overseas installations. Robert Gilpin has stated the dilemma as follows:

The fundamental problem posed for the United States during this period was the asymmetry of the American and Soviet geostrategic positions. The resulting monetary burden of maintaining global hegemony and balancing Soviet power on the rimlands of Europe and Asia was (and is) substantial. Consequently, the balance-of-payments issue was a central one for the United States. How is it possible to pay for the maintenance of large military establishments abroad, to finance and support allies, and generally to cover the costs of far-flung overseas commitments? Such a balance-of-payments problem is not crucial to a strategically well-placed continental power, such as Germany prior to World War I and the Soviet Union since 1945; such continental powers are able to radiate influence from within their own boundaries. But it is of the essence for a sea power trying to balance such a land power. How this problem was resolved is of critical importance for understanding American foreign economic policy in the 1960s and early 1970s.[3]

The United States has achieved some savings in its overseas costs during the past decade by phasing out facilities in Iran, Taiwan, Ethiopia, Pakistan, Libya, and several other countries. But in some cases—many in Europe—base *operating* costs appear to have escalated significantly. Now, costs related to new commitments in Egypt, Oman, Somalia, Kenya, and Diego Garcia are likely to loom equally as large.

On the flip side of this rather indistinct coin, it should be noted that a strictly financial assessment of the cost of a growing overseas basing network to the Soviets is even harder to come by. The USSR, like the United States, utilizes a variety of *quid pro quo* for use of basing facilities—arms sales and aid, low-priced sales of Soviet raw materials, and subsidized purchases of clients' raw materials, for example. In attempting to describe the cost of Soviet access in Cuba, one recent article explained how the Soviets prop up Cuba's economy through purchases of sugar and nickel, despite the USSR's being the world's largest producer of both commodities.[4] Earlier, the Soviets had bought up much of Egypt's and Sudan's cotton crops, often for resale elsewhere. The same article claims that Vietnam has been given markets in the USSR, not only for a variety of light industrial goods but also for Vietnamese vodka: "it's believed the stuff is used for domestic Soviet consumption, thus freeing Russian vodka for export to hard-currency markets." The article concluded that the USSR is paying an increasingly burdensome price for its overseas ventures and access, raising the traditional arguments—familiar to students of theories of imperialism—about whether empires are worth the financial cost. Of course, to the extent that the Soviets have planned upon more global military deployments—in Latin America, southern Africa, the southwest Pacific—the economic advantages accruing to it from a heartland position would dissipate somewhat. This apparently does not, however, apply to balance of payments so much in the Soviet case as it does in the American. Hence, according to Gilpin:

> The Soviet Union, on the other hand, has been generally free of this balance-of-payments problem. The bulk of Soviet military forces have remained within the Soviet Union proper, and foreign aid has been in the form of goods or military equipment. But where the Soviet Union has stationed large military contingents outside the country as in Eastern Europe, it has created a monetary and payments system to support this extension of power. By creating the ruble bloc, manipulating the value of the ruble, and keeping the ruble inconvertible, the Russians have forced the East Europeans to finance their military presence in Eastern Europe. Thus, the extent of Russian influence has been largely determined by the scope of their military rather than their economic power.[5]

Sovereignty versus Security: Base Denial Diplomacy

While the essentially bilateral diplomacy of major powers' basing access has changed in recent years—tilted, in many cases, by the increasing leverage of LDC hosts—the matter has also found its way onto the North-South agenda. Some Third World nations, seeking redistribution of wealth, power, and prestige at all levels—often involving subtle psychological factors as well as more tangible ones—have begun to demand a wholesale removal of the major powers' military presence from the Third World. In that regard, bases have come to be discussed in the context of dependency, along with arms technology transfer, nuclear technology, military uses of the seabed, naval passage through narrow straits and within traditional offshore limits, nuclear "free zones" applying to major power forces, and regional demilitarization.

Thus far, however, more narrowly focused base denial activities have been a far more important part of contemporary diplomacy than the search by the LDCs for still one more global issue with which to belabor the North. A variety of diplomatic instruments have been used to that end: economic and security inducements, threats, propaganda, instigation of indigenous political protest movements, and preemptive base acquisitions, among others. More and more, the United Nations has become a propaganda forum in which efforts have been made to put pressures on rival superpower basing presences in an era when smaller powers are sensitive to charges that they have compromised newly-won sovereignty by supporting a foreign base presence. The Soviets, in particular, have been themselves instrumental in this propaganda effort (through foreign language broadcasts) aimed at creating political pressures on U.S. and other Western basing arrangements by characterizing them as an inherently "capitalistic" phenomenon.

In recent times, the Soviets have placed considerable emphasis on "exposing" what they claim to be developments of new U.S. basing networks and strategies, real or imagined, in a manner that has often revealed Moscow's global cognitive map. For instance, warnings have been issued about an alleged, burgeoning South Atlantic alliance that might provide bases for NATO in a southern arc stretching from Chile to South Africa. Others have concerned the ASEAN grouping in Southeast Asia, where the United States has been allegedly seeking new bases on Morotai Island in the Moluccas group in Indonesia as part of a new fallback, post-Vietnam, Asian periphery strategy. Among the other prominent recent targets of Soviet propaganda have been Oman, Bahrain, Cyprus, Thailand, and Malta.

Oman and Bahrain have been targets of propaganda that harps upon the possible role of their U.S. facilities in support of Israel. According to one Soviet broadcast, "This decision by Sultan Qabus [to allow the U.S. use of Masirah] was received in the Arab world as an act of betrayal of the Arab nation, an act which will result in the Americans dominating not only the Arab sea routes but also the entire Arab world and its natural wealth."[6] And in another, Tass crowed that Bahrain's decision to have the U.S. Middle Eastern naval force removed from the base at Jufayr was "the consequence of the Arab countries' mounting discontent with the American 'gunboat diplomacy,' one of the manifestations of which is Washington's support for Israel's expansionist policy with regard to neighboring Arab countries."[7] Broadcasts aimed at Thailand stress issues of sovereignty and also speak darkly of the lurid activities of American spy planes and other intelligence apparatus. Filipinos are bombarded with broadcasts appealing to their national dignity, filled with data on murders and rapes allegedly committed by U.S. sailors.

Soviet propaganda also highlights statements by various Third World leaders demanding withdrawal of Western bases. In 1976–1977 a great effort was made to amplify complaints from India, Madagascar, Mauritius, and the Seychelles about Diego Garcia and about the asserted desirability of a neutralized Indian Ocean freed of foreign base presences.

The United Nations has become a particularly useful forum for Soviet political efforts directed at getting U.S. bases removed from the Third World. On the one hand, the Soviets continue to profess their goal of a world totally freed of all foreign bases, but then, they have also orchestrated Third World efforts to target specific U.S. bases or countries where military access is now afforded.

In recent years, these efforts have particularly been directed at removing various remnant island dependencies from the United States and Western orbit. Micronesia, American Samoa, Puerto Rico, St. Helena (owned by the U.K.), Guam, Bermuda, Turks and Caicos, Diego Garcia, Tuvalu, Montserrat, the British Virgin Islands, and the Keeling Islands have been among the numerous targets. Such efforts have been pursued relentlessly in the United Nations' "Committee of 24" and in its Subcommittee on Small Territories. These pressures are often seriously considered and reacted to: Britain, after one rancorous session, conceded its willingness in principle to give independence to tiny St. Helena; and the U.S. position in Micronesia has also been under relentless attack in the United Nations, apparently to some ultimate effect as measured by recent independence strivings and the very forthcoming American response.

The United States, as well, has often used both carrots and sticks in its efforts at blocking expansion of the Soviet basing network. Economic aid was earlier dangled in front of Guinea's Sekou Toure in an effort to stop Soviet Atlantic reconnaissance flights out of Conakry, and it may have succeeded to some extent. Earlier, economic aid and perhaps also the prospect of diplomatic recognition entered into implied U.S. bargaining positions related to Soviet basing hopes in Angola. U.S. arms supplies and economic aid have helped pry Egyptian bases from Soviet control, though a similar effort was unsuccessful in the case of Syria. Threats have long been used to restrict Soviet use of Cuban bases, going back to the 1962 missile crisis and reiterated in 1970 when Soviet intentions to use Cienfuegos as a nuclear submarine base began to emerge.

In recent times, the United States has made extensive proxy use of Saudi cash in connection with convergent U.S.–Saudi interests, in order to keep the Middle East free of Soviet bases. The Saudis earlier, of course, had abetted the U.S. bankrolling of Egypt prior to the Camp David accords. Beyond that, Saudi money has also helped to drive the Soviet presence from North Yemen and Sudan (now less certain again in the former case), has been instrumental in the Soviets' being pushed out of Somalia, and has also been dangled in front of radical South Yemen with similar ends in mind.

Oil-rich OPEC nations, too, have now become factors in the

base denial game in a broader context, often in relation to
U.S. desires to maintain the potential for staging arms to
Israel in a future crisis. Arab financial leverage has been
used to jeopardize U.S. use of the Azores and also to block use
of Spanish air bases for possible refueling of Israel-bound
transports. Libyan financial support given Malta was used to
ease the withdrawal of the British presence. Arab oil and
money has also apparently affected future Greek and
Turkish intentions concerning American use of facilities in
some possible circumstances. And, ironically, Saudi Arabia
has apparently offered Oman cash inducements to block expansion of U.S. access there.

In some cases, the timing and pace of Western (particularly British) withdrawals from unwanted or compromised
facilities may have been determined by fears of Soviet take-
over. Earlier, Britain seemed to worry about withdrawing
from Malta more because of fears that it would soon be
replaced there by the USSR than because of the needs of its
own naval forces. Similar considerations were in evidence
with the withdrawals from the Maldives, Seychelles, and
Mauritius, with the Aden denouement serving as a graphic
reminder. France has had similar fears about Djibouti and
Mayotte. While the United States worries about losing some
bases in Micronesia, it perhaps worries even more about
possible later Soviet access there.

China's apparent pressures on Vietnam to deny the USSR
use of former U.S. bases, and India's complaints to the
United States about Diego Garcia and other Indian Ocean
bases, are still further common examples of base denial activities not restricted to the superpowers. In recent times,
Iraq, above all, has become identified with such efforts.

On a more general level—though no doubt with Israel and
the United States still in mind—Iraq in early 1980 floated a
"Pan-Arab Charter" which, among other things, asserted
the need to keep *all* superpower bases out of the region.
Echoing similar regional demands periodically made for

removal of all major powers' basing presences in Africa (by the OAU [Organization of African Unity]), and those made by groupings of Indian Ocean littoral states, the Iraqi charter might presage a more aggressive, organized LDC effort, perhaps increasingly to be surfaced in a variety of international forums as part of a North-South agenda. To the extent successful, it would raise very serious questions about relative advantages and disadvantages for the two superpowers if both were forced by popular demand to retrench significantly from overseas access.

Perhaps only in part constituting a paradox, the recent Third World verbal onslaught upon bases as infringements upon sovereignty and dignity has coincided with some efforts by emerging LDC military powers to acquire access for themselves. Some LDCs have been shedding their long-held role as mere passive actors in the global "game of nations."

India and Iran (under the Shah) began to send small naval flotillas about the Indian Ocean to flaunt a "presence." The large Cuban presence throughout Africa and Southwest Asia and Pakistan's stationing of forces in Saudi Arabia might be perceived as continuing the tradition of mercenary forces; even then, however, they amount to extended extraregional access. Most of all, however, LDCs have entered the access game in the area of acquiring and keeping the staging bases and overflights for their arms suppliers—particularly during conflict—and denying such access to rivals. Hence, the game of sovereignty and leverage continues to be fought out at a microlevel even as the rhetoric about dependency and big power intrusions into potential "zones of peace" drones on.

The Future of Basing Diplomacy in the Third World

Having traced the evolution of recent basing diplomacy through its several phases and dimensions, a few speculations on the future may be warranted. There is, of course, an almost unavoidable tendency to extrapolate the future from the trends of the recent past. Political history, however, rarely can be extrapolated for very long; indeed, the unexpected—and even massive reversals—are more the norm than the exception.

Our previous analysis has touched upon numerous "systemic" factors that have had, and presumably will continue to have, major importance for the global context of basing diplomacy. Among these are evolving developments in military technology (e.g., refueling, ranges, "over the horizon" communications); levels and types of conflicts and in turn their impact on alliances and arms transfer patterns; evolving "norms" regarding sovereignty and permissible degrees of penetration of LDCs; superpower tendencies to intervene militarily under a variety of circumstances; evolving relative military capabilities of developed and developing countries, and so forth.

In analyzing the seemingly important areas of basing diplomacy that would appear subject to heavy influence from these factors, some of the following questions should be borne in mind:

- What will be the future mix of types of bases or facilities required by large powers; critically, the mix of technical and traditional facilities? Will there be an extension of the trend toward increasing importance for the former?

- What will be the nature and amount of *quid pro quo* asked in exchange for access (military and economic aid, protection, markets for raw materials and manufactured goods, Security Council votes or vetoes, pressures on regional foes, technology transfer, etc.)? Generally, what will be the emerging balance of overall leverage between the large and small nations, especially regarding numerous bilateral combinations?

- Will the quest for bases remain primarily a two-nation game, or will multipolarity be reflected in this domain as it is, allegedly, in others?

- What will be the nature of access along the continuum from "bases" to "facilities"?

- How much validity will a heartland/rimland paradigm for basing diplomacy—and global conflict, in general—retain? In that context, what does the future portend for the economics of big power competition for overseas access?

- How will future rivalries over raw materials access—and future shifts in the geography of such rivalries—affect basing diplomacy?

There may be, as indicated, surprises. A tenser, more ideological bipolar struggle could make for a more permissive basing environment, for one or both superpowers. Raw materials rivalries could also, in some circumstances, have the same impact, as witness currently expanded U.S. access around the Persian Gulf. Then too, although not likely, a new era of imperial conquest—perhaps impelled by a struggle for resources—cannot be ruled out. If it occurs, more extensive big power basing networks would presumably automatically follow. But a world that sees twenty to thirty new nuclear powers might also be one where large powers disengage from some areas to avoid being dragged into conflict. Such a world might also see regional LDC basing diplomacy related to possible small powers' nuclear deterrence vis-à-vis superpowers to compensate for the limited striking ranges of the former's delivery systems.

Finally, contrary to present trends, new technological developments resulting in vastly increased access requirements are not necessarily to be ruled out, though that is, at present, unforeseen. It is hard to say what impact on future basing requirements might be wrought by space-based laser stations, massive proliferation of cruise missiles by many nations, or enormous strides in ASW (anti-submarine warfare) capabilities. Quite probably, one way or another, basing matters will remain, as they have long been, a crucial feature of global diplomacy.

IV

The Economic Problem

10

TONY SMITH

The Case of
Dependency Theory

Until recently, literature on the problems of development in
the industrializing areas of the globe—the "South" or Third
World—has tended to concentrate on the *internal* dynamics
of change in these regions: party structures, ethnic and class
conflict, urbanization, land tenure systems, and the like.
Third World countries have been *contrasted* with the industrial societies of the North in the understanding that the
different characteristics of the two regions can be seen as
representative of different "stages" of development. In the
last few years, all this has been called into question by a
group of writers who, whatever their differences, share the
view that the various stages of development among world
societies should not so much be contrasted as *linked,* and

that these linkages should be understood to express the evolution of forces that can be studied only at the level of world, not local, history. To study the Third World is thus to study the history and nature of imperialism as it rose in the North and expanded into the South, shaping local society in its image.

Dependency Theory

This new school of thinking calls its approach *dependency theory,* thereby stressing the way in which the Third World "depends" in its economic, social, and political structures on the formative influence of Northern imperialist domination. From the perspective of dependency theory, the conventional American way of studying Third World "development" or "modernization" is an exercise in ideological obfuscation, deliberate or otherwise, designed to conceal the way imperialism works. Developmentalism does this by focusing theoretical attention on the South alone, as though it can be meaningfully understood apart from the greater global history to which it belongs. In this manner, the imperialistic system. disguises its power, shielding itself from ideological attack.

There is little question that the theoretical underpinnings of professional literature and academic course organization in the U.S. have hereby received a serious challenge. The models of political development, which for nearly twenty years were the stuff of American writing and the foundation of many a brave career, are now disputed in no uncertain terms. This does not seem to be just a coincidence, coming as it does in the aftermath of Vietnam and the rise in petroleum prices; evidently the real power of the Third World in international affairs is coming to be matched by a more aggressive literature on its behalf. As the force of Southern nationalism expresses itself more powerfully in concrete terms, it seeks conceptual arms as well—and finds them in dependency theory. For dependency theory locates the terrible current problems of Third World economic development in past Northern exploitation of the South. The theory calls for a reordering of the international balance of power so that these problems may be solved. In the anti-imperialist struggle, the theory sees the expression of a Southern nationalist determination to achieve genuine independence in the international system and to ameliorate living standards of the poorest in the Third World.

It is important, of course, to recognize the differences among those who can be classified after their Latin American appellation as *dependencistas*. Latin Americans, Asians, and Africans, not to mention North Americans, Europeans, and socialist country experts, figure in their ranks. With so many adherents in so many parts of the world, with a literature in its modern form over twenty years old (although able to trace its lineage back to Lenin and Hobson, if not earlier), and with inevitably different lines of theoretical exposition and sharp disagreements among them, it is nevertheless essential to see dependency theory as a school: whatever the internal differences, it has generally shared assumptions and common enemies. Indeed, the unity and importance of dependency theory's proponents are such that they must be seen as a school in a broader than strictly academic sense. For dependency theory represents the intellectual meeting ground of Marxism and certain important forms of nationalism in the Third World, and it thereby serves as the ideological underpinning of a "united front" among these groups, directed against what it sees as the local power of Northern imperialism. To be sure, the theory contains explicit preferences for the form of domestic social organization it favors for the South—usually some variant of socialism—and thus cannot be expected to attract all Southern nationalists to its banner. But the primary ambition of the dependencistas at this point in time is to struggle at the level of the nation and the international system for what they see as a better world. In this respect especially, dependency theory appeals to a broad spectrum of nationalists in the South.

This chapter is intended neither as a comprehensive survey of dependency theory literature nor as an effort to assess its practical significance as an ideological force mobilizing nationalist sentiment in the South today. Rather, I hope simply to examine what seems to me to be the most important theoretical assumption of this school, and to subject it and its chief corollaries to a thoroughgoing criticism. My concern is not to debunk completely the theory, nor to deny the genuine insights it has into the process of Third World development. Instead, my intention is to show that dependency theory has its limitations in coming to grips with the contemporary problems of the Third World, and that the failure to recognize these limitations converts much of the literature into a partisan ideology every bit as closed to criticism—and ultimately just as unable to see crucial aspects of reality—as the "bourgeois" approach to Third World development the dependencistas so sharply attack. Unless otherwise indicated, the writers referred to all may be considered to belong to the dependency school.

Theoretical Assumptions

The cardinal assumption of the dependency school is Hegel's admonition that the whole has a logic greater than the sum of its parts. Concretely put, this means that whether we are interested in individual psychology or the fate of nations, we must approach our subject by seeing it on the broadest relevant canvas where all the factors influencing its development are present. This is the level of the "whole," the "totality." It is crucial to understand that an analysis conducted at a lower level of interaction, at the level of a "part," will never show us, of itself, this greater pattern. To the contrary, the "part" can only be understood by its place within the "whole," which alone gives it meaning. In the case of

Third World development today, it should be fairly apparent what this approach entails: it means that such issues can only be comprehended *globally*, and this along two dimensions, one of which may be called vertical or historical and the other to be seen as horizontal, or involving the entire international system. Any attempt to see issues of Third World development on a more reduced scale, so the dependency school would hold, must fail, succumbing to the illusion that a "part" is explicable in its own terms alone. In a word, to study the South, one must study imperialism—its origin, its present dynamic, its likely future evolution. In this light it will be seen that *the development and wealth of the North and the underdevelopment and poverty of the South are a function of one another.*

Concrete examples may make this point more clearly. Immanuel Wallerstein, perhaps the dean of the dependency school in North America, has insisted that the dynamism of the West has come precisely from the ability of its economic order to escape local political controls and to work its way on a world level, at which point alone it can be meaningfully studied.[1] Similarly, Samir Amin, an Egyptian with a wide reputation in Western Europe, writes that

apart from a few "ethnographic reserves," all contemporary societies are integrated into a world system. Not a single concrete socio-economic formation of our time can be understood except as part of this world system.[2]

In the African context, for instance, Walter Rodney writes that underdevelopment

expresses a particular relationship of *exploitation:* namely, the exploitation of one country by another. . . . The underdevelopment with which the world is now preoccupied is a product of capitalist, imperialist and colonialist exploitation.[3]

Apparently, even the word "tribe" must be struck from our vocabulary. According to Colin Leys, the word can be used only between quotation marks:

"Tribalism" is a creation of colonialism. It has little or nothing to do with pre-colonial relations between tribes. . . . In neo-colonial Africa, class formation and the development of tribalism accompany each other.[4]

It is in this same vein that André Gunder Frank, writing of Latin America, can speak of the "development of under-development,"[5] while Stanley and Barbara Stein report that, in considering contemporary problems, they

view Latin America as a continent of inadequate and disappointing fulfillment and seek to pinpoint the coordinates of sustained backwardness in examining the process of economic change in a dependent, peripheral, or colonial area.[6]

Asian development can be fitted into the same mold, as Frances Moulder explains; the backwardness of China relative to Japan is attributed to the fact that the former was more incorporated into the European-dominated international system than the latter.[7] Finally, many of these studies refer with praise to Paul Baran's earlier efforts to study Indian economic development in much the same terms:

There can be no doubt that had the amount of economic surplus that Britain has torn from India been invested in India, India's economic development to date would have borne little similarity to the actual somber record. . . . India, if left to herself, might have found in the course of time a shorter and surely less tortuous road toward a better and richer society.[8]

Moral Fractures

The charge, it should be emphasized, is moral as well as historical: the links between North and South, which may be historically demonstrated to exist, are at the same time morally culpable, in the sense of being directly responsible for the widespread misery in the Third World. "The lot of more than a billion people of the developing world continues to deteriorate as a result of the trends in international economic relations," declares the opening sentence of the

Charter of Algiers, founding document of the Group of 77, the name given to the international association of Third World countries (now numbering well over one hundred). A firm example of this process was offered by Salvadore Allende on the occasion of the third United Nations Conference on Trade and Development, held in Chile in 1972. In 1931, Allende declared, foreign copper companies invested about $30 million in Chile. Over the ensuing years, at least $4 billion was repatriated to the United States in profits, but no fresh capital was added to this original sum—and this was in a nation of ten million people, where estimates say half a million children are today mentally damaged as a result of malnutrition. By Allende's account, this development came about when a self-interested local elite, concerned to fill its own pockets but unmindful of the national interest, created a large external public debt to encourage such investment from abroad. Thus, in 1971, some one-third of the total export earnings of Chile had to service a debt, in his words, "largely contracted in order to offset the damage done by an unfair trade system, to defray the costs of the establishment of foreign enterprises on our territory, [and] to cope with the speculative exploitation of our resources."

Such statements could be multiplied many times over by citations from a wide range of Southern writers and politicians and their supporters in the North. These arguments about the character of the international system are ultimately moral: they lodge responsibility for the South's condition on a system of investment, trade, and finance run by the North for its own profit. Thus, the Charter of Economic Rights and Duties of States, voted by the UN General Assembly in January 1975 upon the recommendation of President Echeverriá of Mexico, maintained that the South has the "right" to nationalize foreign investments strictly according to local laws and to enter into commodity cartels to raise and stabilize the prices of raw materials, whereas it is the "duty" of the North to accept such arrangements.

In a formal sense, the argument has merit. Like the claims in the United States today for "affirmative action" and "reparations" by minority groups, Southern countries affirm that the international system has worked to their detriment even as it has furthered the prosperity of the North. The established procedures by which the international economic system is run are only apparently neutral, therefore, and on closer inspection may be seen to serve the interests of one group at the expense of another.

To be persuasive, however, the argument needs to be empirically valid as well as formally sound. Does the international system linking South to North actually exist in the fashion described? The question is, first of all, scientific, and only thereafter normative.

The most fundamental criticism to be made of the world view of dependency theory in this respect is that its manner of exalting what I have called the "whole," the "totality," gives to the international system dominated by Northern capitalism a power far greater and more coordinated than it actually possesses with respect to the "parts," or the countries of the Third World. Not that the system lacks coherence and the means to protect itself. When regimes threaten to nationalize foreign enterprises, for example, they may expect to receive fewer investments of this sort in the future and to suffer international credit restrictions, which may in turn raise the risk of civil disorder as internal economic conditions become unstable. But this is no reason to exaggerate the coordination and power of the international system, which is actually much more fluid than dependency theory allows. Dependency theorists establish a tyranny of the whole over the parts that closer inspection makes difficult to accept.

Even in the heyday of imperialism, there were definite limits on what the Europeans could hope to accomplish, and a clear local component to the character of their rule in the South. Consider, for example, the breathtaking exaggeration of the man generally considered to be the father of dependency theory in the United States, Paul Baran, writing on India under British rule:

Thus, the British administration of India systematically destroyed all the fibres and foundations of Indian society. Its land and taxation policy ruined India's village economy and substituted for it the parasitic landowners and moneylenders. Its commercial policy destroyed the Indian artisan and created the infamous slums of the Indian cities filled with millions of starved and diseased paupers. Its economic policy broke down whatever beginnings there were of an indigenous industrial development and promoted the proliferations of speculators, petty businessmen, agents, and sharks of all descriptions.

And it might be recalled that Baran felt that "India, if left to herself, might have found in the course of time a shorter and surely less tortuous road toward a better and richer society." The obvious objection to this line of argument, however, is that it grants far too much power (for evil or otherwise) to the British, while it gives far too little credit to the power of Indian traditions and institutions. India before the British was not without sin, nor were the British the authors of unmitigated evil. "Parasitic landowners and moneylenders" were present before the British arrival; British "commercial policy" is now believed to have "destroyed" far fewer native artisans than was previously thought; British economic policy certainly did far more to create the foundations for the industrialization of India than to break down "whatever beginnings there were"; British "land and taxation policy," rather than "ruining" the village economy, was surely far less exploitive than that under the Great Mogul in Delhi; and British "administration," far from destroying "all the fibres and foundations of Indian society," in fact adopted the policy of most conquerors of large populations and adapted itself rather well to indigenous ways.

To be sure, India might have fared better; between roughly 1880 and World War I, British policy definitely worked as a handicap on Indian industrialization. But regressive Indian

forces were at work as well. The Great Mutiny of 1857 had
demonstrated to the British that local forces resisting
change had to be handled with care. And the multiple problems of India today, more than thirty years since independence, can only be marginally associated with the British
rule of over a century, evidence again that the British presence did not permeate every level of Indian life.

Accounting for Economic Fluidity

As the case of British India suggests for today, the international system is far less coherent than dependency theorists
allow, and its impact on Southern societies is therefore both
weaker and more varied than they would expect. As a consequence, theoretical room must be made to understand the
real power of initiative that Southern states possess, in
regard both to local affairs and to the international system.
For there is no blueprint, implicit or explicit, that keeps the
South the perpetual "hewer of wood and drawer of water," as
is commonly alleged. Where is the strategy to prevent
Southern industrialization, monopolize raw materials, break
up domestically integrated markets, oppose regional integration plans, accentuate a still greater international division of
labor favoring the developed nations? Where is the strategy
similar to German policy toward southeastern Europe from
the late nineteenth century through World War II or, less
premeditatedly, British policy toward the industrialization of
its dependencies prior to World War I?

To the contrary, as we shall see below, there is strong evidence that most Southern states today enjoy an autonomy
from the influence of the international system that should
not be underestimated (just as it should not be exaggerated).
Indeed, there is reason to believe that this has long been the
case; historians of the Near East, South Asia, and the Far
East have insisted time and again that local cultures have
adapted themselves to the momentary dominance of the

Europeans, only to assert themselves more vigorously as alien power declined. It is an unjustifiable act of condescension to suppose that these local traditions simply disappeared in the face of the European onslaught. It is especially surprising to see those who call themselves Southern nationalists overlook the strength of the identities of these local cultures for the sake of damning the allegedly all-pervasive influence of the North.

The international system might also be called fluid in the sense that, by its very operation, it prepares the ground for changes in the relative power of states within it. For example, World Bank and United States Department of Commerce statistics show that, by the end of 1975, Algeria had run up an external public debt of over $9 billion, and that the United States had become the country's chief creditor and trading partner. Certainly it would be difficult to maintain that Algeria was thereby reduced to a dependent status in the international system, its autonomy diminished and its economy open to exploitation. To the contrary, it would appear that Algeria was practicing that trick of the martial arts whereby the strength of an opponent is turned against himself: Algeria cooperated with the international system in order better to escape its control.

Is Algeria an exception? It would seem not. For perhaps twenty years, as statistics put out by the United Nations and the Organization for Economic Cooperation and Development (OECD) report, manufacturing output in the Third World has increased faster than these economies in general, and faster than the rate of manufacturing output in the capitalist states of the North. One of the principal arguments against colonialism and neocolonialism was precisely that they retarded such progress, but the available figures argue strongly that this is no longer the case.

The most striking demonstration comes from the statistics for the middle 1970s, when the so-called "middle-income" Third World countries—those with per capita incomes of

$200 to $700 a year—managed to increase their manufacturing output by around 8 percent annually, while the OECD
countries registered no annual increase. These figures demonstrate both the vigor and the independence of manufacturing in the Third World.

For so long it was such a sacrosanct article of faith that the
Third World could not develop, given the logic of the international system, that many dependency theorists still simply
deny that Southern industrialization is occurring. They
state—incorrectly—that light, not heavy, industry is the
only growth sector, or that industrial output or employment
is not so dynamic when compared to population growth or
other economic sectors.

Failing these arguments, the dependency theorists may
maintain that there are developments sponsored by the international system that effectively counter whatever favorable trends exist in the South—for example, through "decapitalization" and "denationalization." The preferred manner
of establishing the so-called "decapitalization" of the South
is to present capital flows between North and South, showing
that more leaves the Third World than enters—an apparent
indication of exploitation. Thus, with respect to Latin
America, Dale Johnson writes that "between 1950 and 1961,
2,962 million dollars of U.S. private capital flowed into the
seven principal countries of Latin America, while the return
flow was 6,875 million dollars."[10] But in and of themselves,
what do these figures mean? Unless we know what this balance of $4 billion means in relation either to the size of North
American investment in Latin America or to the amount of
output generated, such sums tell us very little indeed.

Reports by the United States Department of Commerce
provide statistics that suggest how dubious Johnson's
charges are. In 1975, for example, the total of United States
private investment in Latin American manufacturing was
$178 million. At the same time, American corporations
remitted to this country $359 million in profits, and another

$211 million in royalties and fees. Some years do not show such a heavy outflow to the United States, but 1975 would seem to correspond to the dependencista expectation: American firms "decapitalized" Latin America of $392 million that year in terms of manufacturing alone. However, compared to total United States investments in manufacturing of $8.6 billion, the sum repatriated—4.6 percent—hardly represents an extortionist outflow. This sum of $392 million appears all the more trivial when compared to the total sales of North American manufacturing affiliates in Latin America in 1974: $20.9 billion. Either as return on capital invested or on volume of business generated, the amount of money claimed by United States enterprises for use at home can only with difficulty be seen as perpetuating the international second-class status of the South. The opposite could more properly be argued.

A second charge against North American investments is that they "denationalize" industry in the South—that they buy up profitable, progressive firms in the Third World, leaving the less interesting ventures to the local bourgeoisie. Thus, Richard Barnet and Ronald Mueller report that a Harvard Business School study for the period 1958–1967 shows North Americans acquiring Southern property on every side: "About 46 percent of all manufacturing operations established in the period were takeovers of existing domestic industry."[11] Messrs. Barnet and Mueller neglect to inform the reader, however, that this same study shows that through liquidations or expropriations, or sales of an entire affiliate or a considerable portion thereof, United States interests had divested themselves of nearly as many manufacturing concerns as they had acquired: 332 lost versus 337 gained. A more crucial statistic might be the value of affiliates bought and sold, not the number. Here, figures are hard to find, but the Department of Commerce does report that, for 1975 and 1976, United States manufacturing firms sold off about as much in value of their Southern affiliates as they acquired through take-overs.

A final question has to do with the industrial sector in which foreign investments are located. Here again, the pattern seems clear: increasingly in the Third World foreigners are forbidden to invest, except in those domains where local capital and know-how are deficient. This has meant a progressive movement out of some fields and into others by American investors, with the foreigners generally holding the most advanced and remunerative industries. From the perspective of dependency theory, this spells the technological subservience of the South to the North. But it might just as easily be argued that such a strategy is the best way for the South to get technology transferred to it from the North, and that whatever gains the North thereby realizes are small compared with the benefits achieved by the South. It might be recalled that ever since Lenin the Soviet Union has encouraged something like this kind of investment, with the long-range ambition, of course, to emerge technologically superior to the capitalist countries.

It should not for a moment be forgotten that these economic exchanges are occurring within a political context dominated by the American defeat in Vietnam. For the nearly five hundred years of European expansion across the globe, Southern military weakness put a clear limit to political strength. Colonialism's demise may have ended the direct political control of North over South, but there was always the threat of military intervention if Southern regimes failed to respect Northern interests. Thus it had been in Asia since the First Opium War in 1840.

Vietnam meant the end of this tradition, at least on the grand scale, as should be apparent when the current reality is compared with the brave words of George Liska:

The Vietnamese War . . . may well come to rank on a par with the two world wars as a conflict that marked an epoch in America's progress toward definition of her role as a world power. . . .This role implies the necessity to define—by force if necessary—the terms on which regional balances of power are evolved and American access to individual regions is secured. . . . Had it been less dramatized, the Vietnamese War would have been an ideal ground for evolving, training, and breaking in . . . a combined political-military establishment as well as for educating the American people to changing facts of life. It may still prove retrospectively to have been such.[12]

Rising Strength of the South

It was under the shadow of the victory of Vietnamese nationalism that Arab nationalism scored its stunning success in raising petroleum prices late in 1973. In 1972, OPEC states received $29 billion for their exports, some 7 percent of world trade by value; but by 1975 their exports totaled $114 billion, accounting for about 13 percent of world commerce (down from 16 percent in 1974). While OPEC's ability has in certain respects hurt the rest of the Third World, its success is part of the general rise of Southern states internationally, as the figures presented earlier on industrial development pointedly suggest.

How can we best explain the growing relative strength of the South in relation to the North? Any number of factors may be pointed out, including the stimulation of contact with the North through aid, trade, and investment. But the force that appears to me to constitute the single most decisive factor in the emergence of the South internationally is the growing power there of the various state organizations. To an important degree, there has always been genuine political muscle in the South on the part of the local inhabitants. For example, in the case of India, Mahatma Gandhi repeatedly insisted on the absurdity of so few Britons—in the 1930s, some 4,000 civil servants, 60,000 soldiers, and 90,000 businessmen and clergy—billeting themselves upon a country of 300 million persons. British success depended upon a fragile network of local collaborators, including economic elites, warrior tribes, traditional power holders, and minority groups endangered by other Indians. Such a brokerage system between the foreign authorities and the local population could be found throughout the European colonial empires. Its structure was generally a decisive influence on the character of postwar decolonization. From the rise of the Young Turks and the Chinese Republicans under Sun Yat-sen in the early years of this century, the history of political organization in the South has generally tended to confirm the power of local politicians at the expense of the international system. Vietnam and the success of OPEC are only the most dramatic signs of this process.

For the most part, dependency theorists dispute these developments. "The essence of neo-colonialism is that the State which is subject to it is, in theory, independent and has all the outward trappings of international sovereignty. In reality its economic system and thus its political policy is directed from outside."[13] So wrote Kwame Nkrumah before he was toppled as chief of state of Ghana by local political opposition. Most dependency theorists subscribe to this modern expression of Marxism, which sees in ruling groups the expression of class interest, and—in finding the contemporary ruling class to be an international bourgeoisie—sees virtually all state structures, apart from those of resolutely socialist states, as tools of international capitalism.

But it is not only those with a Marxist bias who see the power of the international system throughout the fabric of Southern life. The sheer magnitude of European trade with the Third World seemed to point in the same direction. In 1820, world trade was valued at some 341 million pounds sterling, and British investment abroad—no other country engaged in such activity—totaled perhaps 10 million pounds. But by 1880 world trade topped 3 billion pounds, while British foreign investment came to some 200 million pounds and probably accounted for more than half the European and North American investments abroad. How could such economic dynamism fail to have its impact on the preindustrial areas of the world, seen by these capitalist powers as sources of raw materials and markets as well as geostrategic stakes in rivalries centered in Europe? Virtually any area of the South would show the imprint of European penetration by the end of the nineteenth century, and it is not difficult to establish a *prima facie* case for the point of view of dependency theory. However, when these various Southern areas are placed side by side, and not looked at as separate cases, the differences among them appear as well.

A simple comparison illustrates the point. By 1880, Argentina and Egypt each had received some 20 to 25 million pounds sterling of British investment and each was permeated with the British presence. But Egypt was on the verge of collapse (which came in 1882), while Argentina was moving into position as Great Britain's most important economic satellite in South America. In short, while the outward thrust of European power in the nineteenth century was generally the same (although account must be taken of geostrategic considerations), the European impact varied widely in Africa, Asia, the Middle East, and South America. And to understand the variety of receptions the Europeans got, it is necessary to understand local political conditions and their ability to cope with the foreign challenge. Focusing on the dynamics of European expansion, then documenting its impact on the South, is not enough.

Reconciling Differences

A number of Latin Americanists recently have tried to address the question of the state in order to understand, in terms of dependency theory, the rise there of authoritarian-bureaucratic regimes since the mid-1960s. Even writers who had earlier been critical of the theory have apparently now decided it is a useful tool to comprehend this question. The general schema of their approach has run along the following lines: the international system forced a style of industrialization on Latin America (import substitution) that, by the 1950s, was playing out; the result was increased civil turmoil and a polarization of forces, with the Right backed by the United States. Ultimately, this right-wing action proved successful—at least in the short run—because of the support brought to it by multinational corporations eager to invest in Latin America once stability there was assured. The force of the international system, essentially in its economic relations, thus molded the character of the Latin American state.

Once again, however, the problem is not to determine whether the international system has affected the form of the state in Latin America—surely it has—so much as to evaluate the degree of the contribution and to see it alongside domestic factors. And it would appear that, in their concern to relate local experiences to outside influences, dependencistas have once again systematically underestimated the importance of internal forces. Thus, three hundred years of rule by Catholic Spain and Portugal left Latin America with a legacy of authoritarian government characterized by a corporatist ideology, patron-client relations, and regional *caudillo* authority still alive.

More recent developments have contributed still more importantly to the authoritarian governments of today. World War I and the Great Depression brought such populist leaders as Vargas in Brazil and Perón in Argentina to power, men dedicated to mass mobilization in order to curb the power of foreigners and their local collaborators (chiefly the landed oligarchs of the export sector). In a sense, then, Latin America "decolonized" in the 1930s, with populist nationalism ascendant. The economic crises of the 1950s made these populist coalitions untenable, and the local political situations polarized. But the structures within which these events occurred had been created in a period of opposition to the international system.

Argentina and Brazil fit this pattern, but the case of Mexico is particularly illustrative: the Partido Revolucionario Institucional ruling Mexico since the end of the revolution of 1910–1917 (although under various names) took the most decisive steps in its institutionalization of an authoritarian corporatist structure around 1938, at the very time the Cárdenas government was dramatically expropriating American utility and oil companies in Mexico. It would thus appear that domestic factors, and not simply the dependent status of Latin America internationally, must be respected if one is to understand the current spread of authoritarianism throughout the continent.

Of course, it would not serve our understanding of contemporary international relations to go to the other extreme from dependency theory, to assert blindly the preeminence of local factors in Third World development. For over a century now, Northern trade and investment, combined with occasional military intervention, have indeed vitally affected the economic and political development of the South. Today, most of these countries depend on the international connection for military know-how and espionage services, and for aid, trade, and investment as an integral part of preserving the peace domestically and assuring regional rank. For few of these states have acquired political institutions appropriate to the social forces they must integrate and control. Geographic, ethnic, and class interests are seldom aggregated effectively through party structures, while bureaucracies, which determine the ability of governments to act competently, are often inefficient or corrupt. Conflicts with neighboring states invariably compound these problems, as regional balances of power establish themselves in the wake of decolonization. In such circumstances of incipient civil and regional upheaval, the international connection can take on great political significance. Dependency theory seems to be especially accurate when it speaks of the outcome of these local struggles in terms of their intersection with the forces of the international system.

Conclusion

The point of this chapter has not been, therefore, to deny the interconnectedness of global developments today, nor to doubt the extensive influence the North has on the South by virtue of its far greater relative power and the linkages connecting the two areas. I have tried to establish instead some measure of the South's autonomy from the North despite these factors, some respect for Southern traditions, institutions, and determination, which have historical importance irrespective of Northern imperialism. I have tried to indicate as well the ambiguities and contradictions of the international system, which mean that, even in those domains where the North is strong, the present logic of change may be that it is sponsoring the relative growth in power of the South.

For some two hundred years now, the industrial revolution has been spreading outward from Great Britain. Just as the first nation to gain international predominance as a result of these technological breakthroughs has passed from the center stage of history, so there is good reason to suspect that the future will see the growing importance of states still industrializing. Such developments will result in good measure from the international system itself.

Dependency theory obscures these points, making imperialism more all-pervasive and self-perpetuating than is the case. It may serve the political needs of certain groups to see the power of the North in this light, but there is no reason those of us without such needs should subscribe to a world view so distant from reality.

11

RICHARD E. BISSELL

Political Origins of the New International Economic Order

To the Western mind trained in capitalist economics, the "New International Economic Order" (NIEO) has a reasonably clear agenda: (1) stabilizing commodity prices, (2) controlling the impact of multinational corporations, (3) easing the transfer of technology to developing countries, and (4) increasing the rate of transfer of real resources to developing countries. Despite the existence of real economic problems that fit such categories, solutions have been elusive. Discussions have avoided the underlying political disagreements. Western leaders, following their own training, have con-

sidered economic problems as discrete entities, and Third
World leaders have deliberately avoided bringing their political problems onto the agenda. Because of this, negotiators
find that they are frequently unable to obtain precise defini-
tions of future economic needs in developing countries.

This chapter will contend that such imprecision derives
from readily observable political problems that will never be
addressed by narrowly construed economic discussions. By
using the political bases of the NIEO, the new generations of
political leadership are searching for economic tools to
assure stability of their fragile political orders.

Historical Background

To a large degree, the NIEO is simply a reinvention of the
wheel to carry the burden of social change. NIEOs, in various
forms, have been carried through at historical points in
many societies, generally as a response to unbearable social
tensions. The history of the entrepreneurial middle class is
one of commercial success followed by expropriation by the
ruling classes. Nietzsche was not proposing a new ideology
when he wrote that "merchant and pirate were for a long
period one and the same person. Even today mercantile
morality is really nothing but a refinement of piratical
morality."

The devastating effect of this view can be seen in many
cultural examples. The Chinese evolved a code of social hier-
archies during the Chou dynasty: warrior-administrators at
the top, peasants second, artisans third, with merchants at
the bottom so as to ensure their susceptibility to expropriation. This notion of rights and privileges was transferred to
Japan as well, where the aristocracy exercised its right to confiscate a merchant's wealth when the debt of the upper class
became unbearable—witness the 1705 incident when the
Japanese head of state accused the Yodoya family, richest of
the Osaka merchants, of "unbefitting ostentation," and took

away all of their fortune.[1] Jewish merchants in medieval Europe frequently suffered the same fate, and Ibo merchants in Nigeria encountered the same attitudes in the late 1960s.

The search for an economic scapegoat in human history is as common as crop failures, and where societies are divided into three layers, the temptation to point the finger at the middle is overwhelming. The poor can confiscate from the middleman merchant by riot, and the rich can confiscate by fiat. In the present global economy, where it is manifestly impossible to satisfy the material expectations of all countries, there has been a protracted search for the middleman to blame.

The NIEO is an international attack on the middle-class entrepreneur. The curious aspect of the NIEO, however, is that the attack has been deflected from the rich countries — the greatest pressure has been brought on the Western economic interests in the Third World that play a middle-class role. The entrepreneurial, but physically powerless, roles of expatriate individuals and industries in the national societies of the Third World are being confiscated in an ages-old move to deal with social and political unrest. In the short term, Third World leaders need to find economic scapegoats to explain the unfulfilled expectations to their own people; the long-term effect is to reduce the role of international entrepreneurship, as all commerce is subjected to strict governmental control through each aspect of the NIEO.

Economic nationalism is not a new issue. The growth of autarky in the 1930s is acknowledged to have undermined world peace. Many factors have contributed to this autarky in the past decade, some economic and some political. The economic forces are considered in another chapter. Two political forces will be examined here: the generational changes in the Third World, and the drive for stability by Third World leaderships in shaky nationalistic orders.

The New Third World Leadership

The essential problem of political generations was indicated by Harold Isaacs when he noted that the move from power seeking to power wielding required leaders "to cross the great divide between nationalist dreams and national realities."[2] In effect, "romantic nationalism" gave way to more mundane forces, with Third World elites not fully understanding the extent of the transformation. Those elites felt that it would be possible for the former colonial powers to transfer tangible resources as readily as they had handed over the symbolic trappings of independence. And, for some time after independence, the West did transfer aid and support in a vague gesture of atonement for the colonial period, and in the naive belief that the decolonized areas might need a simple dowry to be pushed along the road to rapid economic development.

Such aid, on a meaningful scale, lasted only until the Vietnam war and 1973 oil crisis. The ambivalence of the West about colonialism—a political order quickly abandoned when the costs of maintaining it put any stress on political and economic tranquility in the home countries—has taken an entirely different form with regard to gifts to former colonies. The developed countries of both East and West are not eager to give away something for nothing, and certainly not in exchange for Third World ideological attacks on "neocolonialism." The current arguments of the NIEO involve both demands for tangible assets and attacks on the legitimacy of Western capitalism, but the developed states cannot concede ground on either issue without imperiling their domestic orders.

A "sea change" is occurring in the training and education of the emerging generation of Third World leaders. Those who took power at the time of independence had been educated in the West—not necessarily at the best universities, but that was not essential. It was a virtual prerequisite that nationalist leaders spend some extended time abroad, forming linkages with exiled fellow nationalists from their own countries and others. The leaders to whom the West was willing to transfer power were those who could speak and understand the vocabulary of Western ideals and institutions. The formative experience achieved by spending years in exile in another, powerful culture with universal influence created a sense of vision in early nationalists that enabled them to transcend many of the discouraging aspects of economic backwardness in their own societies. That distance between the leaders and the people injected a dynamism into the societies that resulted in change and growth.

The leadership class now emerging in much of the Third World, however, is increasingly homegrown. Thirty years have passed since much of Asia achieved independence, and twenty years for most of Africa. Today, time spent abroad is kept to a minimum, for politics have been domesticated. During the tenure of General Acheampong as Ghanaian head of state (1973–1978), people in Accra joked about his unwillingness to travel further than Togo. But the general replied that it had nothing to do with politics or threats to his rule; he simply had no desire to go further.

Domesticated politics also means that aspirant leaders need to remain at home for their training. Even among the military, the focus is increasingly domestic—witness the falloff of interest in Latin America for the Canal Zone school run by the United States for young officers. The growth of service academies and universities in the Third World in the 1960s and 1970s was phenomenal. Inevitably, independence meant founding national universities. The University of Khartoum was established in the Sudan in 1956; in the Ivory Coast, the University of Abidjan in 1964. In Malaysia, universities were founded in 1962, 1969, 1970, and 1973; in Nigeria, although only the university at Ibadan existed at independence, by 1975 the number had increased to fourteen.

To an increasing degree, potential Third World leaders, both civilian and military, are educated at home, and sent abroad only for brief technical training. There is thus no tendency to internalize a Western code of civil and military behavior as had been done by many of the leaders at independence. Ironically, many such "national universities" were funded in the past and currently by universities and philanthropies in the home countries—with apparently little regard for the ultimate political impact of such training.

A second feature of this emerging generation of leaders is their lack of interest in capitalist incentives. The reasons for this are several: the failure to spend extended time in the West, leading to little intuitive understanding of the workings of a capitalist economy; the fact that the ideology of decolonization contained the germ of anti-capitalism, for any aspect of the colonial social order is seen as anathema; a general lack of respect for the concept of contract, the foundation stone of a capitalist economic order;[3] and, perhaps most important, the desire to remove power centers that are potential rivals to the young national governments. Thus, both Third World calls for *authenticité*—reversion to traditional (non-Western) values—and the reaction against European and Western economic institutions are clearly related to a global antagonism toward capitalism. A working capitalist system requires a respect for the long term, a willingness to commit people and resources for the future, the ability to organize a society sufficiently to carry out those commitments, and the strength to compete in an open economic framework. On all four scores, much of the Third World drops by the wayside. Some governments have taken up the challenge—Brazil, Korea, Kenya, the ASEAN (Association of Southeast Asian Nations) states, and others—but in many cases the experiences of the last several decades have eroded the interest of the weaker, domestically oriented leaders in a capitalist order.

The West went through several phases in reaching a functioning capitalist system, including a number of aborted efforts. Thus, there is no reason to assume that the Third World in general will *not* eventually become as capitalist as the West. The creation of numerous fragile political entities since the Second World War, however, has established obstacles to the capitalist development of many societies. Economic power rivals political power, and insecure politicians will exclude the rival entrepreneurial forces to insure their survival. Of greatest interest to us, however, is the absence of conditions in many new nations even to participate in an international capitalist order. Consider, for example, the abrogation of contracts in the last few years in the area of long-term debt. North Korea has simply suspended all debt repayments. Negotiations for rescheduling debts have become routine; the estimated value of multilateral debt reschedulings has risen from about $100 million in 1960 to $800 million annually in the post-1973 period. Such depreciation of debts is a cause for real concern, though not despair. After all, in the nineteenth century both the United States and Russia defaulted with remarkable frequency on European loans (particularly those to railroad-building operations); in one case, the U.S. continued its growth to become the premier capitalist society, and in the other, the capitalist order was demolished.

One must differentiate within the Third World. Some societies have the underlying values to create, eventually, a competitive capitalist order, and others do not. In 1923, the president *emeritus* of Yale, Dr. Arthur T. Hadley, wrote of the character of Americans who developed the Western United States:

They were accustomed to judge men by what they did and not by what they professed. And this saved them from intolerance. They were enthusiastically devoted to their country and to its government; but they asked little of that government except that it should protect land titles and appoint honest judges. They were admirably fitted by temperament and training to carry the theory of free competition to its logical conclusion and reach the kind of result which Adam Smith or John Stuart Mill would have predicted.[4]

In the Third World today there are echoes of that spirit; in both Brazil and South Africa, for instance, there have been calls by significant elites in recent years for a reduction in governmental control after periods of directed economic growth. Their interest in the international welfare state known as the NIEO is of marginal importance.

A third feature of the present generation of Third World leaders is their response to the problem of governing polyethnic societies. At the time of independence, many Third World leaders inherited political institutions with weak domestic legitimacy. In subsequent years, "coming to terms" with the lack of domestic support has resulted in several different kinds of politics: totalitarianism in some cases (with dubious prospects for longevity), and machine politics in others, which attempts to create a political consensus among ethnic groups. The hallmarks of such political systems are patronage, favors, bribery, and other responses to particularistic needs that Westerners would term less-desirable politics. But both Aristide Zolberg and Myron Weiner, scholarly observers of different areas of the Third World, have appropriately identified the utility of the political machine in bringing traditional populations into the same political system.[5] The political machines compensate for the fact that formal legislative mechanisms cannot channel the demands of traditional population groups unfamiliar with democratic, individualistic politics. In providing readily available bargaining groups on domestic political and economic issues, the political machine may not replicate the parliamentary politics of the developed West, but, for the Third World, it is better than no politics at all—i.e., disintegration of the state, or the indefinite perpetuation of authoritarian rule.

What interests us here, however, are the implications of machine politics for the New International Economic Order. They fall into several categories.

1. Since corrupt politics operate at a deficit, the machine politics of the Third World must be subsidized. The price of bringing people into the political process is usually monetary, and the ability of new governments to raise money (presumably through taxation) is limited. Keeping people involved in a political machine requires the government to have more money to hand out to the people than it takes from them. If the government operates without a deficit, in fact, the people have a reduced interest in working within the political system (since their needs are short term), and they are close enough to the subsistence level to ignore the government. In that way, postcolonial attempts in the Third World to continue the European practice of squeezing excess capital out of the farmers has frequently failed, as the farmer simply moved his produce across the border for better prices. At present, Ghanaian farmers are carrying 50,000 to 100,000 tons of cocoa across the border illegally each year.

   Governments faced by such challenges have three choices: do nothing, extort produce from farmers by force (rarely successful), or obtain financial support from overseas to pay farmers and grease the wheels of urban politics. There are short-lived exceptions, of course: the OPEC nations were in the enviable position of extorting money from oil importers for some years after 1973, and some nations have economic sense. In the late 1970s, a report by *West Africa* noted that "the Liberian economy has been badly hit by falling prices for iron ore—its principal export. Government revenue is, surprisingly, standing up well in spite of this because of improved methods of tax gathering and because of high agricultural yields and prices." When the Liberian economy subsequently took a beating from global inflation, the government attempted to pass along real costs to the consumers, and then was overthrown by Sergeant Doe.

2. In the urban areas, Europeans have been replaced by Third World personnel, with important side effects. Dur-

ing the colonial period, various implicit subsidies of colonial operations existed—for example, in the form of
retirement benefits for expatriate civil servants. Thus,
salaries did not have to be appreciably higher than European standards to attract personnel, for there was a long-
term assurance of financial security from the home country. Two conditions have changed. First, external assurance no longer exists for indigenous personnel, and with
the credit-worthiness of many governments uncertain,
governmental elites in the Third World are tempted to establish private pension plans (Swiss bank accounts,
family industries) as compensation. Second, politics are
routinely turbulent, which suggests to elites that their
tenure in office will be short. The societies are not seen to
hold the solutions to their economic problems in their own
hands, and given the vagaries of international politics and
aid flows, any disruption can cause the fall of public
leaders. Thus, the accumulation of "retirement funds"
must be done in a short time, leading to greater demands
on the political machine. It is now unusual for a leader
to be removed without public discussion of financial
irregularities.

3. The instability of external sources of funds for political
   machines in the Third World has led to startling snatch-
   ing of new sources of revenue. The evolution of the
   widespread nationalization of assets owes much to the demands of local political machines. The need for jobs can be
   satisfied in part by placing people in staff positions in nationalized firms. Short-term cash requirements can be
   aided by retaining formerly repatriated profits inside the
   country—at the disposal of the government. The need to
   pay off foreign owners can be avoided by issuing bonds
   and then renegotiating the debt. And the rival power centers represented by foreign investors that dominate the
   cash economies of small Third World countries are thus
   eliminated. In the process, the infrastructure of power

built by foreign entrepreneurs is placed at the disposal of the government and the political machine.

The only problem, of course, is that long-term growth suffers because foreign capitalists lose interest in further investment. Nevertheless, the purposes of the political machine are fulfilled: short-term political gains at the cost of long-term economic growth. Unfortunately, the logical end result of such historical momentum has already happened: Uganda under Idi Amin was reduced to the position of an international bartering agent, with planes carrying twice-weekly loads of coffee beans to Britain and returning with equal amounts of palace goods and essential spare parts. The damage done by such governmental behavior was so great that the Ugandan economy has yet to show any signs of recovery in long-term growth, despite the removal of Amin and the reinstallation of Obote leadership.

The Search For Stability

For their own survival, many Third World leaders attempt to channel all foreign influences through governmental mechanisms. The enhancement of political legitimacy is their overriding objective. Some nations rode the tiger of economic growth and social change, and were successful. Others went for the ride and, to paraphrase the limerick, came back inside. The message from the latter no longer reflects an abiding devotion to economic growth: their dominant concern is regime survival. They feel it would be better for their nations' links with the international system to atrophy than for the government to lose control. The international marketplace is a cacophony of events that is not entirely understood, and the flow of those events must be slowed down by governmental controls. Leaders want to restrict the number of foreign economic influences in their countries, for the number and complexity of those influences can be confusing even to them. The effects of such an outlook on the NIEO are quite evident.

Regarding commodities, the Third World attempts to stabilize export earnings. Since political machines cannot put aside surplus earnings for difficult years, and long-term planning is discouraged, periodic declines in commodity prices precipitate political crises in exporting countries. People with marginal loyalty to the national government are rarely willing to absorb the costs of such export shortfalls themselves, and most governments are not sufficiently developed to enforce the sharing of hard times by the entire population. Under such circumstances, the fragile political coalitions that govern most Third World countries must obtain major subsidies in times of export shortfalls, or the coalitions themselves will fall.

The existence of low internal savings rates exacerbates the situation by restricting the possibilities for financing long-term investment. The people have come to expect governments even to undertake savings plans for the nations. Until "thrift" is given a higher priority in the Third World, as opposed to the present emphasis on "consumption," the developing countries are unlikely to see the transformations of their economies that they so ardently desire. Stabilizing commodity prices ensures consistent levels of consumption-oriented incomes in the Third World— in those well-managed economies, it ensures long-term investment programs—without people having to undertake individual and national measures to cushion the impact of international recessions.

The NIEO also attempts to limit the role of multinational corporations (MNCs) in the global economy. As already mentioned, MNCs threaten the stability of regimes unequipped to deal with the capitalist system. MNCs, in addition, are seen as agents of the former colonial powers, and the goal is to eliminate MNC influence as thoroughly as the world was decolonized. But if the Third World must rely in the long run only on governments and intergovernmental institutions for the necessary investment, they had better be a patient lot. Regime stability and removal of external influences can be achieved, but at a major economic cost.

A major part of the NIEO program deals with the transfer of technology from the developed countries to the Third World. The attempts to regulate such transfers, whether through a generalized "code of conduct" or through the establishment of national screening boards for the import of technology, are additional manifestations of distrust for the capitalist process. There is an abiding suspicion that the Third World is somehow paying "too high a price" for imported technology—and that suspicion is heightened by a general insensitivity to the costs of research and development for new technology (similar to the ignorance of the need for internal savings). The desire to coordinate technology imports at the national level is one more effort to increase the "channeling" role of the political leadership. In many cases, as shown in recent American congressional testimony, such government screenings are actually smokescreens for discreet bribe demands. Those societies with policies of open technology imports, as in Asia, have also been showcases of economic growth.

The last NIEO issue of political importance to the Third World is the transfer of real resources on an increasing scale. The financing of new political elites and growing political machines is becoming more burdensome all the time. If population projections are accurate, the provision of basic services in Third World cities will be a staggering job. The degree of potential social disorder represented by urban populations is a frightening statistic for any Third World leader, for a person in an urban area is by definition a political influence. The money to preserve social order, through the mechanism of local political machines, is rarely being generated internally.

A variety of sleights of hand have been devised to finance

Third World stability. The Third World included in the Law of the Sea Treaty (1982) a provision that some percentage of revenues from mineral mining on the seabed be turned over for Third World development, and at the same time made provision for protection of existing mining operations in the Third World. In the proceedings of the International Monetary Fund (IMF), it has been suggested that the creation of special drawing rights (SDRs) be made an occasion for giving those newly created SDRs to Third World states as one-time donations. The IMF has used profits from gold sales to subsidize borrowings by developing countries from the Fund, and a special oil facility subsidy account was created in 1975 to help African and Asian states pay for the escalating oil costs set by their OPEC brethren. A variety of measures were undertaken after 1973 to renegotiate long-term and short-term debts of some countries, as they began to fail to meet interest payments on an increased scale. A special list of the "most needy"—informally designated the "Fourth World"—was published by the United Nations as a focus of attention, with one proposal being the outright cancellation of all debts held by those countries. And a number of West European countries have agreed to do so, given the growing bankruptcy of the Third World governments in the early 1980s.

Yet there was no suggestion, although it would have possibly been more logical, that the "most needy" might not have the attributes of sovereignty, and that they should therefore be placed under a state of trusteeship by the United Nations. Such a condition is admitted informally, as French advisors remain very much involved in the operations of ministries in the Francophone African states, and Soviet advisors operate the Afghan government. But in formal international negotiations, the only system on the agenda is the manifestly successful economic system of the West—no offer has been made for concessions in the political system of the Third World.

The shape of the NIEO demonstrates the rudimentary awareness among even the poorest of Third World leaders that economic assets can be converted into political power.[6] The golden goose must be carefully tended, however, even while stealing the eggs of gold. The NIEO comes close, even without being implemented, to damaging permanently the global economic machine that has produced the wealth the Third World so much wants to share.

It is unfortunate that the political pressures underlying the demands of the NIEO are likely to increase in the short term. The conflicts between Third World states, and between them and the developed states, can lead to horribly destructive violence. Where economic systems have been destroyed in the past by political and social irresponsibility, it has taken centuries to put them back together again.

12

Beyond the New International Economic Order

The call of the developing countries for the creation of a New International Economic Order (NIEO) has aroused widespread interest. Some observers have gone so far as to advocate that the new order be made the centerpiece of future economic and political relations between the United States and the Third World. Before making such a commitment, however, it is worth considering what would be the likely

I am grateful to the editors of *Foreign Policy* for permission to utilize here material that I previously published in that journal.

effects if the measures of the NIEO were, in fact, implemented. Such an analysis is the first purpose of this chapter.
We then consider the major economic and political shifts
that affected the less-developed countries (LDCs) and the
United States from 1972 to 1978, when the NIEO first
received widespread attention. These changes have had important effects on the place of the NIEO in the international
policy agenda.

For reasons discussed below, U.S. acceptance of the NIEO
would soon lead to a worsening, rather than an improvement, of political relations with the Third World. And the
prognosis for the economic effects is equally pessimistic. Implementation of the various contemplated policy changes—
increases and indexation of prices of primary products,
vastly expanded resource transfers to the Third World,
assured access to technology and markets in the rich countries, and the unquestioned right of LDCs to restructure
their relations with multinational corporations—would not
lead to substantial economic gains for the Third World.
These conclusions may not be intuitively self-evident, so let
us examine the reasoning that underlies them.

Commodity Agreements

International agreements to raise and stabilize the prices of
raw material products exported by the developing countries
have been a prominent theme in the new order. The success
of producer cartels in oil and bauxite has stimulated interest
in similar programs for copper, tin, nickel, and primary products in general. In some cases, such cartels may be implemented by Third World exporting countries acting on their
own. Financial backing from OPEC members with excess
cash would, of course, increase the feasibility of price support
arrangements in more commodities. And active support from
the industrialized countries might in principle raise the
prices of virtually all primary products in relation to prices of
manufactured products.

The potential difficulties involved in maintaining such price support arrangements are clear. Higher and more stable returns would evoke a large increase in world production of primary products. For commodities in which one or two countries are dominant suppliers to the world economy, these countries might be willing to limit supply in the interest of maintaining higher prices. Such curtailment of production would be especially feasible if, as in the case of petroleum, the commodities in question were produced in sparsely populated countries without pressing financial needs. Otherwise, however, an International Price Stabilization Agency would be hard pressed to prevent prices from falling, as supply of primary products increased more rapidly than demand in world markets. Let us assume, however, that with a spirit of international cooperation, and with ample financial support from the developed countries, such problems could be resolved. What would be the effects on the Third World of an increase and indexation of commodity prices relative to prices of industrial products?

It is a misconception, of course, to identify primary product production with the less-developed countries and industrial production with the developed countries. For some commodities—for example, cotton, iron ore, and (beet) sugar—countries like the United States, Australia, and France are major international producers. With higher world prices for primary products, developed countries may well increase their production of these products (or of substitutes), raising the rich countries' share in world trade or, at the least, replacing their own imports from Third World suppliers.

Sufficiently comprehensive international agreements might, of course, bar such perverse effects stemming from a new international order. More important, however, most Third World countries import as well as export primary products. Consequently, the effects of higher commodity prices on individual developing countries will depend on the price increases that are sustained for specific commodities, and on the composition of each LDC's exports and imports. Taking account of the effects of increased *import* prices on developing countries, the net impact of a higher overall level of commodity prices on many Third World countries is likely to be far less favorable than they might expect. The quantitative effects of commodity agreements on income and growth in the developing countries seem to have been seriously oversold.

Increased Resource Transfers

The NIEO would also involve a large increase in resource transfers from the rich to the poor countries. A likely figure for Official Development Assistance under the NIEO would be 0.7 percent of the gross national product of the developed countries, a target that Sweden has already attained. The magnitude of the effective increase in aid would, of course, be larger if the developed countries acceded to another request of the developing countries: cancellation of outstanding Third World debts. For the United States, acceptance of these proposals would involve a rise in public capital flows to a figure greater than $14 billion per annum, more than a tripling of aid from 1977.

Some observers may question congressional willingness to accept so large an increase in aid. Moreover, the conceptual differences from the present aid program involve a shift that is even greater than the change in dollar magnitudes. To facilitate long-term planning in recipient countries, aid would be granted on the basis of a continuing commitment, not subject to congressional vagaries. And, to avoid the manipulation and dependency relations that marred earlier aid relationships, public capital would now be provided without political strings or administrative control. Finally, far from expecting "gratitude" from Third World countries, Congress would be expected to commit aid within a framework of redressing past and present inequities in the international distribution of income.

All of this seems highly unlikely. But let us assume that these problems could be overcome. What would be the likely effects of a massive increase in resource transfers on the international income gap?

A measure of increased aid would undoubtedly accelerate the pace of economic development in many Third World countries. Increases in aid on the scale contemplated by the NIEO, however, would be unlikely to yield commensurate increases in economic growth. Because of human resource and managerial constraints, the capacity to absorb a large volume of investment productively is usually limited.[1] Reflecting limited absorptive capacity, as more and more aid were made available, Third World countries would exhaust their portfolio of high-return investments and would invest in marginal projects that contribute little to growth.

The possibilities for using resource transfers to narrow the international income gap are also limited by other conditions. As proponents of aid have long recognized, even on standard Keynesian grounds a government commitment to a steady flow of aid may well accelerate the pace of economic growth in the developed countries. This may exacerbate inequality in the international distribution of income because, as is well known, the absolute size of the income gap widens if the rich and the poor countries grow at the *same* rate. Further, the prospects for using aid to induce international convergence also depend on such conditions as the pace of population growth in the Third World, and the size of the present difference in income levels between the rich and the poor countries. Given the magnitude of these key parameters, it would be naive to expect that increased resource transfers would narrow the international income gap perceptibly within a time horizon that is politically meaningful.

Improved Access to Technology and Markets

Third World leaders have also emphasized the need for improved access to the advanced technology developed in the rich countries. Compliance with these demands would do little to close the international technology gap, however, unless the LDCs implemented certain changes in their own policies. For example, the knowledge and technology necessary to raise agricultural productivity in some crops has, in fact, been available to Third World leaders for years. They have often failed, however, to create extension services, or to follow the input and output pricing policies that are necessary to diffuse the new technology widely among their agricultural producers. A similar failure to diffuse advanced technology that is already available exists in the industrial sector of many developing countries. Government policies in the allocation of credit and foreign exchange have often created a "dualistic" pattern in which some firms utilize advanced technology and others use backward techniques. This internal technological gap within many Third World countries would not be ameliorated by the measures of the new order.

The demand that the rich countries make their technology more accessible to developing countries has widespread appeal. It is not always clear, however, how implementation of these demands would work in practice. Third World countries already *have* access to advanced technology from numerous sources, such as the consulting and engineering companies that exist in many advanced countries. And, as the relationship between Arthur D. Little and the government of Algeria testifies, such consulting firms have been willing to serve the aspirations even of radical countries in the Third World. Moreover, the number of international consulting firms and potential supplying countries is sufficiently large to preclude effective price collusion or inattention to client needs. Because of these conditions, a Third World country that wants to acquire the advanced technology necessary to build and operate, say, a steel mill or a fertilizer plant can, in fact, do so. Even in more sensitive and esoteric areas, supply conditions are such that China has, for example, purchased advanced technology for undersea petroleum prospecting.[2]

In addition to consulting firms, LDCs at present have licensing agreements, management contracts, and turnkey projects available as alternative sources of advanced technology. Developing countries have complained that the fees charged by such suppliers are excessive. A new order might, in principle, reduce charges. Note, however, that within the present international system, the governments of developing countries can intervene in negotiations for the transfer of technology and press for lower payments and more favorable terms. Even such moderate Third World countries as Mexico and Colombia have already implemented this sort of interventionist policy and have reported large savings in their payments for imported technology.

Further, the measures usually proposed to improve access to advanced technology would do little to help the LDCs achieve another major goal—increasing their competitive capacity in relation to multinational corporations. The multinationals' competitive edge depends not only on sophisticated production technology, but also on management techniques in marketing and accounting. Thus, the most advanced production facilities installed in Third World countries will not yield their economic potential if Third World managers do not utilize modern accounting techniques to control productivity, cash balances, and inventories. Third World leaders have shown little interest in acquiring and diffusing such accounting techniques—which are, of course, easily accessible. The relative unimportance of production technology per se can perhaps best be illustrated with some examples. The Third World already possesses the know-how necessary to produce ball-point pens, rubber-soled canvas shoes, and carbonated beverages. Nevertheless, Parker pens, Ked shoes, and Coca Cola are often preferred products in developing countries. The explanation lies not in the multinational corporations' superior production technology, but rather in their marketing techniques. Implementation of the NIEO would do little to change this situation.

Acceptance of another Third World demand—improved access to export markets in the rich countries—would, however, make an important difference for the pace of economic development, at least in some Third World countries. Greater export sales, facilitated by tariff preferences for developing countries and an end to shameful nontariff barriers in the developed countries, would have a number of beneficial effects. With greater foreign exchange earnings, developing countries could import the larger volume of capital goods and raw materials necessary to sustain more rapid growth of output, income, and employment. There is also evidence that domestic saving in developing countries increases with greater exports, so that more domestic capital formation would also be feasible. Finally, export growth in manufactured products would enable producers in developing countries to attain economies of scale, lowering costs and permitting many consumer products to be brought within the reach of broader masses of the local population.

Notwithstanding these important benefits from improved market access, we should also note some potential problems. Some developing countries are more industrialized than others. Brazil or Taiwan, for example, would be better able than, say, Ghana or Sri Lanka to take advantage of the opportunities that tariff preferences would open for expanding sales in the rich countries. Consequently, a generalized tariff preference scheme might not help all—or, indeed, many—developing countries. The more industrialized Third World countries would appropriate the lion's share of the benefits, with little accruing to the poorer majority. Another possibility would be to equalize opportunities for the diverse set of LDCs by creating categories for differential rates of tariff preference. Such a system would not be easy to administer. It would also involve rivalry between Third World countries, and an opportunity for the rich countries to exercise "leverage" against individual developing countries by controlling access to their domestic markets. These political effects of equalizing opportunities would go counter to the whole spirit of the new order.

Further, the place of multinational corporations (MNCs) in improved market access would also have to be clarified. As is well known, despite the many barriers they encounter, exports of manufactured products from the LDCs to OECD (Organization for Economic Cooperation and Development) countries have, in fact, grown rapidly over the past twenty-five years. Multinational corporations with "sourcing" subsidiaries located in the Third World have had a large role in this expansion of manufactured exports from developing countries. Presumably, these corporations with subsidiaries in the Third World would also want to participate in the advantages of generalized tariff preferences. Note also that in negotiations over such participation, MNCs have an important bargaining card that is not under the control of the Third World—the possibility of direct sales to their companies' worldwide production and marketing networks. Inclusion of multinational corporations in the benefits of improved market access, however, is not what Third World leaders mean when they speak of a new order.

Multinational Corporations

A major redressing of the balance of forces between Third World governments and multinational corporations is, of course, a prominent theme of the NIEO. The proposed restructuring is reflected clearly in the *United Nations Charter of Economic Rights and Duties of Nations.* Article 2 of the charter declares unequivocally that every state has the right

to nationalize, expropriate, or transfer ownership of foreign property in which case appropriate compensation should be paid by the State adopting such measures, taking into account its relevant laws and regulations and all circumstances that the State considers pertinent.

These provisions may be juridically unimpeachable. In the present context, however, the question is: what would implementation of these conditions imply for the Third World's economic development?

The present lack of international legal sanction for nationalization on terms they themselves decide has not been a major factor deterring Third World countries from expropriating multinational corporations. Rather, in cases where Third World governments have been deterred, it has been mainly because they have felt that they would lose more than they would gain. And, in the post-Suez world, the potential losses to be considered are largely economic—the inflow of new investment and international credits. The numerous examples of expropriations successfully carried out in recent years suggest that, with favorable economic conditions, developing countries will nationalize as they see fit. Universal acceptance of article 2 in the new order would not change very much the actual practice of Third World governments.

Increasing juridical recognition of the right of Third World countries to expropriate and compensate as they like would, however, enhance the legitimacy of such actions. Consequently, the NIEO would increase the risk that multinational corporations perceive in the developing countries. This would affect their decisions with respect to new investments and to existing activities in the Third World. Confronted with increased legitimacy for discretionary expropriation, foreign companies would hardly be motivated to take a long-term perspective in efforts at investment, human resource development, and technology transfer. Further, greater risk can also be expected to reduce the flow of new investment to the Third World. As some Third World governments have seen, imposing conditions that worsen the investment climate for multinational corporations in their countries is often feasible. Unless its country is blessed with special resources like petroleum, however, the LDC government cannot also be assured that foreign firms will actually invest in the country.

From some perspectives, a sharp decline in multinational corporate investment in developing countries might be a good thing. It is unlikely, however, to accelerate the pace of economic development in the Third World. That foreign multinational corporations can be a powerful force for economic development can best be inferred from the behavior of some governments that have been without foreign investment and that now solicit it actively—for example, Egypt and East Bloc countries. The experience of India is also instructive here. India has been very successful in safeguarding its rights vis-à-vis multinational corporations. For example, because the government considers the division of the gains it was offered to be inequitable, it has rejected more than one proposal by foreign firms to build modern fertilizer factories in India. The Indian experience also indicates, however, that independence from multinational corporations is not always associated with economic and technological dynamism. Implementation of the new order's principles with respect to multinational corporations may be expected to lead to a generalization of the "Indian model" to other Third World countries.

The Overall Economic Impact

We can now summarize our discussion concerning the likely effects of the New International Economic Order on economic development in the Third World. An increase in public resource transfers to the developing countries would certainly be helpful. Because of limited absorptive capacity, however, increases in aid on the scale contemplated should not be expected to yield commensurate acceleration in the pace of economic development. Other measures such as assured access to technology developed in the rich countries would change little in substance unless developing countries revised some of their internal policies. Similarly, acceptance of the right of Third World governments to nationalize multinational corporations as they see fit would also modify little, for juridical considerations have not been the operative constraint on Third World decisions in this area.

Other new order policies, such as improved access to export markets in the rich countries, could be expected to yield major benefits to some Third World countries and negligible gains to others. Measures to raise prices of primary products would also have differential effects on various developing countries. Individual commodities vary greatly in the extent to which they satisfy the ideal conditions for a Third World producers' cartel—for example, in the availability of substitute products, in the participation of rich countries as competitive suppliers, and in the possibilities for controlling production. Consequently, the price rise that is sustainable will vary among different primary commodities. Moreover, developing countries import as well as export primary commodities. Hence, the net gains to individual Third World countries will be appreciably less than the rise in overall commodity prices.

The foregoing leads to a basic conclusion concerning the likely economic effects of the New International Economic Order: implementation of the various measures that constitute the NIEO will not lead to a marked narrowing of the international income gap, or to the major economic gains that Third World leaders have been led to expect.

Political Relations

One may well object that the preceding discussion has missed the essence of the story: the New International Economic Order has to do less with economics than with politics. Thus, it has been suggested, elites in the Third World may have little interest in such Western values as economic growth. Rather, Third World pressures for a new order are essentially an effort at emotional gratification and enhanced status. Consequently, gestures of accommodation on the part of the United States and the developed countries would answer their needs. And even if the NIEO did little for the developing countries economically, United States support for such policies would have the enormous benefit of improving political relations with the Third World. In this perspective, even if it yields no economic benefits to the Third World, a new order may be amply justified by giving several years of respite to American officials who must deal with the developing countries.

These views may have a great deal of validity. They also have important limitations. For, although some Third World elites may disdain economic growth per se, they may nevertheless be keenly interested in some things that economic growth permits. Furthermore, in view of the rapid increase of population in the developing countries, pressures would inevitably make themselves felt for more jobs. Economic growth can be helpful in creating additional employment opportunities. Willy-nilly, Third World leaders must be concerned with economic growth or its absence. Consequently, it does not seem productive to base United States relations toward the developing countries on a set of policies—the new order— that would do little to accelerate economic developments.

Furthermore, it is hardly realistic to assume that Third World leaders can be appeased by gestures of accommodation. American policymakers may believe that, by accepting negotiations on the new order, they can use talk to deflect Third World pressures. Such an approach, however, would involve a serious underestimate of the competence of Third World diplomacy. Leaders of the developing countries are fully capable of understanding such stalling tactics. They can also be expected to use such negotiations to their own advantage. Recent experience in negotiations with Third World countries, beginning with Teheran in 1971, suggests that Third World negotiators have, in fact, been far more skillful than some observers in the developed countries ever expected. Those observers have apparently underestimated the negotiating prowess of the developing countries, missing the masterly diplomatic skill that is the reality behind the rhetoric of Third World spokespersons.

Exhibiting this skill, Third World diplomats have already executed the classic maneuver of isolating the "extremists" (U.S. conservatives) and aligning many "moderates" (U.S. progressives) and opinion leaders on their side of the new order debate. The LDCs can be expected to be no less adroit in actual negotiations on a new order. Consequently, such negotiations would likely take on their own momentum and lead to concessions much more far-reaching than American policymakers may expect. Alternatively, negotiations would degenerate into a forum and focus for Third World hostility against the United States.

Finally, and perhaps most seriously over the longer term, United States acceptance of the principles and measures that constitute the new order would itself raise economic expectations in the Third World. For the reasons discussed earlier, however, the actual experience under the new order is not likely to satisfy these hopes. Such a conjunction of heightened expectations and poor experience can be expected to generate disillusion and frustration in the Third World, leading to markedly worsened relations with the United States. If the new order indeed led to such an outcome, it would hardly serve American political goals.

Learning from Experience

The scenario outlined above may seem unnecessarily pessimistic. It is supported, however, by the denouement of an earlier experience of United States policy toward Third World countries, the Alliance for Progress. In that case, too, the United States reacted to a perceived challenge (Fidel Castro) by switching from rejection to espousal of ideas and measures that Latin American leaders had earlier propounded. The alliance was duly launched, in an atmosphere of good intentions and dedication to a new era in U.S.–Latin American relations. Further, the United States committed itself to provide $20 billion—a large sum in terms of preinflationary purchasing power—in order to accelerate economic and social development in Latin America. The alliance also embodied significant multilateral elements (the Comité Interamericano Alianza para el Progreso [CIAP], the Inter-American Development Bank, and support for the Latin American Free Trade Association), and it contained important institutional innovations such as the Social Development Trust Fund and the Peace Corps.

The Alliance for Progress may well have helped promote important economic achievements in Latin America. Nevertheless, and notwithstanding its good intentions, we must recognize that the alliance failed to achieve its political objectives. The effects in terms of relations between the United States and Latin America were distinctly negative. Promulgation of the alliance led to heightened expectations that could not be sustained, and in Latin America it was soon judged a failure. The ensuing aftermath of disillusion led to a souring of United States/Latin American relations.

The experience with the Alliance for Progress suggests three important conclusions that are relevant in the present context. First, the United States cannot assure, by its own policies, satisfactory economic and social development in Third World countries; policies implemented by the developing countries themselves are also necessary. Second, to the extent that the United States (or a multilateral agency such as a regional development bank) attempts to influence the developing countries to implement such policies, it creates an intrusive dependency relationship that is intolerable to local elites. Finally, to prevent disillusion and ensuing hostility, the United States should not promise what it cannot deliver. In this perspective, United States acceptance of the New In-

ternational Economic Order appears even less desirable, for
political rather than for economic reasons.

U.S. Policy and the Third World

Humanitarian reasons suggest that it would be desirable for
the United States to offer international aid that would reduce pauperism in the poorest developing countries. As the
efforts at famine relief in Ethiopia show, however, such
measures may not always be feasible. Effective administration of large-scale humanitarian programs may well conflict
with the preferences of Third World elites for autonomy and
an end to foreign meddling in their affairs. Less grudging U.S.
acceptance of such measures as the International Development Association (IDA) and improved access to markets in
the rich countries would also be useful, particularly if they
are *not* cast in a new order framework that would raise Third
World expectations.

It would also be helpful for the United States to convey to
Third World elites the postcolonial perception that their
countries' economic and social progress depends most fundamentally on their own decisions with respect to mobilization
and utilization of their domestic resources. Such an approach
does not imply bleak prospects for development in Third
World countries. As in the past, Third World countries that
maintain development-oriented investment and exchange
rate policies will experience economic growth. And if
autonomy and self-esteem rather than renewed dependency
are the object, economic development that is achieved
through domestic efforts will be all the more meaningful.

It may well be disagreeable for American spokespersons to
address Third World leaders on the virtues of self-help in
such areas as domestic savings, internal technology policy,
and exchange rates. Americans who find uncongenial a
stress on self-reliance rather than external support for
development can, however, draw intellectual and ideological

support from the works of radical political economists, who have also emphasized the advantages for Third World countries of autonomous development rather than international entrapments.[3] The Chinese, too, have advocated an ideology urging self-help for Third World countries that seek meaningful development. Ideological legitimacy and support from the Chinese for the United States in a reorientation of American economic policies toward the Third World could prove to be an unexpected benefit of the Washington-Peking rapprochement.

Finally, for the reasons we have discussed, U.S. acceptance of the NIEO would soon lead to worsened political relations with the Third World. At the same time, the NIEO would do little for economic development. Indeed, by diverting developing countries from necessary policy measures that are within their own control, the NIEO might well be counterproductive. As such, taking the NIEO as the lodestar for a new era in U.S. relations with the Third World would be a movement in the wrong direction. This may be a disagreeable conclusion. However, as the experience of the Alliance for Progress showed, policies conceived with the noblest of intentions but grounded in illusion do not lead to a happy outcome for anyone.

Economic Shifts Since Promulgation of the NIEO

Since the twenty-sixth session of the United Nations, and the ensuing Third World pressures in 1972–1976 on behalf of the NIEO, major international economic and political shifts have occurred. These have changed the policymaking environment both for the United States and for the LDCs. Some discussions of the new order, however, have ignored the fact that these changes have rapidly altered the international policy agenda, including perspectives on the NIEO.

As is now well known, the countries most severely affected by OPEC's quintupling of petroleum prices were the oil-importing LDCs. The sharp rise in oil prices meant a drastic increase in the foreign exchange receipts necessary for sustaining high rates of economic development. With petroleum costing so much more, LDCs have much less foreign exchange available to pay for the imports of the raw materials and intermediate products that they require for economic expansion. As the experience of the 1950s and 1960s demonstrated, even a process of development based on import substitution necessitates a growing volume of imported inputs.

LDC governments reacted quickly and effectively to the newly imposed import constraint on their development. They borrowed heavily in the Eurocurrency markets in order to finance higher import levels and thereby obtain higher rates of output growth than would otherwise have been possible. The sharp increase in the LDCs' external debt during 1974–1977 thus enabled them to stave off temporarily the impact of higher oil prices on the pace of development.

This policy option for maintaining rapid economic expansion is becoming increasingly unavailable. As Third World debts reach high levels, a flow of new loans to sustain development at the earlier pace appears increasingly unlikely. This is because continuing high rates of output growth in the LDCs require ever-higher levels of imported inputs and hence ever-increasing absolute magnitudes of foreign borrowing. New loans to the LDCs will be negotiated, if only to "roll over" old debts and avert defaults. But the net volume of imports financed through Eurocurrency borrowing is unlikely to increase sufficiently to enable most LDCs to maintain high rates of economic development.

Developing countries with highly diversified manufactured and agricultural exports may be able to avoid extreme economic slowdown. Diversification is important here, for it permits an LDC to expand its export receipts and import volume without impinging excessively on individual markets in the developed countries and thus evoking higher tariffs or quota restrictions. Brazil is perhaps the prime example of an oil-importing LDC that has followed such a strategy to mitigate the import constraint on its development. But notwithstanding record-breaking export growth and foreign borrowing, Brazil's rate of GNP growth dropped sharply from 10 percent in earlier years to 5 percent in 1977.

The impact of higher oil prices comes home to roost in LDCs in a special institutional form. The import constraint on development generally manifests itself through an International Monetary Fund (IMF) policy package to stabilize the LDC's balance of payments and internal inflation. The typical package usually involves an austerity budget, tight credit, and constricted wages. Such measures are designed to reduce the growth of domestic demand and monetary expansion in accordance with the LDC's foreign exchange availability. The adjustment to lower economic growth is thus implemented via policy measures dictated by an agency of international neocolonialism, the IMF.

Blaming the IMF for the austerity program, however, would be equivalent to condemning the messenger for the message. To see this, imagine the situation of the LDCs facing high petroleum prices, but without the IMF. The LDCs would still have to make the macroeconomic adjustment to a tightened import constraint. Indeed, without the IMF, Third World countries would be worse off, for they would not have access to the fund's low-cost loans. The full economic (and political) burden of adjustment would thus fall completely on themselves. The problem that the oil-importing LDCs now face is not the IMF, but rather the low growth caused by high petroleum prices.[4]

Finally, foreign exchange receipts of the developing countries have also been hurt by the oil-induced slowdown of the OECD economies. As balance-of-payments constraints have reduced growth rates in Western Europe, the imports of these countries from the Third World have also fallen. The prospect is now for intensifying protectionism against many of the products that the oil-importing LDCs export.

Possibilities for an Exit

As the somber economic growth prospects of the LDCs have loomed more sharply, international policy discussions have proceeded in search of solutions. For reasons considered below, the measures stressed in the NIEO—commodity agreements, indexation, increased aid—have not received much attention in these deliberations. Rather, the focus has shifted to "technology," and particularly to narrowing the international technology gap. This theme was highlighted in the 1979 UN Conference on Science and Technology for Development.

Notwithstanding its magical, "black box" properties, technology is unlikely to solve the short- and medium-term growth problems of the LDCs. The probability of finding "appropriate technologies" that would markedly accelerate the pace of economic expansion in the LDCs is low.[5] In addition, proposed changes in the present system for transfer of technology to developing countries also have their problems. Measures that would reduce the price paid for know-how may in some cases also reduce the quantity and quality of the technology transferred. Policies to increase Third World control over technology transfers may also diminish the flow of new know-how for economic development.

Moreover, the most serious technology gap that LDCs face is usually not international, but internal. In most sectors, there are firms in the developing countries using technology that is up to international productivity levels. The problem is the technology gap within the LDCs—the multitude of other firms that in a dualistic pattern of development utilize far less productive techniques. This internal gap is the major technology condition that keeps productivity and living standards low in the developing countries, and international policy measures can do little to narrow it. Indeed, for their own reasons, many LDCs have rejected an innovative policy development by the United States—the Peace Corps—which was set up to accelerate the diffusion of modern technologies within the LDCs.

Further, as the pace of economic development has slackened, the trade-offs between economic growth and reducing external dependency have become increasingly painful. Dependency with the high rates of economic growth of the pre-1974 era was one thing. Dependency is perceived to be less harmful, however, if it involves possibilities for maintaining expansion in an otherwise bleak economic situation. This shift in LDC perspectives is clear in the treatment now being accorded to multinational corporations. As foreign exchange constraints intensify, some Third World countries are increasingly welcoming MNCs, with their capacity for investment and export promotion. In some cases, the new treatment includes bending, waiving, or reversing measures implemented in the earlier epoch to control MNC activities.

The changing climate for MNCs in the Third World is best understood as a new cycle around a trend. The long-run trend in Third World–MNC relations has been toward increasing LDC self-assertion. The milestones of that trend are clear: Mexico's petroleum expropriations of 1938, Egypt's seizure of the Suez Canal in 1956, and OPEC's pricing moves in 1973. But within the long-run movement, cycles are also evident in which LDCs alternatively welcome or squeeze foreign investors. Many oil-importing LDCs are now entering a welcoming phase because, in their present predicament, they find the reduced-dependency theme of the NIEO unhelpful.

If LDCs were to orient their development strategies toward increased economic cooperation among themselves, they might be able to relax the present import constraint on their development. There is little indication, however, that LDC economic policymakers are taking seriously the 1975 Lima Declaration in this regard. Similarly, another possibility might be for Third World countries to adopt a "basic needs" development strategy. This might reduce the dependence of their economies on imported inputs, and enable them to attain higher growth rates despite the limited foreign exchange they can expect to have available. The elites who control most LDCs, however, have shown little interest in pursuing vigorously a development strategy focusing on basic needs. Moreover, it is not even clear that such a strategy would, in fact, lead to high rates of economic expansion. Sri Lanka, a country noted for its basic-needs approach, has not had rapid economic growth. And despite its commitment to providing basic necessities rather than useless gadgets for its population, Cuba has not been able to avoid heavy dependence on a continuing flow of foreign capital.[6]

Thus, not only have perspectives in the developing countries altered considerably since the heyday of the NIEO, but policy measures for escaping from slackening economic growth are not at hand. And even if one is not concerned with growth per se, markedly slower rates of economic expansion in the LDCs have obvious implications for increasing unemployment and hence widening internal income disparities.

The Changing International Context

The international political context within which the New International Economic Order was proposed has also changed drastically. First, within the United States, positions on policies vis-à-vis the LDCs have shifted. With stagflation continuing, and longer-term economic prospects worsening in the industrialized world, U.S. policymakers have lost whatever interest they may have had in the cost-raising measures of the NIEO. The main hope of pro-LDC officials in the U.S. government is now to prevent new barriers from being erected to restrict LDC exports, not to dismantle old ones.

Further, important ideological shifts have also occurred in

the U.S. These have undercut the philosophical basis for the massive U.S. resource transfers that were an integral part of the NIEO. U.S. supporters of the developing countries have belatedly come to recognize the importance of reducing LDC dependence for Third World aspirations and for U.S.–LDC relations. They have also come to recognize the inherent inconsistency between a large U.S. developmental role and a reduction in LDC dependence. As the reality of "aid as imperialism" has become clear, the position of liberals like Frank Church toward the LDCs has moved close to a Moynihan policy of benign neglect. This change is ironic, inasmuch as it is out of phase with the present position of LDC policymakers. Irony apart, the current American stance hardly provides the political basis for a vigorous U.S. commitment in support of the NIEO.

The focus of the U.S. development community has, in fact, shifted to a new set of themes: basic needs, human rights, employment growth, and income redistribution in developing countries. Unfortunately, governments in the LDCs do not share U.S. enthusiasm on these issues. The result has been an erosion of dialogue and of a consensual basis for fruitful collaboration on behalf of the NIEO or in support of the LDCs in general.

Authoritarian governments in the Third World have been incensed by U.S. efforts, especially during the Carter administration, at promoting human rights in their countries. In the case of Brazil and Chile, this anger led to the rupture of some political and military links. At the same time, LDCs that do guarantee human rights have been put off by the moralizing, interventionism, and inconsistencies of American policy.

Despite lip service to the goal of reducing unemployment, LDC governments have not been willing to make job creation a central part of their development strategies. Their lack of enthusiasm in this regard is best seen in the meager policy response to the recommendations of the International Labor

Organization's employment missions to Colombia, Kenya, and the Dominican Republic. Similarly, LDC governments have shown a decided disinterest in the American initiative on basic needs. For one thing, such a development pattern does not accord with the consumption preferences of the elites in most LDCs. For another, LDC governments have construed a basic-needs strategy as condemning them to the status of permanent welfare clients, with no prospect for developing to high consumption levels.

The U.S. focus on the highly skewed income distributions of most LDCs has also intensified U.S.–Third World conflict. The LDCs' negative reaction here clearly reflects their elites' economic interests and their hostility to American interventionism. In addition, emphasis on the social and economic inequalities that prevail within individual LDCs has an important implication in the context of international negotiations on a New International Economic Order. LDC negotiators feel that, with attention drawn to the inequalities rampant in their own societies, they lose the moral advantage that aids them in pressing for a reduction in international inequalities in the distribution of income.[7]

Finally, positions have also changed within the Group of 77. Divergent views have developed as the higher-income LDCs, like Brazil and Korea, have done better in surmounting economic difficulties than have the poorer LDCs. Such a split is evident in the differing positions within the Third World camp on the issue of international debt moratorium. Lack of unanimity as compared with the 1972–1976 years has also appeared, as individual LDCs have scrambled for international investment and export markets.

Most important, it is increasingly clear to oil-importing LDCs that the function of the NIEO issue in international diplomacy is now very different from what they first expected. In the present international context, the prospects for achieving the NIEO are dim. Continued focus on the NIEO issue has thus come to fill a different international role: providing LDC political support to OPEC for its oil-pricing policies. With superb diplomatic skill, OPEC has succeeded in maintaining the allegiance of the oil-importing LDCs—despite the impact of higher petroleum prices on Third World economic growth, foreign debt, and external dependency. OPEC has achieved this feat not by selling the LDCs oil at substantially concessionary prices, but by offering its support to them on behalf of the NIEO.

As expectations concerning the NIEO have become less sanguine, the illusory nature of OPEC's *quid pro quo* is becoming apparent to the LDCs. Keeping the pot of the NIEO issue boiling is now essentially a tactic for sustaining Third World support of OPEC. The LDCs are increasingly aware of just who is being boiled in that pot.

The Need for Nonintervention

The main economic objective of the LDCs is now maintenance of a rising flow of imported raw materials, intermediate products, and capital goods in order to sustain their economic development. Because of the severe impact of OPEC's oil prices on the LDCs, that goal is increasingly harder to attain. From 1974 through 1977, many LDCs avoided a drastic drop in economic growth by borrowing in the Eurocurrency market to finance a higher level of imports than would otherwise have been feasible. As external debt has mounted, however, that option is no longer open to most developing countries. The continuation of high rates of economic expansion requires ever-growing absolute levels of imported inputs. Foreign loans to sustain a net flow of imports in the necessary magnitudes are not likely to be forthcoming in the future.

For most LDCs, therefore, the prospects for attaining high rates of economic growth in the face of the oil-price import constraints are bleak. International policy measures to permit an exit from this situation are not at hand. Escape via the

NIEO is also unlikely. In effect, the economic and political changes that have occurred since 1972—1976 have removed the NIEO from the international policy agenda insofar as one is concerned with helping the developing countries.

What are the realistic possibilities for U.S. policy in this context? We could bar, at the outset, forceful U.S. action to lower the relative price of oil to its pre-1974 level. That would enable the oil-importing LDCs to resume economic development at high rates without increasing debt. But it would also disturb our Saudi friends. Consequently, the only course that seems open is monetary and fiscal policy that maintains American economic growth and a buoyant world economy for LDC exports. This is hardly a bold new demarche in U.S.–Third World relations. But it does have the advantage of being feasible.

U.S. economic policies toward developing countries will often face a trade-off between promoting either economic growth or a dependency relationship that engenders resentment. The United States can do little on its own to accelerate the social and economic development of Third World countries. Our resources and leverage are limited, while the LDCs often have their own preferences and priorities. Consequently, a nonintrusive approach might be, in general, the best overall course for American policy. Such a hands-off stance may not be congenial to traditional American values of activism and involvement. But a nation that has learned to say "No more Vietnams" should profit from a parallel experience to say "No more Alliances for Progress." Otherwise, U.S. policymaking will resemble the post-Napoleonic Bourbons, who "forgot nothing and learned nothing" from their experience in a world that did not conform to their assumptions and preferences.

U.S. policies toward developing countries have, in fact, taken a definite new turn. Broad economic and political commitments have been replaced by specific actions based on perceptions of mutual strategic interests in individual countries.

This is what the U.S. has been doing; it might even be the wisest course to follow. Policy pronouncements, however, have not yet caught up with this new reality. As a result, confusion has sometimes been engendered among observers, and perhaps even among participants. Clearer statements on the reality of U.S. policy are, therefore, desirable. U.S.–LDC relations are an issue area where much would be gained from a de-escalation in rhetoric and a fostering of realistic expectations.

13

WILSON E. SCHMIDT

The Role of Private Capital in Developing the Third World

It is obvious to all that the incomes of the poor people of this world could be increased if they had more capital and know-how with which to work.

It requires only a casual review of the facts to see that the volume of government aid—aid in the sense of gifts and loans at very low interest rates and long maturities—has been stuck at $13 to $14 billion per annum in real terms since the early 1960s. Despite the enormous growth in the real income of the rich countries' governments, they have not been willing to give more. This is a reality.

The outlook for stealing is also limited. After their success in forming the OPEC cartel and the less substantial achievements of the International Bauxite Association, the poor countries have few commodities left that are so readily cartelizable. This, too, is a reality.

Faced with these facts, the poor countries have gone to collective bargaining for a New International Economic Order (NIEO), demanding of rich governments in a variety of international forums almost every conceivable dispensation, subsidy, and privilege one could imagine. Their efforts to gain more aid receipts, starting with the United Nations Conference on Trade and Development in 1964, failed; it is doubtful that the new efforts will be more productive, for the myth that it is better to give than to receive has been broken.

The Possibility of Mutual Gain

The problem lies in the fact that there is no mutual gain in aid except in patently political situations. The donor gives up real resources; the poor country gains real resources. It is sometimes thought that by accelerating economic growth abroad through aid, we increase the market for our exports. Higher incomes abroad no doubt do increase our exports. But the absurdity of an argument that aid somehow, therefore, pays for itself is revealed by the fact that private merchants or manufacturers give only samples to their customers; aid to develop their customers is not part of their marketing strategy. The outlook for intergovernmental transfers of resources is grim indeed.

What, then, should the poor do? The answer is for them to give something in return for what they need—something that is tangible, real, and worthwhile, so that the *private* sector of the rich world is co-opted into their progress. The idea of mutual gain is fundamental to energizing the rich to help the poor.

Both the opportunity provided by this prescription, and the poverty of the aid approach, can be demonstrated by a simple numerical example. Suppose the return on capital in a poor country is 20 percent, while the return on capital in a rich country is 10 percent. If the rich country's government gives the poor nation $5 per annum for each of the next twenty years, the rich country is poorer by that amount, while the poor country is equally richer. If the rich country's government loans $25 for twenty years at zero interest, the poor country gains $5 per annum by investing the $25 at 20 percent; the rich country loses $2.50 per annum, because it could have invested the $25 at home at 10 percent. *But* if the rich country were to loan $100 at 15 percent interest for twenty years, the poor country would still gain $5 per annum (investing the $100 at 20 percent, but paying 15 percent interest), *and* the rich country would gain $5 per annum, earning $15 on the loan as compared to $10 at home. Only in the last example is there mutual gain. It hardly takes much understanding of human behavior to see that the transfer of resources is much more likely to materialize when there is mutual gain.

What is required for mutual gain is that the return on capital in the poor countries exceed that of the rich countries, and there is a fair amount of evidence that such is the case. At least, this is what can be deduced from a casual reading of project feasibility reports of the World Bank over the years, and the observation seems to be supported by at least some of the literature surveyed by Nathaniel Leff.[1]

The Burgeoning International Capital Market

There is a great deal of money to be had out there. What does not seem to be fully recognized by the poor countries is that there is an international capital market open to them as well as to the rich, from which they can borrow on terms more cheaply than they can invest at home. In 1977 alone, $74 billion in capital was transferred among countries through international bond issues and Eurocurrency credits.

This international capital market has exploded from a mere $8 billion in 1970. The poor countries began to catch on to it in 1968, when the Ivory Coast borrowed $10 million. Use of the market by the poor countries grew from $375 million in 1970 to $16.2 billion in 1977, far faster than that of the rich countries. What is striking, however, is that two countries — Brazil and Mexico — accounted for almost half of the borrowing by the poor countries in 1977 and have, in fact, dominated the figures through much of the last decade. Some countries do not even want to borrow on this market. The Indian government in 1973 limited such borrowing for fear of alienating lenders who offer soft terms — low interest rates and long maturities — which is surely a comment on the donors' policies, if not on the Indians themselves. Clearly, there is money out there for qualified borrowers who desire it.

To qualify, a nation needs to convince the creditor that it can repay the debt and cover the interest in the currency of the lender. If it can do this continually, it need never really repay, because the creditor will be eager to repeat and expand the loan or credit when it comes due.

What makes a country credit-worthy in the eyes of private international lenders is complicated. It includes a variety of measurable features of the borrower, such as the portion of a nation's foreign currency earnings that needs to be set aside to cover the amortization and interest on existing external debt. It also includes a variety of features that are truly immeasurable, such as how good the financial managers of the government are, and how ready their access is to the chief of state.

Cutting through all of the details, the real issue in creditworthiness is whether the borrowing nation can be expected to come up with the foreign currency to repay the principal and cover the interest. This, in turn, depends on the condition of its balance of payments — the flow of foreign currency in and out of the country.

The two keys to a country's balance of payments are (1) its exchange rate system, and (2) the productive use of externally borrowed funds.

Most of the poor countries maintain fixed exchange rates. They far too often employ exchange controls to limit their citizens' demands for foreign currency and, in doing so, maintain overvalued currencies that in turn restrict their exports because their prices are too high in foreign markets. They seem forever short of foreign exchange. Needless to say, this makes them less credit-worthy.

A costly side effect of the fixed exchange rate system employed by so many poor countries is that these countries waste their own resources. Their central banks hold foreign currency reserves of around $50 billion (this figure excludes members of the OPEC countries). This is partly for the protection of their exchange rates; they can draw upon these reserves when export receipts fall or import requirements rise instead of allowing the exchange rate to depreciate. Such reverse investments to the rich countries probably yield from 6 to 10 percent—there are no figures—which means, in this world of inflation, a zero real return. Were these resources invested at home by the poor, they would, at 20 percent, yield $10 billion per annum, a figure not far from recent aid levels of $13 to $14 billion. (This, of course, is a rough figure open to a number of objections, including the possibility that, if these funds were not held by central banks, private citizens would instead have to hold them. But such an objection is doubtful when one considers that the simultaneous removal of both the fixed rates and exchange controls would bring home capital illicitly kept abroad by residents because of the exchange controls.) No one forces the poor nations to fix their exchange rates. Since April 1978, each country has been free under the rules of the International Monetary Fund to choose its own exchange rate system. Most of the rich countries have wisely chosen to allow their currencies to float, albeit in a managed way.

The second requirement for credit-worthiness is that the borrowed funds be employed productively—either directly or indirectly. This, in fact, is intimately related to repaying the funds in foreign currency and to the exchange rate system. To repay the borrowed funds and the interest, the debtor nation must raise its exports or cut its imports to gain the foreign exchange to repay the debt. This, in turn, means that it must produce more goods and services than it previously used at home in order to create a surplus to be exported. By employing the borrowed funds productively, the national output will be smoothly converted into foreign currency.

The seeming contradiction with an earlier point by Nathaniel Leff (chapter 12) is thus also reconciled. He has argued that the "continuing high rates of output growth . . . require ever-higher levels of imported inputs and hence ever-increasing absolute magnitudes of foreign borrowing" (p. 256). The availability of capital to finance such imports is indeed limited, as he has argued, but with floating exchange rates an adjustment in import levels would be automatic.

A number of the poor countries have unwisely restricted the use of international capital markets to fund projects that would directly yield foreign exchange, either by substituting for imports or by expanding exports. In doing so, they have greatly constrained their borrowing opportunities. Such policies rest on a lack of understanding of how the balance of payments adjusts to exchange rate changes. If the externally borrowed funds are used wisely in projects unrelated to trade, they will yield a return in local currency; when that currency is used to buy foreign exchange to repay debt, the debtor's exchange rate will depreciate, automatically stimulating exports and constricting imports. The export surplus provides the required foreign exchange. There is no requirement that external funds generate foreign currency directly, as long as the authorities are willing to let the exchange rate change.

Multinational Corporations

The other major source of resources that has been less than fully exploited is the multinational corporation. Because they are large and transcend national borders, these corporations have access to enormous amounts of capital. In the early 1970s, such companies in market economies had $165 billion invested abroad. Perhaps a fourth of this was in poor countries. American companies alone had invested $30 billion in the poor nations, out of a total of $137 billion invested abroad by the end of 1976.

The benefits that accrue to the poor countries go well beyond the provision of capital. Multinational corporations provide jobs: a recent estimate put the jobs generated by American multinationals in poor countries at 1.5 million. They provide training to local citizens. They provide scarce entrepreneurial and managerial talent. They provide production know-how, market information, and sales organizations. They provide markets for local suppliers. Because they are multinational, they connect the poor with the world, widening their horizons and increasing their opportunities. And they even provide a conduit for tax funds from the rich nations; e.g., under U.S. law, a multinational corporation's tax liability to the Internal Revenue Service (IRS) is reduced, within limits, to the extent that it pays income taxes abroad.

Despite these benefits, the normal rhetoric of the day has the multinational corporation as the villain of the piece. The catalog of charges: stifling local entrepreneurs, employing too little labor per unit of capital by virtue of transferring excessively advanced technology; evading taxes; producing products that the poor buy but ought not to be allowed to have; charging excessively for know-how; absorbing poor countries' savings through local borrowing; using bribery; charging extreme prices behind tariff protection; depending on head-office decisions that can adversely affect the jobs,

foreign exchange receipts, and real income of the host nation, etc.

It is difficult to feel sorry for a corporation—after all, it is
not a natural person. But sometimes it is subject to absolutely ludicrous complaints.

Some of the charges appear to be flat wrong. Some are
right, but only if one grants certain assumptions about the
good society, assumptions that are arguable. Some are right,
but miss the culprit. Some are, in fact, backhanded compliments, for they amount only to the argument that the host
country is not getting as much as it should from the multinational, rather than that the multinational is doing harm.

The charge that the multinationals use more capital-
intensive techniques of production, implying fewer jobs in
the host countries, appears to be wrong. A number of studies
confirm this conclusion. A particularly interesting one reports that multinationals from both the West and the East
exhibited lower capital/labor ratios than their domestic
counterparts in over two hundred manufacturing firms in
Thailand.[2]

The charge that the multinationals produce goods that
people ought not to have—e.g., Coca Cola—somehow misses
the misery of the poor, the relief that such simple pleasures
provide from grinding poverty. I doubt that those who make
such charges would wish to dictate or even comment on the
religious choices of the poor; why should they dictate or comment on their other consumption patterns?

Tax evasion is said to arise through transfer pricing. For
example, if a foreign affiliate of an American parent corporation produces a product that becomes a component of
another product produced by the parent in the United States,
the price charged for the component determines where the
profit is. Opportunities for profit shifting, and thus tax evasion, occur as long as these are not arm's-length transactions. But research in the area fails to point in any particular
direction. In any event, since it is clear from the data that the

host countries receive substantial revenue from the subsidiaries of multinationals, this is the backhanded compliment that the host countries do not get enough.

The complaint that multinationals charge excessive prices behind protection from imports misses the culprit. Added to this complaint is the argument that the excessive profits are then taken out of the country. This at first appears to be correct, because we have shown that the external funds must be used productively if they are to provide the extra goods and services required to increase exports in order to pay the earnings transferred abroad. The proper answer to the charge is that if, in fact, the protection reduces the real income of the country, it should not have been afforded to the product in the first place by the host government. Furthermore, the fact that the income may be taken out of the country is irrelevant; if local investors instead of foreign investors provide the resources, the country's real income is still reduced, because the local investors' investible funds are wasted in projects with artificially inflated returns.

Bribery obviously does exist. The odd element in the picture is that it is the multinationals, and not their critics, who should complain. Unfortunately, in many poor countries corruption in government is the norm. To get action, a bribe must be paid. Because this raises the costs to the multinational, the necessity to bribe is a deterrent to investment. It is indeed unfortunate that the laws, regulations, and procedures of many poor countries put officials in a position to demand bribes. The thief is the one who accepts the bribe, or the government that gives such people positions of power.

There are a variety of methods by which the poor countries deter the inflow of capital and know-how through multinational corporations. One is plain, if perhaps unintended, harassment. For example, a number of years ago I had a casual conversation with an American middle manager in a very poor country. He told me that he had just solved a very serious problem—namely, getting a work permit for a highly skilled welder to come into the country for a brief period of time. He had solved his problem by bribing the clerk at an airline company to inform him when a certain high official of the government would next be flying out of the country. When he got that information, he further bribed another clerk to reserve a seat next to the official. In the course of the flight, he raised the problem of the work permit, the official invited him to visit his office when he returned from the trip, and after that meeting the work permit was issued. It struck me as a hard way to do business.

Another deterrent is the threat of expropriation. During 1946–1973, no less than $2 to $3 billion of U.S. investment in poor countries was expropriated (not including the nationalization of Middle East petroleum producers). Presumably, the risk of appropriation deters some investments altogether. In other cases, it causes the multinational to commit less capital to the host country while still achieving the scale of operations it desires. It can do this, for example, by borrowing capital in the host country for some of the investment in plant and equipment, thus reducing the amount of the parent's assets at risk. Alternatively, it can sell equipment to a host country leasing corporation, which leases the equipment to the parent's subsidiary. Both techniques reduce the net transfer of capital to the poor country. By borrowing locally, it does not put its money into the country in the first place. By leasing, it gets its money for the equipment immediately by selling it to the local leasing company.

Obviously, multinationals do not like to have their assets expropriated. But if they are, they would then like fair compensation for them, as is thought to be the rule of international law. This, however, has been a serious problem. One estimate puts uncompensated losses at $6 billion in the postwar period. As one United Nations study recently put it:

Although compensation in the event of nationalization is usually guaranteed under investment laws, legislation tends to be vague concerning the criteria for the assessment of compensation and the modalities of compensation payments. Consequently, disagreements over the amount of compensation due to a nationalized enterprise have become a frequent source of investment disputes.[3]

Another deterrent to multinational investment is the frequent requirement in the poor countries of some minimum amount of local control and ownership (sometimes majority)—by either the host government or local nationals—of foreign-owned subsidiaries. Clearly, all other things being equal, a parent corporation would prefer to own 100 percent of its foreign subsidiary, if for no other reason than that it makes the operation simpler. The adverse effect of Colombia's requirement, along with other restrictions under the Andean Common Market, that foreign corporations divest their majority ownership, is shown by the fact that in the four years after the decision (in December 1970), registration of new foreign investments in Colombia averaged $31.4 million per year, compared with $114.7 million per year in the preceding four years. The sad part of this is that the host country puts up cash that it needs badly for other purposes, and puts it in the place of funds that otherwise would be available from abroad. For example, there was one government in a poor country that insisted on owning half of a small refinery that the foreign investor was willing to carry 100 percent. The government's presence surely would not have made it more efficient, and thus added nothing to the national welfare. What the government wanted was the income, when projects elsewhere in the economy cried out for financing. One would have thought that, in its own national interest, the government would have at least insisted that the foreign investor put the relinquished funds somewhere else in the economy.

Still another deterrent is the limitation imposed by some governments of poor countries on the transfer of profits of foreign subsidiaries to their parent corporations, and thus to their stockholders. Some impose limits on payments of royalties for patents and know-how. Some restrict the payments of externally owned debt. And some place limits on the repatriation of capital originally invested.

Obviously, all of these controls limit the freedom of action of the multinationals and, therefore, make foreign investment less attractive to them. More specifically, the delays in the repatriation of profits have dramatic effects on the rate of return from foreign investment, because compound interest takes its toll. Thus, an American parent corporation able to invest at home at 15 percent will find that its yield on foreign investment whose income is blocked for five years will fall by 25 percent, as compared to the situation in which it can repatriate the foreign income annually. Future managers of multinational corporations are now being tutored in the concept of the terminal rate of return—the return they obtain after the profits are unblocked. As foreign investment decisions are most often based on rates of return, such restrictions markedly reduce the incentive to invest.

As explained above, what is so senseless about restrictions on the repatriation of profits is that profitable foreign investment produces a rise in the national output that, if the exchange rate is allowed to move, automatically transfers the profits at no net cost to the nation. The multinationals are often charged with taking more money out of the country than they bring in. Even if such were the case, this argument shows that it is costless as long as the original capital investment is employed productively.

Finally, many of the poor countries prohibit foreign investment in selected areas. Some of these may make sense, such as national defense industries. But others, like banking and insurance, do not. The capital and money markets of many of the poor countries are sorely underdeveloped; the presence of more bank and nonbank financial institutions would help to relieve the glaring defects in the mechanisms for allocating scarce capital within those countries. Particularly objectionable are the restrictions—such as those imposed in India and in the Andean Common Market countries—on foreign investment in industries already "adequately serviced" by existing enterprises. By dulling the threat of competition, the performance of the existing countries clearly is worsened.

Having mentioned the wide variety of restrictions on foreign investment imposed by poor countries, one should note the incentives that many of those same countries provide to foreign investors. These often take the form of exemptions from various import duties on raw materials and components, as well as income tax holidays. As anyone familiar with the notion of gains from trade knows, the exemptions from import duties are, with or without foreign investment, a step in the right direction from the standpoint of the poor country. The income tax holidays are, however, a useless incentive, as we shall see below.

The Problem of Subsidies and Mutual Gain

We began by emphasizing the importance of mutual gain if the private sector of the rich countries is to be co-opted into the progress of the poor. When looked at from the standpoint of the rich countries, the extent of mutual gain is suspect by reason of the policies of their governments.

The United States government has for years provided insurance to American foreign investors against losses due to wars, civil disorders, expropriation, and currency inconvertibility. In 1974, Congress mandated that the Overseas Private Investment Corporation (OPIC) increase private participation in these activities and ultimately withdraw completely from direct underwriting of these risks by 1979–1980. Subsequent to the mandate, OPIC made major efforts to gain the participation of private insurance companies in its portfolio, but this has largely failed, presumably because the risks are too great given the premiums. The Carter administration recommended that OPIC be continued without the mandate for privatization. In 1981 the Congress, with Reagan administration support, lengthened the list of OPIC insurable risks to include civil strife and extended the agency's underwriting authority to late 1985.

Failure to attract private insurers suggests that there is no true mutuality of interest. In effect, OPIC is a subsidy. The rate of return to the United States, given the risks, does not exceed the rate of return on investments at home. If it did, OPIC would not be necessary. In such circumstances, *if some public purpose* is served by providing help to the poor countries where investors will not go without such guarantees, the optimal policy is no investment at all. Instead of subsidizing private investment by continuing OPIC, the Reagan administration should replace it. It is cheaper to simply apply a straight grant to the poor, as a simple numerical example will show.

Reversing the constellation of yields on investment assumed earlier, imagine that the return on capital in the poor country is 10 percent, while in the rich country the return is 20 percent. Clearly, there is no loan or investment that will benefit both the rich and the poor country simultaneously, inasmuch as the lender (investor) would require 20 percent or more, whereas the poor country would gain only if the charge for the capital were less than 10 percent. If the rich country's government were to subsidize the loan (investment) to the extent of 11 percent, both the *private* lender (investor) and the poor country would gain. For example, the lender (investor) could charge 9.5 percent on a loan of $100; the poor country would gain $0.50 per annum by investing the funds at 10 percent, and the private lender (investor) would gain $0.50 with a 9.5 percent return, plus the 11 percent subsidy included, compared with a 20 percent return at home. But the true cost to the rich *nation* is $10.50 per annum, because it obtains a return of 9.5 percent from abroad but foregoes a return of 20 percent at home on the $100 loan or investment. It would, in fact, be far cheaper simply to give the poor country $0.50 per annum. There is no loan on any terms that would benefit the poor country and also cost the rich country less than $0.50. Subsidized loans or investments are not the economical option when the yield on capital in the poor country falls short of that in the rich country. Hence, even if some public purpose is served, OPIC is not the answer.

The other reason why the notion of mutual gain is suspect stems from the U.S. tax code. As suggested earlier, the multinational corporation provides the poor with a conduit to the U.S. Treasury. Within certain limits, the Internal Revenue Service permits American investors to take a credit against their U.S. income tax liability for income taxes levied by foreign governments on the income they earn abroad. The consequences of this for mutual gain can also be seen from another numerical example.

The United States actually loses real income on some of our investments, because multinationals choose between foreign and domestic projects on the basis of their comparative returns after taxes. For example, suppose a multinational had a choice between a domestic and a foreign project, both of which yielded $100 before taxes, and both of which required the same investment. If the foreign corporate tax rate were 40 percent, while the U.S. corporate tax rate were 50 percent, the domestic project would yield $50 to the company (with the other $50 going to the IRS), while the foreign project would yield $50 (with $40 going to the foreign government and, because of credit, only $10 going to the IRS). Here we see that the U.S. credit would decline if the host country provided an income tax holiday, so that the $40 foreign tax would fall and the after-tax profit on the foreign project would remain unchanged, making the tax holiday ineffective.

Since the after-tax return would be the same, the multinational would be indifferent between the two projects. But if the company flipped a coin and the foreign project won, America would lose. The reason is that the United States gets only $60 of foreign currency with which to buy foreign goods and services from the earnings of the foreign project, whereas it gets $100 of additional goods and services from the domestic project. The total amount of goods and services available to Americans as a whole is $40 lower than it could be. In effect, foreigners take $40 of the output in one case, and none in the other. If the investment were made at home, our taxes could be $40 lower.

This situation would be rectified if the U.S. tax code were amended to reduce the U.S. corporate tax rate on income from domestic investments to offset the effect of the credit. The same result could be achieved if the code allowed the American corporation to deduct as costs (rather than credit) foreign taxes in computing its tax liability to the IRS. In that event, the investment committee would be choosing between a foreign project that yielded only $30 after all taxes ($100 gross income minus $40 foreign taxes equals $60 net income before U.S. taxes; $60 less the U.S. corporate income tax rate of 50 percent equals $30) and a domestic project that yielded $50 after all taxes. It thus would prefer the domestic project; therefore, the United States' real income, measured in terms of goods and services available to it, would be higher than it otherwise would be.

One estimate, clearly rough, suggests that annual American investment in the poor countries would decline by half if the deduction were substituted for the credit. That still leaves a substantial flow of capital to help the poor, a flow that would be enhanced if the poor would reduce their restrictions on private foreign investment. After adjusting the U.S. tax laws and rescinding OPIC, there would be a mutuality of gain.

Development Strategies and Obstacles

Benjamin Franklin may have been a great diplomat, a fine editor of the Declaration of Independence, and perhaps a superb flier of kites, but he was a lousy economist: "He that goes aborrowing goes asorrowing." "A man may, if he knows

not how to save as he gets, keep his nose to the grindstone."
Franklin obviously did not perceive the value of capital
markets. He did not see that, by borrowing the savings of
others, the grindstone and the nose are soon parted.

As long as the rate of return on capital in the poor countries is higher than in the rich countries, a fact for which
there is fairly persuasive evidence, there is a possibility of
mutual gain by the transfer of capital from the rich to the
poor countries. By offering a tangible return to the rich, the
poor can co-opt the private sectors of the rich countries into
their progress, gaining the benefits of their capital and
know-how. With aid levels roughly constant in real terms
since the early 1960s, and with the outlook for further stealing limited, capital transfers that provide mutual gain are
the most viable option to enhance the economic well-being of
the poor.

Unfortunately, the poor countries have not taken full advantage of the international capital market, which has grown
rapidly in the 1970s. Because they employ fixed exchange rate
systems in so many cases, their ability to repay debts is
weakened and their credit-worthiness impaired, making them
less attractive to lenders than they otherwise would be.

Furthermore, the poor countries have imposed a variety of
obstacles to investment by multinational corporations, institutions that have great access to capital and knowledge
that could be put to work in the poor nations to the benefit of
both. Complaints about the performance of the multinationals are flat wrong, miss the culprit, or are really backhanded compliments amounting to the charge that they do
not do enough for the poor.

To insure mutual gains to the rich countries, some adjustment in their tax systems is required, along with the cessa-
tion of such subsidies as insurance against various losses.

V

Conclusion

14

W. SCOTT THOMPSON

A World of Parts

A policymaker might derive a variety of lessons from this new edition; most differ from those of the first volume only by degree. The principal lesson now, as then, is that we live not in a bipolar world of North and South, but rather in a world of many heterogeneous parts. For analytic, political, or even policy purposes, the Third World is merely a term of convenience, more a metaphor than a descriptive reality.

Although it is in our interest, and in the interest of the West in general, to deal separately with each of the discrete regions and countries that constitute this fictitious entity, it is important that each area's separate policies and relations be unified by a clear and consistent strategic principle. The Carter administration's attempts to use human rights as its unifying policy suggest the difficulty of synthesizing a strategy with principles that are less than absolute.

More specific lessons can be organized around the three functional themes of the book itself.

Political Order

The most striking recent change in the Third World since this book first appeared has been the almost complete decomposition of its ideological foundations. This means several things. First, in reassessing their own ideologies, the more thoughtful leaders in the less-developed countries (LDCs) are timidly but increasingly turning to the sources of Western values—i.e., eighteenth- and nineteenth-century liberalism—as they reevaluate the relevance of Marxism, which has so long informed their thinking. Sometimes unwittingly asserting liberal principles rather than more egalitarian ones in international forums, the Third World intelligentsia is slowly realizing that "the revolution" is not so much a historical necessity as it is a historical myth.

The shift may be subtle. But one began to see it by midpoint in the Reagan administration—for example, in the delegates whom the American mission's assertive staff at the United Nations was beginning to win over to its causes. It has also been evident in the lack of universal support for the Law of the Sea Treaty and, more generally, in a world that is more inclined to support the causes of the growing number of democratic regimes. Specific examples may not abound, but few actors have failed to detect the change in the air.

Survey data indicate the same trend. Third World answers to questions such as "For which nation do you have the most respect?" suggest that the United States has held and even slightly increased its large favorable margin over the Soviet Union as well as over countries such as West Germany, Canada, and Great Britain. Perhaps more importantly for the policymaker, although less encouraging for the Western interest in general, the most recent polling data also suggest that when queried whether the decade of the 1980s will be one in which America or Russia will increase her relative power, the LDCs still seem to feel that the Soviets will remain more serious and formidable. The Third World, while seemingly favoring Western political principles and economic prosperity, in the end is concerned with the ultimate military balance.

This attitude, discussed by Lord Beloff herein, is not merely a function of the balance of materiel levels; it is, more importantly, a measure of Soviet willingness to project power directly and indirectly throughout the world.

Secondly, the decomposition of ideologies bears on what is perhaps the single largest problem in the Third World: the problem of political and social order. In places where the problem of order is most critical, ideologies with a quasi-religious character—whether Marxism or more traditional religious forms, such as those in Iran—can be effective tools for maintaining order and animating public spirit. But the militancy of these quasi-religious governments implies and justifies a strong role for the armed forces—as the experience of both Iran and the Marxist states shows.

The critical problem in political order is *consent;* and, in order to encourage democratic forms, an important role may be played by expanded education about the benefits of democratic principles and practices and their related economic policies. But it is also important that Western policymakers not allow themselves to have unrealistic expectations about the capacity of countries lacking democratic traditions to reform instantly their institutions. In the West, democratic institutions required centuries to evolve to their current levels of consent. To expect instant democracy in the Third World today often will only upset a fragile balance of order and thus encourage introduction of an extreme authoritarian or even totalitarian regime to restore the order that the state cannot exist without.

This brings us to the problem of human rights. Although not dealt with specifically in any particular chapter, the issue of human rights demands more attention in the wake of the excessive expectations encouraged by several recent administrations. We said in the first edition of this book in 1978, and can say again, that the principal problem with human rights *qua* foreign policy is a preoccupation with leverage. It does little good to ask an authoritarian government—let alone a totalitarian one—to cease being authoritarian and to release political prisoners (whose imprisonment is a critical manifestation of the order problem discussed above) unless one has the power to back up such a demand. Small wonder, then, that the American human rights policy in the Carter administration—for all its noble idealism—was effective for the most part only in relatively powerless Third World countries and among our allies and close friends from whom Washington could withhold credits, arms, and state visits. It is impossible to influence those who do not care about Washington's good opinion. The point is best seen with respect to the Soviet Union, which has increased its violence in Southwest Asia and has continued to oppress its East European satellites. This problem of influencing certain countries is made even more difficult when domestic interest groups in the United States oppose measures that might bring effective pressure—as the banking community did, for instance, in opposing restriction of credits in the past several years.

The point about where human rights pressure can be effective and where it cannot is especially evident in the Third World. In the case of the Philippines, U.S. pressure was one reason for President Marcos's decision to release numerous political prisoners there. On the other hand, we have had no success whatever in influencing Tanzania, which has poor relations with the U.S., to release any of that state's several thousand political prisoners. This asymmetry is ironic, considering Marcos's reputation as an unbending authoritarian, in contrast to Julius Nyerere's reputation as exemplary for his humanity and compassion.

In another example of this problem, the People's Republic of China, recipient of much American attention recently, has yet to provide the State Department's human rights bureau with sufficient evidence to come to a ruling as to the status of the political freedoms in that country.

But the problem of human rights is riddled with many other difficulties as well. Most of the conventions on the subject are politically slanted, and enforcement is often selective. The Human Rights Commission and the UN Committee of Twenty-Four refuse to investigate the status of the Central Asian colonies of the Soviet Union and the condition and origin of the laborers working on the Yamal pipeline. There is no intrinsic reason why a UN committee cannot put a superpower in the dock; the Committee of Twenty-Four has been investigating the status of Puerto Rico for many years in spite of the fact that the freely elected governor of that territory has repeatedly testified as to the position of the body politic therein. A consistent U.S. policy on these issues would insist on more evenhanded behavior by these agencies as a condition of full U.S. contributions to the United Nations. The important point about human rights, in any case, is that they are *derivatives* of democracy—the objective of President Reagan's "Project Democracy."

One final note—it might be prudent to talk less and do more. A Somali, clarifying what he charged as Ethiopian genocide in the Ogaden, once remarked, "We had some trust in the international advocates of human rights. But we found that their concern was hollow. *They are the empty vessels which make the most noise.*"

Economic Management

By now there should be little doubt as to what *works* in the economic development of Third World countries. One need not confine his view to the miracle economies of free-market Asia. One can look to a jaunty little country like Tunisia which, despite the absence of many natural resources or more oil than suffices for internal needs, has joined the four major African natural resource exporters who maintain an average per capita income of over $1000 per year. Tunisia is in the same class as Algeria, not because of vast deposits of gas, but because of a freer economy and better use of manpower.

One can compare the Ivory Coast with two countries that started out at roughly the same level. Guinea broke with France in 1958, when the Ivory Coast chose continued association. Guinea's Marxist government has superintended an almost continuous slide downhill for its people ever since. The regime survives because a capitalist enclave supplies enough bauxite to maintain the state's international commitments. Ghana started out as the richest country in black Africa but chose various forms of managed economies over the years, and its position relative to the Ivory Coast has slipped continuously. The most basic commodities have long been unavailable, the currency is almost worthless, and the most important export, cocoa, is smuggled out through neighboring Togo and the Ivory Coast in large quantities owing to the unrealistic internal market price. The historic bet Ghanaian founder Kwame Nkrumah made with Ivory Coast's leader Houphouet-Boigny, as to which system would bring more benefits to its respective peoples, was lost long ago by the Ghanaians. It might have been arguable fifteen years ago that the Ivory Coast's conspicuous wealth in the capital did not trickle down to the villages, but it is clear today that the modern infrastructure and its amenities have spread to every corner of the country.

However, in spite of the increased impact of Western ideologies on Third World thought, the predisposition against free-market economic policies still persists. As Richard Bissell points out, this predisposition in itself is essentially political rather than economic. The problem of political order, mentioned above, is its generic source. Establishing and maintaining power is the first concern of many Third World leaders—a concern not generally consistent with the tendency of markets to decentralize power. Centralized economic control may not be efficient, and it may be difficult to reconcile with strong economic performance; but it does act to consolidate power. In the long run, however, economic performance will tend to matter a great deal to the continued political support of LDC leadership. Therefore, encouraging economic efficiency through markets may become critical to many political leaders. Understanding their stake in allowing markets to allocate resources to their most valuable uses will remain difficult for leaders universally aware of the tenuous nature of their regimes and the frequency of threats to their legitimacy in affairs political, economic, and military. To convince this mindset that growth, stability, and prosperity are products of minimal control completely opposes all of their natural political instincts.

The same is true of the counterintuitive analysis of aid programs put forth in this book by Professors Bauer and Yamey and by Wilson Schmidt. Although their economic arguments are negative on foreign aid, in some cases good political arguments may support it—for example, to save in the short term a government that might otherwise fall, leaving the country open to external manipulation. Certainly, this is the best case that can be made for the bailout of Zaire's government in the aftermath of the Cuban-aided invasion of Shaba province in 1978, or the economic aid to Salvador after the free elections of 1981 (given the continuing Cuban aid to the opposition in that country). But such situations are exceptional at best.

It is interesting, from the other side of the coin, that the absence of aid programs has never prevented other great powers from garnering influence in the Third World. The Soviets, for all intents and purposes, have ceased to grant purely economic aid to LDCs save direct subventions to Cuba, technical assistance to client governments like those in

Ethiopia and Afghanistan, and loans (to be paid back in much-needed Western currencies) to purchasers of their oil and gas. All totaled, the amount is no more than a tiny fraction of all American aid. Moscow has made a virtue of necessity. It proclaims that it has no responsibility to help poor countries, having had no responsibility in "hamstringing the social and economic effort of the developing countries" originally, as one Soviet writer has put it.

Moreover, the Soviet example is not exclusive; the paradigm of Gaullist France is worth considering, at least from the perspective of one Tunisian diplomat who argued in 1966:

France is the only country that openly breaks the UN embargo on the sale of arms to South Africa. It defies Africa and tests its nuclear weapons on the Sahara. It maintains a string of neo-colonized states to whom it gives its only aid, in the form of budgetary subventions. And yet which major power is the most prestigious in the Third World? France. Which leader most influential? Charles de Gaulle.

De Gaulle's style, it is worth noting, was attentive to Third World aspirations without pretending an ability to solve their problems—and all the while forthrightly looking to French interests. The United States need not tackle every problem of the developing world to sustain a position of respect.

Recalling Lord Beloff's maxim—that the Third World will follow the likely winner of the strategic competition between the superpowers—one realizes how important our own self-esteem is in garnering respect in the Third World. Because of the *political* nature of the Third World's economy, it is evident that purely economic problems are the least important factors in the matrix of elements constituting economic development. A return to the classical formulation of political economy might be both the most instructive as well as the most useful direction for policymakers.

Military Factors

In one of the most thought-provoking chapters in this book, S. E. Finer explains why the military dimension of Third World politics will not soon disappear. Given the problem of order discussed above, the military will remain the most effective ordering mechanism in LDC countries. Of course, its effectiveness is a two-edged sword, as it may be employed only at great risk. There are few Third World countries in which the armed forces are employed even marginally in enforcing justice, even as the vanguard. The central role of the military, rather, will continue to be either to guarantee or to subvert the legitimacy of regimes.

Attempts to change this role often founder. For example, it is still unclear whether attempts to prevent arms purchases address symptoms or causes of the problem. It is clear, however, that the refusal to sell arms to an American friend may, in fact, increase international insecurity, especially where our friend's adversary is being supplied by the Soviets. The fact that the Soviet Union now substantially outstrips the U.S. in total arms transfers to the Third World does not bode well for a policy of Third World disarmament.

It is U.S. policy to encourage military regimes to civilianize themselves, but such has to be done with care: a clear view of political reality should encourage an understanding of why it is so difficult to lower the profile of the military in the Third World, given the weakness of all other institutions.

This is no brief for military rule. Indeed, the decision of the Reagan administration to put its campaign for democratic values at the forefront of its diplomacy demonstrates the sincere commitment of America to democratic rule. But this is something that can best be achieved, in many cases, by working with existing elites, including the military, whose power is too well grounded in the society to disappear overnight; new values need to be inculcated and reinforced before social change can be constructive.

The example of the fall of the Shah is frequently cited to illustrate the futility of attempting to undermine weak leaderships without viable alternatives. But it does little good to assess guilt in this situation. Scholars of the area have pointed out that the signal to the Iranians of the American withdrawal of support for the Shah (or, at the least, the ambiguity of our commitment) was eloquent. Iran had been a regional peacekeeper and yet we argued endlessly over the merits of arms sales to the Shah's regime; now his theocratic successors use those arms to advance the cause of Islamic fundamentalism throughout the region. Adequate arms sales alone, obviously, are not a prudent policy without some care taken to insure that the regime remains friendly.

One hastens to note as well that an American withdrawal from Third World arenas will not encourage their leaders to solve differences peaceably, whether or not we have sold arms. When their arsenals were empty and the West's hand was reasonably strong in the Third World, piety was the order of the day. With the breakdown of colonial and now postcolonial constraints, Third World governments are free to use military force to achieve conventional goals such as the acquisition of land and resources, or to settle longstanding ethnic disputes. The clearest example of this is also in the Persian Gulf, where Iraq and Iran have attempted to destroy each other's economies after wriggling free of their respective patrons' leashes. The wishful thinking that characterized the "post-Vietnam" foreign policy of the United States has been proved wrong by recent events.

Geopolitical Ramifications

This leads us naturally to examine the larger picture and the role of the Third World in the world's geopolitical fabric. The West, it cannot be overemphasized, is intrinsically involved in the security of the Third World as an extension of its own security and its own political and economic interests. Even NATO (of which Turkey, a very poor country, is a member) in recent years has been concerned with support on its southern flanks—from Africa across the Persian Gulf. This has been an essential part of its strategic planning. Two Third World states—Iran and Saudi Arabia, both of whom outrank many industrial states in gross national product—are among the most important states in the geopolitical order from a Western point of view, and moreover are much-sought-after prizes from the Soviet point of view. Another Third World country—China—is considered by many as the central geostrategic nexus in the world today.

The Soviet Union, for its part, is building an alliance system in the Third World. It is no mirror image of the West's; the Soviets cleverly determined it would be cheaper and more expedient to avoid those exposed dimensions of the Western security system that hobble it. They employ surrogate troops, they prohibit shore visits by Soviet sailors, and they eschew formal, explicit alliances where treaties of friendship and political sympathies will do. The geographic advantage of the Soviet Union resulting from its proximity to the Western Sea Lines of Communication (SLOCs) between the Persian Gulf and its industrial customers can hardly be taken for granted. Ethiopia and Afghanistan are only two geographically well-placed allies.

Ironically, despite the fact that most of the conflict acted out on the battlefield since World War II has taken place in the Third World, it became fashionable in Washington in the late 1970s to say that these areas were not strategically significant. It was a misperception to have seen them as such, and to have fought over their loyalties or over the endurance of one regime or another—or so the argument went. Misperception or not, it is, alas, not something that can be decided unilaterally. Those who yesterday said Angola was "not important," and who prevented an effective American response to Soviet-Cuban aggression, were simply ignoring the Communist perception—which was the opposite.

Today the most critical region in the world may be the Persian Gulf. It is there, rather than on the Central European front, that sparks might most easily light a world war. And this is a region in which no peaceful changes of power have occurred in memory. So, the Third World is acquiring even more strategic pertinence.

The irony in the Soviet challenge to the West in the Third World is that it has any credibility at all. Western experience and involvement—both political and economic, throughout Asia, Africa, and Latin America—is greater by many orders of magnitude in most countries there. Where the methods of communism have been applied to the economies, disaster has uniformly resulted. If resentment of the role of the colonial powers exists in places, it is nevertheless a diminishing asset for enemies of Western–Third World partnership, as the disparity between colonizer and former colony continues to narrow. Perhaps Western political models have only limited relevance to these pluralistic, unstructured states, but the Western tradition of freedom at least sets a standard whereby Third World states can minimize abuses of authority as they struggle to find indigenous and satisfactory solutions to the problem of order.

It is time to face reality. The Soviet Union is a failure on almost all counts. It was long an economic irrelevance, despite the continuing embers of socialist commitment in various voluble Third World states. By the late 1970s it had become a political irrelevance, as all but a handful of self-serving dictators, using Leninism as a tool of survival, rejected the Soviet model. And by the 1980s the Soviets had become a problematic military factor.

Consider the lessons of the 1982 Middle East war. The PLO was decimated, as were the Syrian armed forces, by the American-equipped Israelis. What Washington lost in Europe and the Third World from Israeli excess was, at least in the latter areas, compensated for in large measure by the respect accruing to the United States for backing a winner. A Syrian diplomat said in June 1982, "We sided with the Soviets not because of their economic or political relevance but because they supplied us with arms. Unfortunately, the arms didn't work."

But this is not a situation Western strategic planners can be complacent about. The Soviets are building up their power projection capability apace and narrowing the American lead in that one last arena of Western military superiority. Moscow can still intervene with sufficient ruthlessness (as shown in Afghanistan) where it considers its own strategic interests to be directly engaged, and can succeed where in times past it dared not venture. Further, Soviet strategic power casts a shadow on the Eurasian land mass, affecting all crises there, even where (as in Syria) Russian arms, incompetently used, still present a threat.

Restoration of American will in the 1980s, providing the achievement of a military balance overall, continues to be a priority of the U.S. government. This dedication gives a happier outlook for Western interests than seemed possible a decade ago. The new willingness to assert the relevance of our values, and the growing evidence that Third World leaders themselves are searching for elements in liberal models that can achieve both legitimacy and order for their regimes, are good omens. "Democracy" is not going to thrive overnight where order has long been so fragile, but the very fact that values associated with democracy have become the alternative to "the state of nature," much as Marxist variants were in earlier decades, is of great import. Soviet military power might be the overwhelming and immediate threat to many Third World arenas, but ideas nurtured in the West might, with a little luck, turn out to have far more relevance in the years ahead.

Notes

Contributors

Index

NOTES

1. W. Scott Thompson: "The Third World Revisited"

1. W. Scott Thompson, "The Need to Take Stock," in *The Third World: Premises of U.S. Policy,* ed. W. Scott Thompson (San Francisco: Institute for Contemporary Studies, 1978), p. 4.

2. For other implications of this attitude, see Robert Conquest, et al., *Defending America* (New York/San Francisco: Basic Books/Institute for Contemporary Studies, 1977), chs. 2, 13; and W. Scott Thompson, ed., *National Security in the 1980s: From Weakness to Strength* (San Francisco: Institute for Contemporary Studies, 1980), ch. 13.

3. Allan E. Goodman: "Myth versus Reality in 'North-South' Negotiations"

1. Branislav Gosovic and John Gerrard Ruggie, "On the Creation of a New International Economic Order: Issue Linkage and the Seventh Special Session of the UN General Assembly," *International Organization* 30 (Spring 1976): 309.

2. World Bank, *World Development Report 1982* (New York: Oxford University Press, 1982), p. 1.

3. Ibid., p. 9.

4. Friedrich Ebert Foundation, *Towards One World? International Responses to the Brandt Report* (London: Temple Smith, 1981).

5. Mahabub Ul Haq, *The Poverty Curtain: Choices for the Third World* (New York: Columbia University Press, 1976), p. 2.

6. For an excellent source of this and subsequent G−77 documents, see Karl P. Sauvant, ed., *The Collected Documents of the Group of 77,* 7 vols. (New York: Oceana, 1981).

7. A. W. Clausen, "Global Interdependence in the 1980s," remarks before Yomiuri International Economic Society, 13 January 1982, p. 2.

8. David Rockefeller, "U.S.−Third World Relations: Time for a New Assessment," 14 September 1981.

4. Dennis Austin: "Prospero's Island"

1. The first conference was in 1966, when 77 nations joined together. They were as diverse as Afghanistan, Brazil, El Salvador, India, Saudi Arabia, Togo, and Yugoslavia. Others joined subsequently, to bring the number to over 100. By 1974, there was a good deal of talk about a "New International Economic Order," and distinctions began to be drawn between subcategories of the more- or less-developed countries; but still the

basis of diplomacy and organization remained that of the notion of there being two or three "worlds."

2. O. Manoni, *Prospero and Caliban* (New York: Praeger, 1956).

3. A few simple statistics. Monthly wage rates in the textile industry in 1977 were: Japan £269, UK£180, Hong Kong £76, South Korea £59. Steel output per man-year: Japan 690 tons, UK 116 tons, South Korea 280 tons. Costs of steel production per ton: South Korea (hot-rolled steel) $180, UK $300; South Korea (cold-rolled steel) $230, UK $385. Present plans include the production of 2 million cars by 1991, including 40 percent for export. See "The Awakening Industrial Giant," *Times* (London), 15 and 16 August, 1978.

4. John Maynard Keynes, *General Theory of Employment, Interest, and Money* (London: Macmillan, 1961), p. 374.

5. As in the West Indies. "In global terms, Jamaica and Trinidad are microterritories, but in the Commonwealth Caribbean they are giants without which the less-developed countries of the eastern Caribbean cannot survive" (A. J. Payne, *Caribbean Integration* [Manchester: University of Manchester Press, 1978]).

6. "Since 1974 there has been no available information on the composition of the cabinet except for the reported deaths of several cabinet ministers (description of the government of Equatorial Guinea under Francisco Nguema in Amnesty International, *Africa South of the Sahara 1977–1978* [London: Europa Publications, 1978], p. 303).

7. Quoted in Edwin J. Feulner, Jr., *Congress and the New International Economic Order* (Washington, D.C.: The Heritage Foundation, 1976), p. 12.

5. S. E. Finer: "The Military and Politics in the Third World"

1. On the mechanics of the coup, see S. E. Finer, *The Man on Horseback: The Role of the Military in Politics,* 2nd ed. (London: Penguin Press, 1976); and especially Edward Luttwak, *Coup d'Etat: A Practical Handbook* (London: Penguin Press, 1969).

2. "It is a partnership in all science; a partnership in all art; a partnership in every virtue and in all perfection. As the ends of such a partnership cannot be obtained in many generations, it becomes a partnership not only between those who are living, but between those who are living, those who are dead, and those who are to be born" (Edmund Burke in *The Philosophy of Edmund Burke, A Selection from His Speeches and Writings,* ed. Louis I. Bredvold and Ralph G. Ross [Ann Arbor, Mich.: University of Michigan Press, 1960], p. 43).

3. S. Decalo, *Coups and Army Rule in Africa* (New Haven, Conn.: Yale University Press, 1976).

4. W. R. Thompson, *The Grievances of Military Coup-Makers* (Beverly Hills, Calif.: Sage, 1973), pp. 29–31.

5. A. Bebler, *Military Rule in Africa* (New York: Praeger, 1962), pp. 203–4.

6. Eric Nordlinger, "Soldiers in Mufti: The Impact of Military Rule Upon Economic and Social Change in the Non-Western States," *American Political Science Review,* vol. 64, no. 4 (December 1970): 1131–48.

7. R. D. McKinley and A. S. Cohan, "Military Coups, Military Regimes and Social Change," mimeo prepared for delivery at the APSA annual meeting in September 1974; and idem, "Performance and Instability in Military and Nonmilitary Regime Systems," *American Political Science Review,* vol. 70, no. 3 (1976): 850–64.

8. R. W. Jackman, "Politicians in Uniform: Military Governments and Social Change in the Third World," *American Political Science Review*, vol. 70, no. 4 (1976): 1078–97.

9. Philippe Schmitter, "Military Intervention, Political Competitiveness, and Public Policy in Latin America, 1950–1967," in *On Military Intervention*, ed. M. Janowitz and J. van Doorn (Rotterdam, The Netherlands: Rotterdam University Press, 1971), pp. 493–94.

10. José Nun, "The Middle Class Coup," in *The Politics of Conformity in Latin America*, ed. C. Veliz (Oxford: Oxford University Press, 1970), pp. 66–118.

11. Manfred Halpern, "Middle East Armies and the New Middle Class," in *The Role of the Military in Underdeveloped Countries*, ed. J. J. Johnson (Princeton, N.J.: Princeton University Press, 1962), pp. 278–79; and idem, *The Politics of Social Change in the Middle East* (Princeton, N.J.: Princeton University Press, 1963), chs. 4 and 13.

12. Samuel Huntington, *Political Order in Changing Societies* (New Haven, Conn.: Yale University Press, 1969), ch. 4.

6.   Peter T. Bauer and Basil S. Yamey: "Foreign Aid: What Is at Stake?"

1. Where the political survival of a newly created country is widely doubted, it may not be able to raise capital even if it can use capital productively. These apparent exceptions to the rule that development does not depend upon external aid are plainly irrelevant to the case for global transfers to the Third World.

2. According to Kuznets, the contribution of the increases in material capital (both reproducible and nonreproducible) to the increase of per capita income over long periods in major developed countries was limited, "ranging from less than a seventh to not much more than a fifth" (S. Kuznets, *Postwar Economic Growth* [Cambridge, Mass.: Harvard University Press, 1964, p. 41]). Much more important were improved efficiency in the use of resources and the movement of resources from less productive to more productive sectors. See also P. T. Bauer, *Dissent on Development* (London and Cambridge, Mass.: Harvard University Press, 1971), ch. 2, and *Equality, the Third World and Economic Delusion* (London and Cambridge, Mass.: Harvard University Press, 1981), ch. 14.

3. This effect of aid is discussed in Hans O. Schmitt's "Development Assistance: A View from Bretton Woods," *Public Policy*, Fall 1973.

4. This political reality has been recognized by others. Governments "genuinely committed to improving the material standards of life of the mass of their population" are "rare in the Third World." C. H. Kirkpatrick and F. I. Nixson, "The North-South Debate: Reflections on the Brandt Commission Report," *Three Banks Review* (London, September 1981), p. 39.

5. The economic policies and achievements of Kenya and Tanzania, and also official Western attitudes to these countries, are compared briefly in Gunter Krabbe, "East Africa and Double Standards," *Encounter*, October 1981.

6. The decision to build a new capital from scratch in the center of the country was political, not economic or social. Instead of unifying the peoples of Nigeria as some of its proponents hoped, the project has already proved to be highly divisive. Critics complain that $9 billion has been spent to date "and that much of this has vanished without pro-

ducing visible results"; as yet, "the new capital exists only on paper" (*The Economist*, 3–9 October 1981, p. 56). Yet, more was budgeted for Abuja (*Süddeutsche Zeitung*, 22 September 1981).

7. An officer of the government agency in charge of "transforming Dodoma from a semi-arid railway crossroads to an elegantly planned headquarters for the nation" said recently: "I believe Dodoma is rapidly approaching a crisis. It will have to be abandoned or else saved by a major international rescue operation." An Australian aid official, who serves as information director and business manager for the new capital, is reported as saying: "Even if the project were given more money, I doubt whether it could all be spent. We cannot get enough cement, enough steel, enough diesel to run the trucks. But it is not only a question of financial resources and building materials, the country basically does not have enough skilled people to properly run the place" (*The Times* [London], 23 December 1981).

8. In 1979 the official development assistance given by aid-giving OECD countries included loans that on average had a grant element of 61 percent (an average that corresponds to a loan at 3 percent with a grace period of 10 years and a maturity of 40 years). In the same year, the grant element in grants and loans combined came to 90 percent (*Development Co-operation: 1980 Review*, Paris, 1980, p. 103).

9. Willy Brandt and Anthony Sampson, eds., *North-South: A Program for Survival* (*The Brandt Report*), London, 1980, pp. 290–91.

7. Kenneth L. Adelman and Marc F. Plattner: "Third World Voting Patterns at the United Nations"

1. U.S. Department of State, Bureau of Public Affairs, "Current Policy #257," Washington, D.C., 9 January 1981.

2. Free, of course, to the users and benefactors of such services; not free to all. The U.S. pays 25 percent of these expenses —more than all of the NAM combined—since it pays 25 percent of the UN regular budget.

3. The twenty-fourth OECD country, Switzerland, is not a voting member of the United Nations.

4. The 0.8 percent exception was on a vote on U.S. membership in the International Civil Service Commission. The Soviets were obligated by the Permanent Members' Convention to side with us, even though they hoped we would lose (and we did). So they instructed their Pact colleagues to vote against us, and thus against them.

5. The membership of the G–77 is larger than 120 because it includes both Koreas, which are not full United Nations members, and Romania, despite its ties with the Soviet bloc.

6. Only three NAM states voted with the Soviets *less* than 75 percent of the time: Jamaica, Malawi, and Liberia. The statistics on group voting patterns within the NAM in this article are taken from a forthcoming book by Richard Jackson of the U.S. Mission to the UN entitled *The Non-Aligned Movement and the UN* (Praeger).

8. Daniel Pipes: "The Third World Peoples of Soviet Central Asia"

1. A. Nove and J. A. Newth, *The Soviet Middle East* (London: George Allyn and Unwin, 1967), pp. 97, 125.

2. Ibid., p. 45.

3. Michael Rywkin, *Moscow's Muslim Challenge: Soviet Central Asia* (Armonk, N.Y.: M. E. Sharpe, 1982), p. 57.

4. M. M. Shorish, "Soviet Development Strategies in Central Asia," *Canadian Slavonic Papers* 17 (1975): 412.

5. Nove and Newth, pp. 138–39.

6. R. A. Lewis, et al., "Modernization, Population Change, and Nationality in Soviet Central Asia and Kazakhstan," *Canadian Slavonic Papers* 17 (1975): 293–94.

7. Rywkin, p. 117.

8. Karl H. Menges, "People, Languages, and Migrations," in *Central Asia: A Century of Russian Rule,* ed. E. Allworth (New York: Columbia University Press, 1967), pp. 79–82.

9. A. J. E. Bodrogligeti, "The Classical Islam Heritage of Eastern Middle Turkic as Reflected in the Lexikon of Modern Literary Uzbek," *Canadian Slavonic Papers* 17 (1975): 475–91.

10. This is true without even considering the European republics (Estonia, Latvia, Lithuania, White Russia, the Ukraine, and Moldavia) or the satellites in Eastern Europe (Poland, East Germany, Czechoslovakia, Hungary, Romania, Bulgaria) and Mongolia.

11. The People's Republic of China rivals in size the Soviet empire. It includes some 40 million non-Han Chinese, including Manchus, Mongols, Koreans, Turks, and Tibetans. As in the Soviet Union, Turks constitute the largest minority. The Chinese case also fits classic colonial patterns, perhaps more closely than the Soviet Union, although the Chinese, of course, are not Europeans.

12. For an informed discussion, see Rywkin, pp. 69–83.

9. Robert E. Harkavy: "Military Bases in the Third World"

1. Alfred T. Mahan, *The Influence of Sea Power upon History, 1660–1783* (Boston: Little, Brown, 1890).

2. P. M. Dadant, "Shrinking International Airspace as a Problem for Future Air Movements — A Briefing," Report R–2178–AF (Santa Monica, Calif.: Rand Corporation, 1978).

3. Robert Gilpin, *U.S. Power and the Multinational Corporation* (New York: Basic Books, 1975), p. 152.

4. "Soviet Imperialism Is in the Red," *Fortune,* 13 July 1981, pp. 107–8.

5. Gilpin, pp. 173–74, footnote 14.

6. Foreign Broadcast Information Service, "Oman's Qabus to Allow U.S. to Use Al-Masirah Base," *U.S.S.R. International Affairs* (Middle East and North Africa), 26 January 1977, p. F5.

7. Ibid., "Bahrain Reportedly Asks U.S. to Close Naval Base," *U.S.S.R. International Affairs* (Middle East and North Africa), 10 January 1977, p. F6.

10. Tony Smith: "The Case of Dependency Theory"

1. Immanuel Wallerstein, *The Modern World-System: Capitalist Agriculture and the Origins of the European World-Economy in the Sixteenth Century* (New York: Academic Press, 1974).

2. Samir Amin, *Accumulation on a World Scale: A Critique of the Theory of Under-development,* vol. I, trans. Brian Pearce (New York: Monthly Review Press, 1974), p. 3.

3. Walter Rodney, *How Europe Underdeveloped Africa* (London: Bogle L'Ouverture, 1973), pp. 21–22.

4. Colin Leys, *Underdevelopment in Kenya: The Political Economy of Neo-Colonialism, 1964–1971* (Berkeley, Calif.: University of California Press, 1974), pp. 198–99.

5. André Gunder Frank, "The Development of Underdevelopment," in *Dependence and Underdevelopment: Latin America's Political Economy,* ed. James D. Cockcroft, et al. (New York: Anchor, 1972).

6. Stanley J. Stein and Barbara H. Stein, *The Colonial Heritage of Latin America: Essays on Economic Dependency in Perspective* (New York: Oxford University Press, 1970), p. viii.

7. Frances Moulder, *Japan, China, and the Modern World-Economy: Toward a Reinterpretation of East Asian Development* (New York: Cambridge University Press, 1977).

8. Paul Baran, *The Political Economy of Growth,* 2nd. ed. (New York: Monthly Review Press, 1962), p. 150.

9. Ibid., pp. 149–50.

10. Dale Johnson, "Dependence and the International System," in Cockcroft, et al., p. 75n; repeated with other dates, p. 94n.

11. Richard Barnet and Ronald Mueller, *Global Reach: The Power of the Multinational Corporation* (New York: Simon and Schuster, 1974), pp. 154–55.

12. George Liska, *Imperial America: The International Politics of Primacy* (Baltimore: Johns Hopkins Press, 1967), Preface (unpaginated) and p. 180.

13. Kwame Nkrumah, *Neo-Colonialism: The Last State of Imperialism* (New York: International Publishers, 1966), p. ix.

11.   Richard E. Bissell: "Political Origins of the New International Economic Order"

1. Edwin O. Reischauer and John K. Fairbank, *East Asia: The Great Tradition* (Boston: Houghton Mifflin, 1958), pp. 55, 636.

2. Harold R. Isaacs, "Fathers and Sons and Daughters and National Development," in *Political Generations and Political Development,* ed. Richard J. Samuels (Lexington, Mass.: Heath, 1977), pp. 39–56.

3. See Adda Bozeman, *The Future of Law in a Multicultural World* (Princeton, N.J.: Princeton University Press, 1971).

4. Arthur Twining Hadley, *Economic Problems of Democracy* (New York: Macmillan, 1923), pp. 36–37.

5. Aristide Zolberg, *Creating Political Order: The Party-States of West Africa* (Chicago: Rand McNally, 1966), and Myron Weiner, *The Politics of Scarcity* (Chicago: University of Chicago Press, 1962). See also James C. Scott, "Corruption, Machine Politics, and Political Changes," *American Political Science Review* 63 (1969): 1142–58.

6. For some descriptions of the NIEO, see William G. Tyler, *Issues and Prospects for the New International Economic Order* (Lexington, Mass.: Heath, 1977); Jagdish N. Bhagwati, ed., *The New International Economic Order: The North-South Debate*

(Boston: MIT Press, 1977); Edwin J. Feulner, Jr., *Congress and the New International Economic Order* (Washington, D.C.: The Heritage Foundation, 1976); and Karl P. Sauvant and Hajo Hasenpflug, eds., *The New International Economic Order: Confrontation or Cooperation between North and South?* (Boulder, Colo.: Westview, 1977).

12. Nathaniel H. Leff: "Beyond the New International Economic Order"

1. Richard S. Eckaus, "Absorptive Capacity as a Constraint Due to Maturation Process," in *Development and Planning,* ed. J. N. Bhagwati and R. S. Eckaus (Cambridge, Mass.: MIT Press, 1973).

2. See S. Harrison, "Time Bomb in East Asia," *Foreign Policy* (Fall 1975).

3. See, for example, Samir Amin, *Accumulation on a World Scale: A Critique of the Theory of Underdevelopment,* trans. Brian Pearce (New York: Monthly Review Press, 1974).

4. See Inter-American Development Bank, *Latin American Energy and Oil: Present Situation and Prospects* (Washington, D.C.: Inter-American Development Bank, 1978).

5. Richard S. Eckaus, *Appropriate Technologies for Developing Countries* (Washington, D.C.: National Academy of Science, 1977).

6. David Morawetz, "Economic Lessons from Some Small Countries," paper presented to the American Economic Association, December 1977.

7. I owe this observation to Graciella Chichilnisky.

13. Wilson E. Schmidt: "The Role of Private Capital in Developing the Third World"

1. Nathaniel Leff, "Rates of Return to Capital, Savings, and Investment in Developing Countries," *Kyklos* (December 1975).

2. D. Lecraw, "Direct Investment by Firms from Less-Developed Countries," *Oxford Economic Papers* (November 1977).

3. Center on Transnational Corporations, *National Legislation and Regulations Relating to Transnational Corporations* (New York: United Nations, 1978), p. 10.

CONTRIBUTORS

KENNETH L. ADELMAN is deputy permanent representative of the United States to the United Nations. Prior to this appointment, he held positions in the Department of Commerce, the Office of Economic Opportunity, and VISTA, and most recently served as assistant to the secretary of defense. His publications include *African Realities* (1980) and a host of articles on the Third World in *The Wall Street Journal,* the *Washington Post,* the *New York Times, Harper's,* and *Foreign Affairs.*

DENNIS AUSTIN, professor of government at the University of Manchester in England, is well known for his studies of African and Asian nations formerly associated with Great Britain. His most recent books include *The Commonwealth in Eclipse* (1972) and *Politics in Africa* (1978).

PETER T. BAUER is professor of economics at the London School of Economics and Political Science, University of London, and a Fellow of the British Academy. His primary interest is in the economic development of underdeveloped countries, a subject of many of his books and articles published within the past twenty years. He is the author of *Dissent on Development* (1976), and his latest book is *Equality, the Third World, and Economic Delusion* (1982).

LORD BELOFF has been a Conservative life peer since 1981. His previous academic career included seventeen years at All Souls College, Oxford, as Gladstone Professor of Government and Public Administration; he was also the first principal of the University College at Buckingham. Lord Beloff's many books include *The United States and the Unity of Europe* (1963); *Imperial Sunset: Volume 1, Britain's Liberal Empire, 1897–1921* (1969); and, with Gillian Peele, *The Government of the United Kingdom* (1980).

RICHARD E. BISSELL, professorial lecturer at the Johns Hopkins School of Advanced International Studies, formerly taught at Temple University and the University of Pennsylvania, and was managing editor of *ORBIS.* He is the author of *South Africa and the United States: Erosion of an Influence Relationship* (1982) and editor of *Strategic Dimensions of Economic Behavior* (forthcoming), among many books and articles.

S. E. FINER, F.B.A., is Gladstone Professor of Government and Public Administration at the University of Oxford, and former chairman of the Political Studies Association at the United Kingdom. He just completed a term as Visiting Albert Schweitzer Professor in the Humanities at Columbia University, New York City. Dr. Finer's many publications include *A Primer of Public Administration* (1950), *Comparative Government* (1970), *Adversary Politics and Electoral Reform* (1975), *The Man on Horseback: The Role of the Military in Politics* (second edition, 1976), and *Britain's Changing Party System* (1980). He is currently engaged on *The History of Government: From the Earliest Times.*

ALLAN E. GOODMAN is associate dean and director of the Master of Science in Foreign Service program at Georgetown University. Prior to joining the Georgetown faculty in 1980, he served as presidential briefing coordinator for the director of Central Intelligence, special assistant to the director of the National Foreign Assessment Center, chairman of the Department of Government and International Relations at Clark University, and National Fellow at Stanford University's Hoover Institution. Dr. Goodman is a specialist on Asia and on the theory and practice of international negotiation, and has written over thirty articles and five books on international affairs.

ROBERT E. HARKAVY, associate professor of political science at Pennsylvania State University, is spending the 1982–83 year as visiting research professor, Strategic Studies Institute, U.S. Army War College. He is the author of numerous works on international affairs, including *The Arms Trade and International Systems* (1975); *Spectre of a Middle Eastern Holocaust: The Strategic and Diplomatic Implications of the Israeli Nuclear Weapons Program* (1977); and *Great Power Competition for Overseas Bases: The Geopolitics of Access Diplomacy* (1982).

NATHANIEL H. LEFF is professor of business economics and international business at the Graduate School of Business, Columbia University. He has published widely on the economics and politics of the developing countries, and his latest book is entitled *Underdevelopment and Development in Brazil* (1982).

DANIEL PIPES, formerly of the University of Chicago, where he specialized in Middle Eastern and Islamic affairs, is presently serving on the policy planning staff at the Department of State. His articles have appeared in many leading magazines and newspapers, and he is the author of *Slave Soldiers and Islam* (1981) and the forthcoming *Season of Discontent: Islam in Modern Politics.*

MARC F. PLATTNER, adviser on economic and social affairs at the United States Mission to the United Nations, formerly served as program officer at the Twentieth Century Fund and as managing editor of *The Public Interest.* He is the editor of a forthcoming volume of essays entitled *Human Rights in Our Time* and the author of *Rousseau's State of Nature* (1979), as well as numerous articles on public policy issues.

WILSON E. SCHMIDT was professor of economics and director for international programs in the Center for the Study of Public Choice at Virginia Polytechnic Institute and State University prior to his death in June 1981. Formerly a consultant to government agencies on policy questions of international finance and economic development, his many writings include "Trade Regulation: Areas of Conflict and Congruence," in *Latin American–United States Economic Interactions: Conflict, Accommodation, and Policy for the Future,* edited by Robert Williams, W. S. Glade, and Carl Schmitt (1974), and "U.S. Capital Export Policy: Backdoor Mercantilism," in *U.S. Taxation of American Business Abroad* (1975).

TONY SMITH is professor of political science at Tufts University. He is the author of *The French Stake in Algeria, 1945–1962* (1978) and *The Pattern of Imperialism: The United States, Great Britain, and the Late-Industrializing World Since 1815* (1981).

W. SCOTT THOMPSON is on the faculties of the Fletcher School of Law and Diplomacy and Georgetown University, where he teaches courses in international politics and security studies. Formerly a delegate to the special session of the United Nations General Assembly on Disarmament (1982) and assistant to the secretary of defense (1975–76), he is currently associate director for programs at the United States Information Agency. Dr. Thompson has written widely, and his numerous books include: *The Fulcrum of Power: The Third World Between Moscow and Washington* (1983), *The Lessons of Viet Nam* (1977), *Unequal Partners: Philippine and Thai Relations with the United States* (1975), and *Ghana's*

Foreign Policy: Diplomacy, Ideology, and the New State (1969). Professor Thompson also edited the first edition of this book (1978) and *National Security in the 1980s* (1980), both published by the Institute for Contemporary Studies.

BASIL S. YAMEY is professor of economics at the London School of Economics and Political Science, University of London, and a Fellow of the British Academy. He was a member of the official British Monopolies and Mergers Commission from 1966 to 1978, and has published a number of books and articles on economics and related subjects. He is the author of *The Economics of Futures Trading,* published in 1976.

INDEX

Abramowitz, M., 122
Afghanistan, 15, 27, 31–32, 146, 172, 179–180, 236, 294, 297
Agency for International Development (AID), 191
Algeria, 46, 96, 213, 244
Allende, S., 209
Alliance for Progress, 253, 255, 264
Amin, Idi. *See* Uganda
Amin, S., 207
Amnesty International, 69
Andean Common Market, 277–279
Angola, 32, 185, 187, 196, 297
Arab League, 140
Argentina, 15, 87–88, 104, 111, 140, 180–181, 219, 220. *See also* Falklands
ASEAN, 51
Austerity programs, 257

Bahrain, 95, 144, 194–195
Bangladesh, 70, 96, 105, 111
Baran, P., 208, 210–211
Barbados, 60, 71
Barnet, R., 215
Bases (military, naval, air), access via overflights, 184–185, basing assets rivalry, 178, 191–196, communications and intelligence facilities, 183–185, 200, factors affecting user-host relations, 186–187, technological changes in basing needs, 181–185, 200
Basic-needs development strategy, 260

Bauer, P. T., 140–141
Benin, 82, 97
Biafra, 93–94, 111
Bolivia, 82
Borrowing, in Eurocurrency and international capital markets, 256, 263, 269–271, 282–283
Brandt Commission, 41, 134
Brazil, 40, 43, 92, 96, 98, 102, 188, 228, 230, 257, 261, 262, 270
Bribery, 275
Burke, E., 110–111
Burma, 70, 89, 96–98, 100–13, 105
Burundi, 70, 93

Cairncross, Sir Alec, 122
Cambodia, 23, 146
Cancun summit, 49
Carter administration, 6–7, 27, 179, 261, 279, 287, 290
Castro, Fidel, 8, 252
Central African Republic, 58, 84, 96
Chenery, H. B., 115
Chile, 85, 106, 209, 261
China, 24, 59, 184–185, 197, 291, 297
Church, F., 261
Clausen, A. W., 46
Collectivization, forced, 123, 125, 164
Colombia, 83, 104, 262, 277
Colonial rule, contrasts in, 60–63
Conference on International Economic Cooperation (CIEC), 38
Costa Rica, 77

Creditworthiness, 270–272. *See also*
  Borrowing
Cuba, 8, 21, 27, 60, 252, 293, 297,
  bases, 178, 184, 187, 196, 198,
  foreign aid, 119–120, 260
Cyprus, 60, 79, 187, 194

Debt rescheduling or cancellation,
  229, 236, 242, international debt
  moratorium, 262
Decalo, S., 93
Denison, E., 112
Dependency theory, 11–13, 42,
  204–222, decapitalization,
  214–215, "denationalization,"
  214–215, warranted concessions
  to, 221–222
Diego Garcia, 181–182, 192, 195,
  197. *See also* Indian Ocean,
  Bases
Diversification, 256
Dominican Republic, 262

Ecuador, 82
Education, higher, in Third World,
  227–228
Egypt, 48, 92, 96–97, 99, 103, 179,
  188–189, 192, (1880) 219,
  (1956) 259
Equatorial Guinea, 84, 96
Eritrea, 6, 23
Ethiopia, 6, 23, 90, 92, 106, 111,
  178, 185, 187, 192, 291, 294, 297
Exchange rate policies, 254, fixed
  rates, 271
Expropriations, 259, 247–248,
  276–277
Expulsion, expropriation of
  productive minorities, 123, 125,
  131

Falklands, 15, 87–88, 140, 180–181
Foreign aid, 115–135, 293, as
  obstacle to development, 10–12,
  123–128, for emergencies,
  134–135, justifications offered
  for, 129–130, level of total

foreign aid 1960–1980, 267,
  limited aid absorption capacity,
  243, 249, reform of aid policies,
  133–135, restitution, 131–133,
  242
Frank, A. G., 208

Gabon, 87
Gambia, 69
Gandhi, M. K., 22, 217
General Agreement on Tariffs and
  Trade (GATT), 190
Ghana, 28–29, 87, 101, 292
Gilpin, R., 191–193
Governmental instability, 8, 66–68,
  230–234, 289, 295–296,
  abandonment of competing-
  parties framework, 77–78. *See
  also* Military governments
Grenada, 71, 178, 180
Group of 77 (G–77), 41–46, 145
Guinea, 196, 292

Hadley, A., 229–230
Haig, A., 139–140
Haiti, 58, 84
Halpern, M., 110
Harberger, A. C., 11
Hong Kong, 64, 132
Human rights campaign, 69–72,
  173, 179, 261, 287, 289–291
Huntington, S., 110

Import constraints, 246–247, 256,
  exemption on import duties, 279
Import substitution, 256
Imported technology, price of, 235
India, 71, 77, 112, 121–123, 128,
  187, 211–212, 249, 270, 278
Indian Ocean, 181, 195, 197. *See
  also* Diego Garcia
Indonesia, 102–103, 105, 184, 188,
  194
Inflationary pressures, 124,
  stagflation, 260
Inter-American Development Bank,
  253

International Bauxite Association, 268

International Civil Service Commission (ICSC), 148

International Development Association (IDA), 254

International Labor Organization, 261–262

International Monetary Fund (IMF), 38, 54, 144, 236, 257, 271

Investible funds, volume of, 121–122, 275, rate of return on capital invested, 283, reverse investments, 271

Iran, 124, 179, 184, 189, 192, 198, 289, 296–297

Iran-Iraq war, 142, 296

Iraq, 82, 92, 96–99, 179–180, 187–188, 197–198

Ireland, Northern (Ulster), 85

Isaacs, H., 226

Israel, 21, 48, 142, 143, 147, 148, 289–299

Ivory Coast, 40, 65, 78, 104, 126, 270, 292

Jackman, R., 108

Japan, 48, 51, 62, 182

Johnson, D., 214

Kampuchea. *See* Cambodia

Kenya, 60, 65, 78, 126, 189, 190, 262

Keynesian views, 65, 243

Korea, North, 70, 229

Korea, South, 10, 40, 43, 64, 97–99, 262

Kuznets, S., 122

Law of the Sea Treaty, 236, 288

Lebanon, 88, 93, 298–299

Leys, C., 207

Liberia, 87, 231

Libya, 6, 83, 105, 140, 187, 188, 192

Lima Declaration, 259

Liska, G., 216–217

Little, Arthur D. (Corp.), 244

MacArthur, D., 89–90

McKinley, R. D., 108

McNamara, R., 40

Malawi, 62–64

Malta, 194

Marketing and accounting know-how, 244–247

Marshall Plan, 128

Mexico, 76, 112–114, 209, 220–221, 239, 270

Micronesia, 127, 147, 195–197

Military Assistance Program (MAP), 191

Military governments, coups, 78–114, class antagonisms within, 92–93, conditions favoring coups, 85–86, dismantling of military governments, 104–112, formats and styles, 94–100, modernizing influence, 93, 106–111, number of troops involved, 87, political and social order as priority, 289, 295, prospects for Third World disarmament, 295

Morawetz, D., 42

Morocco, 83, 120, 178, 183, 187, 191, Western Sahara, 140

Moulder, F., 208

Moynihan, D., 261

Multinational corporations, 234–283 *passim,* accusations against, 273–274, bribery, 275, preferred areas of operation, 132, responses to expropriation threat, 276–277, restrictions on, 277–278

NATO, 177, 183, 297

"Neocolonialism," 132, 218, 226, 257

New International Economic Order (NIEO), 13, 37, 41–44, 47–48, 60, 73, 144, 223–237, 238–265, 268

Nicaragua, 6, 7, 71–72, 180

Nietzsche, F., 224
Nigeria, 28–29, 46, 70–71, 88,
    93–94, 101, 111, 225
Nkrumah, K., 218
Non-Aligned Movement, 8, 140, 142
Nordlinger, B., 107–108
Nun, J., 109–110

OAU (Organization of African
    Unity), 140
Oman, 95, 144, 194, 197
OPEC, 12, 34–37, 43, 119, 140, 196,
    217–218, 226, 231, 236, 240,
    256, 263, 268, 271
Opinion polls, Third World leaders,
    289–290
Organization for Economic
    Cooperation and Development
    (OECD), 38, 48, 142, 213–214,
    244, 257

Pakistan, 85, 90, 184, 192, 198
Palestine Liberation Organization
    (PLO), 147, 298
Pauperization, perpetuated,
    126–127
Peace Corps, 253, 259
Philippines, 46, 48, 77–78, 95, 189,
    190, 290
Point Four program, 118
Poland, 27, 83
Politicization, 226–237, economic
    scapegoats, 224–225, long-term
    and short-term goals, 231–236,
    losers' attitudes, 233–234,
    multi-ethnic machine politics,
    231–234
Portugal, 90, 93
Prestige projects, 120, 126, 260
Price indexation, 240, 258
Price supports (for primary
    products), 241
Pricing, transfer, 274–275
Protectionism. *See* Import
    constraints
Puerto Rico, 291

Race, 21, 26–27, 30–31
Reagan administration, 179,
    279–280, "Project Democracy,"
    291, 295
Rockefeller, D., 50
Rodney, W., 207
Rumania, 21
Rwanda, 63, 96

Salvador, 14, 96, 147
Saudi Arabia, 179–180, 188–189,
    196, 264, 297
Schmitter, P., 108–109
Sierra Leone, 70
Singapore, 43, 64
Somalia, 142, 143, 147, 230, 294
South Africa, 142, 143, 147, 230,
    294
Southeast Asia Treaty Organization
    (SEATO), 177
Soviet Central Asia, 155–174, 291,
    centralization of power, 162,
    165, collectivization, 164,
    compared to colonies, 160–169,
    compared to Third World, 164,
    demography, 170–171,
    education, literacy and
    alphabets, 166–169,
    input/output, 164–165, Islam,
    167, local Slavic/indigenous
    relations, 163, 165–166,
    motivations attributed to USSR,
    158–159, openings for U.S.
    meddling, 171–173, productivity
    and standards of living,
    163–166, 171, Tsarist rule,
    157–158
Spechler, M., 165
Special drawing rights (SDRs), 13,
    37, 236
Sri Lanka (Ceylon), 60, 77, 95, 112,
    187, 260
Stein, B., and Stein, S., 208
Sudan, 82
Syria, 76, 82, 92, 96, 98, 187, 189,
    196, 298–299

Taiwan, 64, 192
Tanzania, 70, 78, 125, 129, 290
Taxation, exemption on import
    duties, 279, income tax holidays,
    279, 281, IRS, 273, 281–282,
    OPIC, 279–281, tax evasion and
    multinationals, 274–275
Technology gap, internal, 258
Technology transfer and access,
    235, 243–245, 258
Thailand, 82, 96, 100–102, 191, 194
Trinidad, 65
Tunisia, 291–292, 294
Turkey, 84–85, 95, 104, 184, 297

Uganda, 23, 29, 61, 63, 93, 106, 233
UNCTAD (UN Conference on Trade
    and Development), 37–38, 44,
    48, 56, 132, 145, 268, Charter of
    Algiers, 218–219
United Nations. *See* UNCTAD.
    Group of 77, voting patterns in
    UN, 139–149, Table 1

Upper Volta, 66
Uruguay, 97

Venezuela, 104, 112
Vietnam, 119–120, 125, 146, 147,
    178, 180, 183, 189, 192, 197
Vietnam-U.S. war and aftermath,
    25–26, 29, 204, 216–218, 226,
    296, domino theory, 26

Wallerstein, I., 207
Weiner, M., 230
World Bank, 38–40, 213, 269

Zaire, 24, 29, 97, 125, 293
Zambia, 78
Zimbabwe, 27, 29
Zolberg, A., 230